Vichara

Self Enquiry

Who am I?

Vichara

Self Enquiry

Who am I?

A Selection of Self Enquiry Teachings
From Bhagavan Sri Ramana Maharshi

OPEN SKY PRESS
www.openskypress.com

A Selection of 5* Reviews

Aham Sphurana – A Glimpse of Self Realisation

Published in 2022

Three years ago, we published *Aham Sphurana – A Glimpse of Self Realisation*, the first volume in the *Aham Sphurana* trilogy based on Gajapathi's diaries. It was enthusiastically received by many Ramana devotees worldwide.

Solomon Katz, Harvard, USA, September 2023

In telling people about this book, I've compared it to unexpectedly finding a lost Shakespeare manuscript! While there has been some controversy about the authenticity of the notebooks, the voice of Bhagavan and the value of the instruction seems unmistakable. The notebooks from which this book is edited comprise a newly found treasure trove of Bhagavan's teaching, and his voice comes alive. For any serious student of the Maharshi, this book is essential.

Paul, August 2022

This book is an edited version of *Aham Sphurana* which only takes the relevant text from *Aham Sphurana* and leaves out the portion of no interest. What remains is a great text in the style of *Talks* but immensely better than the more popular *Talks*.

Reading the comments by Sri Ramana from this book I get the impression that *Talks* must have been edited heavily since this book gives more elaborate details of various topics of Sri Ramana's teachings like Self-enquiry, surrender and much more. *Talks* seems to leave out certain details since there is also content in *Talks* from July 1936 which is different than this account.

The author, a lawyer visiting the Ashram from July-December 1936, gives an incredible record not only of the teachings but also of Sri Ramana's reactions to day-to-day life including never before published tales from Major Chadwick and S. Cohen who were present at the Ashram at the same time. This book, is a must for any sincere devotee of Bhagavan!

E.W., December 2022

The core theme of the book is the fundamental question of life: Who am I? Sri Ramana Maharshi makes it clear – the answer to this question is not explanation but experience! In this book, The Experiential Presence is so clearly perceptible and supports the reader for a direct experience of self-knowledge. Deep gratitude to all who have contributed to the publication of this book and have widened the door of grace for self-awareness a little more.

Swami Hamsananda, Tiruvannamalai, January 2024

In my opinion, *Aham Sphurana – A Glimpse of Self Realisation*, will become a Treasure Trove of Wisdom to the Seekers of Truth in general, and particularly to the devotees of Bhagavan.

A.G., September 2022

Aham Sphurana is gem of a book, an offering par excellence for all seekers. The editing done by your team is great effort for making this knowledge available for all seekers in a simplified manner. The printing and paper quality is excellent, done with love and care. Sincerely hoping for the rest of the volumes to be published.

Noah Arc, July 2022

Aham Sphurana is the most profound, subtle and practical version of Ramana Maharshi. When you read this book you realise just how diluted, vague and lacking are most of the books published in the name of this great sage of Arunachala.

It is not an easy new age read, it is the real deal with all its subtleties and intricacies. Our role is to develop a profound, sensitive and subtle mind and heart to understand and absorb these teachings.

The persons who wrote and published this book faced fierce objection from many people and are no less than warriors of spiritual truth.

Their devotion and respect to Ramana Maharshi made them fight this war and they deserve our appreciation and respect for making these rare teachings available to us.

Johannes Kiffer, August 2022

It seems this manuscript has captured a huge variety of dialogues and meetings with Sri Ramana - in incredible detail. The book is nicely set out in different chapters so you can read it according to a particular interest, but it also has the character of a diary which really allows a deeper glance into how Bhagavan responded to situations and questions. I can highly recommend it.

Sri Ramanacharana Tirtha Swami (formerly Sri Nochur Venkataraman), January 2024, Tiruvannamalai

Thanks for presenting the book. I went through the book and it is indeed a good read. As you have mentioned, certain portions are controversial. However, many portions on Self-enquiry (genuinely in Bhagavan's words) are profound and helpful to the seekers. Pranams

Amazon Customer, November 2022

I made several attempts to write an appropriate and meaningful review after I finished this book. But words cannot describe the true treasure of these records. The reader can only experience this for themselves. The dialogues with Bhagavan Sri Ramana Maharshi are clear and provide deep insight into his spiritual teachings. It wasn't just the written text that gave me deeper insights, but also the transformative energy that revealed itself to me behind the written words. A book that a spiritually open person should not miss.

Customer, October 2022

I have always appreciated the clear words in the works on Ramana Maharashi. In the manuscript *Aham Sphurana*, the presence of Ramana becomes even more palpable. I have rarely been so moved. The description of Ashram life is unadorned and very authentic.

As always, the words of wisdom are timeless – but this time they have been particularly well chosen. The previously available notes from 1936 have finally been expanded. So, you can read and learn a lot of new things – although the message remains the same, of course.

I have been reading *'Talks'* regularly to gain inspiration for everyday life and to constantly remind myself of the truth. Now, I will rather turn to *Aham Sphurana,* as it is not so overloaded and makes the teachings of Ramana Maharshi even clearer and adds new insights.

And for all doubters: if you don't believe that the manuscript is authentic, just read it and see if it resonates with you. It certainly did for me right from the start. For me, the words are unmistakably from the same source as all of Ramana Maharshi's other works.

Arvind, October 2022

This is an outstanding effort by the German Ramana and Papaji Satsang group, called Open Sky House, to bring out the material in the *Aham Sphurana* manuscript, in a more readable form to the general public. The layout is well done and pleasing.

The inclusion of photos of the handwritten material also inspires confidence in the authenticity of the work, as do the results of the scientific testing of the manuscript's fragments in a laboratory facility: confirming that the fragments are really old as claimed, and there is no 'hoax' really involved, as suggested by people elsewhere.

Also looking forward to the remaining manuscript material getting published! And truly hats off to the Open Sky team for the effort made so far!

Ingo, December 2022

The diary of Ramana Maharshi's teachings has been my almost daily companion for several months. In an amazingly condensed form, the guru repeatedly points out the essentials, which is a very pleasant reflection for me, a daily reminder of the reality beyond my 'everyday reality', a mantra.

What I also find very remarkable – and here I perceive a clear difference to the other books by / about Ramana Maharshi that I know – is that the person Ramana comes very close here. Thus, I can confirm what can be read in the introductory words of the book: that here the image of the 'world-distant saint' receives an essential addition. In my view, this book is more suitable for advanced people on the path. Basically, what the guru conveys here is very tough stuff. To really take this in means nothing less than a complete collapse of our learned ideas, our ego bubble. My heartfelt thanks to the publishers of Open Sky House.

After a year of intensive study: *Aham Sphurana* is undoubtedly still the spiritual book that fascinates and accompanies me the most. It conveys the essence of the teaching as well as the nature of the person and the guru. In this wholeness, it touches me more deeply than his best-known book *Nan Yar* and many other spiritual books.

Vichara
Introductory Texts

Bhagavan Sri Ramana Maharshi

30.12.1879 – 14.04.1950

Unselfish Love, Motiveless, Incessant, Intransigent Love,
is the key that unlocks the Gate of the Heart once and for all.

Vichara – Self Enquiry, Who am I?

A Selection of Self Enquiry Teachings
from Sri Bhagavan Ramana Maharshi

Published by Open Sky Press GbR
office@openskypress.com
www.openskypress.com

First Edition 2025

ISBN: 978-3-943544-81-7

Cover design by Om
Photographs from Bhagavan's Ashram Archives
All other photographs from Open Sky House archive

Printed in Poland

OPEN SKY PRESS
www.openskypress.com

Bhagavan's Life Events

1879 Dec 30.......	Born in Tamil Nadu, South India, as Venkataraman
1896 July............	Spiritual Awakening aged sixteen
1896 Sept 1.........	Arrived at Arunachala
1898...................	Moved to Gurumurtham
1899...................	Moved to Virupaksha Cave aged nineteen
1901...................	First recorded teaching Who Am I? aged twenty-one
1906-07.............	Recovered his speech
1907...................	Given the name Bhagavan Sri Ramana Maharshi
1916...................	Mother arrived to live at Virupaksha Cave
1917...................	Moved to Skanda Ashram aged thirty-seven
1922 May...........	Mother died and later Sri Ramana moved down the hill
1920s.................	Sri Ramana rewrote and published Who Am I?
1920s.................	Simple bamboo ashram buildings constructed
1927-1942.........	Stone ashram buildings constructed
1930s.................	Paul Brunton visited
1940s.................	New granite Hall built in front of Mother's Shrine
1949..................	Cancer appeared on Sri Ramana's arm
1949..................	Moved very ill to live in Samadhi Room
1950 April 14......	Sri Ramana passed away at 8.47 pm

1902

Earliest known Portrait
Taken at Virupaksha Cave, Age 22

1950

Mahasamadhi
At Sri Ramana Ashram, Age 70

Acknowledgements

Suddenly in October 2021 a friend sent me news of a huge manuscript, *Aham Sphurana*, a diary of Sri Ramana Maharshi's meetings and the day-to-day life of the Ashram in 1936. It had been published on Amazon, and I urgently downloaded it.

When I shared the *Aham Sphurana* texts with my students, and in particular the residents of Open Sky House, they gave me the needed response and encouragement to choose and edit around fifty texts. Ole in particular introduced me to texts written about the daily Ashram life, and how Bhagavan used the different situations to show a practical teaching. Also, Indira pointed out the insights that different visitors painted of Bhagavan and the Ashram. She has been one of several proof readers.

I wish to thank the members of Open Sky Press (OSP) who have, over the years, published over thirty spiritual books and films, my own but also Papaji's own books and several Ramana Maharshi books, notably a superb Art Quality version of *Nan Yar, Who am I?*. These were published in three Indian languages and four European languages. As a small spiritual publisher, Open Sky Press has been supported financially by the residents of the Open Sky House Community for eighteen years. They donate their time, seeing it as their way to thank Existence for all the benedictions received whilst living in the community. Now the whole community wished to support the publication of *Aham Sphurana* and so we contacted those responsible for putting the manuscript out in the world. Now, in 2024, we have decided together to publish this new book of selections of *Vichara* teachings.

At a moment of personal doubt, I met Swami Hamsananda of Athithi Ashram at Arunachala who talked with me about the material and convinced me to publish the whole manuscript in several volumes. He continued to act as a valuable adviser through the editing process.

As Bhagavan spoke Tamil and naturally used India's spiritual language, Sanskrit, we had great need of translation help. In January 2022 OSP had just published our Art Quality book *Nan Yar* in Tamil, Hindi and Telugu and S. Nagarajan, a Tamil scholar, devotee of Bhagavan and a writer, gave hours of his time to help us translate Tamil and Sanskrit. He has generously continued his wonderful contribution to *Vichara*.

My ex-wife and friend, Sally, has diligently proofed all my edited texts and given invaluable help in the preparation of this book in so many different ways. I would like to extend my gratitude to Dominik, whose meticulous last-minute proofreading has polished the book into a professional marvel.

The whole OSP team has worked intensely together over four weeks at Open Sky Oasis in Denia, Spain. Over six months a team of six people have freely given days of their time to bring Bhagavan's valuable teaching into the public realm. Special mention to Om for his brilliant cover designs and his constant computer help to the whole team. He has formatted the book and readied it as an e-book and a print book for publishing.

I would also like to thank Pravin Anand from the Indian law firm Anand & Anand who is an expert in copyright issues and provided us top quality legal advice.

A big thank you to Athreya and Nalini for all their devotion in being the midwives of this important manuscript. Athreya's mother, Nalini, typed up the whole manuscript some years ago before her passing. As she is so lovely, I decided to publish this photo of Nalini and allow that the rest of the family are also wonderful people. They requested the following acknowledgement:

This work is dedicated to Bhagavan Sri Ramana Maharshi, the peerless Master of Non-duality, who, for more than half a century, silently poured out his Grace on all sentient beings that came to him and who uninterruptedly shines forever as 'I'-'I' in the Heart-lotus of all, as the One Perfect Reality.

In conclusion I would like to thank the Ashram management for their tireless efforts to maintain the Ashram as a service to the thousands of devotees who feel a deeper connection to Bhagavan while spending some time inside this hallowed place.

I would particularly like to thank the amazingly strong, divine, beautiful energy which has surrounded me, and in fact the whole team, in the last months. I have become so intimate with Bhagavan and the daily life around him that often I felt I was in the Ashram Hall basking in his light. So, to him a huge thank you for touching my life so deeply.

John David, Director, Open Sky Press, March 2025

Disclaimer

News of the manuscript brought great excitement and it was immediately downloaded, only to discover that it was an unformatted continuous stream of text which was painstakingly difficult to read. In the process of preparing this formatted and edited book *Aham Sphurana – Vichara*, it has felt as if destiny has worked to make this treasure available to a wider public.

We have felt surrounded by an energy which has brought us closer to Bhagavan, sometimes as if we were sitting in the Hall. We hope that all readers of the book will experience something similar.

It soon became apparent that *Aham Sphurana* is a controversial manuscript. Due to its age, it has proven impossible to authenticate directly. However, we are in possession of a few original notebooks which purportedly formed part of the original manuscript. When tested in a laboratory, the paper appears to be from the 1930s. The antiquated English is reminiscent of something that would have been written 100 years ago.

We approached the Ramana Ashram President, Dr. Venkat S. Ramanan in two separate years with a list of questions. Our aim was to inquire whether the ashram's archive contains records of the original six-month manuscript and the 1936 group photograph. Unfortunately, both times we received no interest in engaging with us. Despite this, the overwhelmingly positive feedback from devotees encouraged us to proceed with making this second selection available.

Many experts agree that especially the teaching dialogues in this manuscript carry the unmistakable spiritual clarity that is characteristic of Bhagavan. These dialogues form the majority of this current book.

So even without a clear resolution on its origins, we feel confident that this second selection of teachings will bring tremendous value to those who are open to receiving Bhagavan's grace and guidance. We invite you to explore this book with an open heart and mind, and to treat it as a profound treasure and a mysterious gift. Athreya, the young Indian man from whom we have received the manuscript, wrote the following in the introductory pages of the original manuscript:

'I simply carried out the task of digitisation of this work's contents, and have no idea about their authenticity or otherwise. I believe that the work should be made public and the final decision as to the truthfulness or otherwise of the work's contents ought to be left to the individual reader into whose hands the work might happen to fall.'

Open Sky Press Team, Cologne, March 2025

Foreword

Sri Ramaswamy Reddy

O. P. Ramaswamy Reddy *was a prominent Indian National Congress politician and freedom fighter, former Premier of Madras State, where he was noted for his compassion, and a devoted admirer of Sri Ramana Maharshi. Reddy held Bhagavan in great reverence and visited Sri Ramanasramam, where he sought spiritual solace.*

In 1950 Swami Rajeshwarananda, a resident of the Ashram, received a manuscript from his friend Sri Gajapathi. He planned to arrange publication and so invited Ramaswamy Reddy, a close devotee of Bhagavan, to write the following short foreword. ED

As a devotee of Bhagavan Sri Ramana Maharshi I consider it my blessed God-given opportunity for performing obeisance to him to be given the good fortune of penning a foreword to this book. According to the writer, Sri Gajapathi Aiyyer, he stayed at Sri Ramana Ashram from 5 July 1936 to 31 December 1936 and made notes of the various spiritual advice and anecdotes graciously shared by the Master. I have gone through a few leaves from this manuscript and find the Master's winsome words full of spiritual nectar. I am confident this book will exude utility even beyond the limited circle of Sri Bhagavan's immediate followers. I am looking forward to seeing this book in print and wishing all success to the writer, Sri Gajapathi, and the editor, Swami Rajeshwarananda in all their current and future endeavours.

My humble pranams to Sri Bhagavan Ramana, the embodiment of compassion.

O. P. Ramasamy Reddy (Former Premier of Madras State), 1950

Foreword

Ken Wilber

***Ken Wilber** is a renowned American philosopher and the founder of Integral Theory, a comprehensive framework that seeks to integrate diverse fields of knowledge and human experience. Wilber's Integral Theory aims to bridge the gaps between different world views and encourage a more inclusive, integrative approach to personal growth and global transformation. His work synthesises insights from psychology, philosophy, science, and spirituality, offering a holistic view of human development and consciousness.*

The Sage of the Century

That non-dual vision in the form of *Vedanta*, is the precious gift of India to the world, and it found its purest, most elegant, most brilliant expression in the simple sage of Arunachala, Sri Ramana Maharshi.

His realisation came to him fully formed – or perhaps we should say, fully formless – and therefore it needed no further growth. He simply speaks from and as the absolute, the Self, the purest Emptiness that is the goal and ground of the entire manifest world, and is not other to that world. Sri Ramana, echoing Shankara (Indian sage), used to say:

The world is illusory;
***Brahman* alone is real;**
***Brahman* is the world.**

This profound realisation is what separates Sri Ramana's genuine enlightenment from today's pretenders – deep ecology, Gaia revivals, Goddess worship, ecopsychology, systems theory, web-of-life notions – none of which have grasped the first two lines, and therefore, contrary to their sweet pronouncements, do not really understand the third.

It is for all of those who are only in love with the manifest world – from capitalists to socialists, from green polluters to green peacers, from egocentrics to ecocentrists – that Sri Ramana's message needs so desperately to be heard.

What and where is this Self? How do I abide as That? There is no doubt how Sri Ramana would answer those – and virtually all other – questions: Who wants to know? What in you, right now, is aware of this page? Who is the Knower that knows the world but cannot itself be known? Who is the Hearer that hears the birds but cannot itself be heard? Who is the Seer that sees the clouds but cannot itself be seen?

And so arises Self-enquiry, Sri Ramana's special gift to the world. I have feelings, but I am not those feelings. Who am I? I have thoughts, but I am not those thoughts. Who am I? I have desires, but I am not those desires. Who am I?

So you push back into the Source of your own awareness – what Sri Ramana often called the 'I'-'I', since it is aware of the normal I or ego. You push back into the Witness, the 'I'-'I', and you rest as That. I am not objects, not feelings, not desires, not thoughts.

But then people usually make a rather unfortunate mistake in this Self-enquiry. They think that if they rest in the Self, or Witness, they are going to see something, or feel something, something really amazing, special, spiritual. But you won't see anything. If you see something, that is just another object – another feeling, another thought, another sensation, another image. But those are all objects; those are what you are not.

No, as you rest in the Witness – realising I am not objects, I am not feelings, I am not thoughts – all you will notice is a sense of Freedom, a sense of Liberation, a sense of Release – release from the terrible constriction of identifying with these little finite objects, the little body and little mind and little ego, all of which are objects that can be seen, and thus are not the true Seer, the real Self, the pure Witness, which is what you really are.

So you won't see anything in particular. Whatever is arising is fine. Clouds float by in the sky, feelings float by in the body, thoughts float by in the mind – and you can effortlessly witness all of them. They all spontaneously arise in your own present, easy, effortless awareness.

And this witnessing awareness is not itself anything specific you can see. It is just a vast background sense of Freedom – or pure Emptiness – and in that pure Emptiness, which you are, the entire manifest world arises. You are that Freedom, Openness, Emptiness – and not any little finite thing that arises in it. Resting in that empty, free, easy, effortless witnessing, notice that the clouds are arising in the vast space of your awareness. The clouds are arising within you – so much so you can taste the clouds, you are one with the clouds, it is as if they are on this side of your skin, they are so close. The sky and your awareness have become one, and all things in the sky are floating effortlessly through your own awareness. You can kiss the sun, swallow the mountain, they are that close. Zen says *'Swallow the Pacific Ocean in a single gulp'*, and that's the easiest thing in the world when inside and outside are no longer two, when subject and object are non-dual, when the looker and looked at are One Taste.

And so: The world is illusory, which means you are not any object at all – nothing that can be seen is ultimately real. You are *neti-neti*, not this, not that. And under no circumstances should you base your salvation on that which is finite, temporal, passing, illusory, suffering-enhancing and agony-inducing.

Brahman [absolute reality] alone is real, the Self (unqualifiable *Brahman-Atman*) alone is real – the pure Witness, the timeless Unborn, the formless Seer, the radical 'I'-'I', radiant Emptiness – is what is real and all that is real. It is your condition, your nature, your essence, your present and your future, your desire and your destiny, and yet it is always ever-present as pure Presence, the alone that is Alone.

Brahman is the world, Emptiness and Form are not-two.

After you realise that the manifest world is illusory, and after you realise that *Brahman* alone is real, then you can see that the absolute and the relative are not-two or non-dual, then you can see that *nirvana* and *samsara* are not-two, then you can realise that the Seer and everything seen are not-two, *Brahman* and the world are not-two – all of which really means, the sound of those birds singing! The entire world of Form exists nowhere but in your own present Formless Awareness: You can drink the Pacific in a single gulp, because the entire world literally exists in your pure Self, the ever-present great 'I'-'I'.

Finally, and most important, Sri Ramana would remind us that the pure Self – and therefore the great Liberation – cannot be attained, any more than you can attain your feet or acquire your lungs. You are already aware of the sky, you already hear the sounds around you, you already witness this world. One hundred percent of the enlightened mind or pure Self is present right now – not ninety-nine percent, but one hundred percent.

As Sri Ramana constantly pointed out, if the Self (or knowledge of the Self) is something that comes into existence – if your realisation has a beginning in time – then that is merely another object, another passing, finite, temporal state. There is no reaching the Self – the Self is reading this page. There is no looking for the Self – it is looking out of your eyes right now.

There is no attaining the Self – it is reading these words. You simply, absolutely, cannot attain that which you have never lost. And if you do attain something, Sri Ramana would say, that's very nice, but that's not the Self.

So, if I may suggest, as you read the following words from the world's greatest sage: If you think you don't understand Self or Spirit, then rest in that which doesn't understand, and just that is Spirit. If you think you don't quite 'get' the Self or Spirit, then rest in that which doesn't quite get it, and just that is Spirit. Thus, if you think you understand Spirit, that is Spirit. If you think you don't, that is Spirit. And so we can leave with Sri Ramana's greatest and most secret message: The enlightened mind is not hard to attain but impossible to avoid.

Ken Wilber

Foreword

Pravrajika Divyanandaprana

***Pravrajika Divyanandaprana** is a monastic of Sri Sarada Math and Ramakrishna Sarada Mission. She is a respected teacher and spiritual guide, specialising in Yoga-Vedanta and the teachings of Sri Ramakrishna and Sri Sarada Devi.*

With extensive study in classical texts such as the Bhagavad Gita, Yoga Sutras, *and the* Upanishads, *she has lectured at prestigious institutions like MIT and Princetown University. She is the editor of the English journal* Samvit.

Various levels of knowledge arise from human observation and experience. Classified and categorised they fall under the landscape of the different sciences – objective and subjective. Mind sciences and life sciences have arrived at the fringe of concepts like *prana* [life force], will or intent and consciousness. But what the reader will find in this book is mind-bending. The book, which is a compilation of Sri Ramana Maharishi's teachings drawn from the notes of Gajapathi Aiyyer, during his six-month stay in 1936 at Bhagavan's feet, presents a completely new paradigm, a revolutionary view from a vantage point quite beyond mind. It reveals stunning insights into the very core of human consciousness – a peak into the Unchanging Self. Beyond logic and intellectualising, way beyond our persona and thinking faculties, lies the *Atman*, the True Self of man, which is most immediate and direct, and yet utterly beyond cogitation and speculation.

Bhagavan Sri Ramana Maharishi embodied pure Self-knowledge, the condensed essence of the *Upanishads* [sacred scriptures] and the *Vedic* [most important scriptures in Hinduism] wisdom. Radiant with the light from the very source of all knowledge, the silent Sage of Arunachala offers incisive pathbreaking insights into the fundamental ground of all perception, cognition and – mentation – Pure Being. For the seeker or *sadhaka* the Maharishi's words are pure nectar coming from the very fount of existence. Openly direct and convincing, they speak to the soul rather than the mind.

"Do not go on discussing or talking about it. Do not tell yourself, *'First I shall obtain intellectual mastery over the technique and subsequently shall begin the application thereof.'* Instead – plunge into the practice HERE and NOW; stick to the teachings of any one *Mahanubhavar* [Great Enlightened Being], and all will come right in the end."

Masters are there only to show you the way. Man fogs the fulfilment of their purpose by merely theorising or intellectualising about their respective lives, advents and teachings, such as asking:

"Is this one or that one a Siddhapurusha *[Perfected being],* Muktapurusha *[Liberated soul], or an* Avatarapurusha *[Divine incarnation]*?"

Of course, these are your mental concepts only. In fact, the Master, being not at all different from the formless Absolute seated in the tabernacle of the Sacred Heart of Man, is really synonymous with your own True Self. Being so, why seek him anywhere else?

The path of Ramana Maharishi yields the experiential feel of pure Being. It is gained through incisive Self-enquiry. It is not the path of belief nor of concepts or processes. When asked if the highest state of realisation could be made possible by giving up the idea of individuality, the Maharishi answers:

"You may persuade yourself into believing, *'I am not the body but the Self.'* The consequence will be that your troubles will only increase. One set of mental concepts has been substituted with another."

The questioner counters, *"What* sadhana *[spiritual practice] should I do then?"*

And the light shines forth, **"You need not do anything except to dwell incessantly and intensely on the inner sense of 'I'. That is good *sadhana*."**

Thought, ideation, mentation and memory have all been put into place by the might of the Maharishi's Realisation. When asked, *"Is it not good to remember all the time that I am the Self?"*

He answers, **"And who is the one who is doing the remembering? He is not the Self. He is an arbitrary mental conceptualisation of the mind masquerading as the actual Real Self."**

Bhagavan did not just put the mind in place, but also the visions born of long meditative practices. On page 56 of this book we have the experience of such a devotee. Bhagavan's words sent him into a paroxysm of joy and bliss before the very eyes of those present in the hall:

Later, when Bhagavan was asked, *"This fortunate man who left now – did Bhagavan just give him an experience of the* Sahajastithi *[natural state]?"*

Bhagavan casually replied, **"His mind began to subside in the Heart, and the bliss was objectified as the object of his long contemplation or meditation, manifesting externally as a stupefying vision of mesmerising charm. If the bliss is understood to be not apart from one's Self, one will stop attempting meditation and simply resolve oneself into THAT WHICH IS."**

The uniqueness of the *Upanishadic* path unfolds in the Maharishi's acute observations:

"Asking 'Who am I?' is the only *sadhana* which is such that the one making it is the same as the one in relation to whom it is made. The snake bites its own tail."

The milestones along the path of *Vichara* are clearly outlined – *"How will the 'I'-'I' consciousness manifest itself when the Heart is reached? Will I recognise it?"*

Bhagavan replies, **"Certainly, as pure Subjective Consciousness, free from all thought. It is pristine, unbroken awareness of the Beingness of the Self; there is no mistaking it when it remains uncontaminated by thought or by the faculty of the intellect. When the *Aham Sphurana* actually flashes forth, you will know it alright. Cognition of the *Aham Sphurana* is not based on intellectual corroboration. It is a direct experience of the Self, inferior only to the *Sahajastithi* of the *Jnani* [the Self-realised Sage]."**

Q: Is the Aham Sphurana *something that is felt only by ripe souls?* Bhagavan replied: **Yes.** *Q: What are the others to do then?*

B: (smiling) **Ripen themselves!** *Q: How?* ***B: Vichara abhyasa*** **[Self-enquiry practice] is the way.**

There are faculties higher than the intellect that hold the power to penetrate the laws of existence. Intuition is one such faculty manifest in a developed mind and heart. Our intuition knows and points at things which our informed mind and logic can never know nor explain. With this power up his sleeve, Bhagavan would effortlessly harmonise the paths of *Bhakti* [devotion] and *Jnana* [spiritual knowledge].

"The secret of *Jnana* is *Bhakti*. Unselfish love, motiveless, incessant, intransigent love, is the key that unlocks the gate of the Heart once and for all."

That immortal love which swallows up all the cares and worries of life and liberates the mind unasked, comes into the life of the sincere aspirant as the very fruit of *Jnana*. The *Jnani* radiates this divine love by his very presence and purifies and unifies our divided world. This book in the hands of the reader is a work of such power. The pristine, pure mind of the Master that speaks through this profound volume is bound to bring us to an awakening into the most obvious yet hidden truth of our own existence. Om Sri Ramanaya Namaha!

Pravrajika Divyanandaprana, Sri Sarada Math,
Ramakrishna Sarada Mission, Delhi

Contents

Introduction

John David

***John David** is an English spiritual teacher in the lineage of Sri Ramana Maharshi and Papaji. He is the founder of the international centres for Self-realisation, Open Sky House near Cologne, Germany, and Open Sky Oasis near Valencia in Spain. Both provide a vibrant space for people of all ages and backgrounds to explore spirituality, with a focus on Meditation, Self-enquiry, and Community Living, with the intention to reach Self-realisation.*

As an author and filmmaker, John David offers a transformative approach to Self-realisation, guiding individuals to break free from the limitations of the mind and uncover their True Nature.

After the enthusiastic interest from Bhagavan devotees to our first book from the *Aham Sphurana* Manuscript, namely *Aham Sphurana – A Glimpse of Self Realisation* – which is a selection of Bhagavan's teachings from 5th July 1936 to 31st September 1936 (available on Amazon, with glowing reviews) – we are delighted to present this new volume. This book focuses on Bhagavan's renowned teaching of *Vichara*, the practice of Self-enquiry encapsulated in the fundamental question: Who am I? While this volume is being published, work continues on a third book, *Sharanagati, Surrender*, which will complete a trilogy of invaluable teachings from the *Aham Sphurana* Manuscript. In 2025 the trilogy will be available as a special box set.

Since I came in contact with this manuscript in October 2021, I have been filled with an unstoppable energy to edit this jewel into readable books. It has been a miraculous journey seemingly orchestrated by Bhagavan himself. I was deeply touched by the detailed quality of how Gajapathi reported the teachings. Key elements of Bhagavan's guidance are highlighted, such as the pivotal role of a Master, and surrender as the direct path – both deeply challenging and transformative for most seekers. The manuscript also provided fresh details about his central teaching of Self-enquiry, making this volume indispensable for devotees and seekers alike.

This manuscript captures fascinating dialogues with mature Western seekers, unveiling many lesser-known details about Bhagavan's teachings. The tremendous global interest in Bhagavan's wisdom has led us to publish translations in German, Spanish, Russian and Tamil. French and Dutch translations are currently in preparation. Perhaps you would like to help with translation or proofreading?

In the first months of working with the manuscript selections were made spontaneously, many of which were shared on my website blog, where you can also find a special Bhagavan Sri Ramana Maharshi page. Over time, these were edited and became the basis for the selection found in this book. Initially, only one-on-one teaching dialogues were chosen. Then gradually it became evident that the quality of the detailed reporting of daily life around Bhagavan was seen to reveal new insights into him and it became apparent that these glimpses also contained very valuable practical teachings.

The year 1936 was influential for Bhagavan's teachings. Following the publication of Paul Brunton's *A Search in Secret India* in 1934, many seekers arrived inspired by the complimentary portrait of Bhagavan painted in that book. Major Chadwick (Sadhu Arunachala) arrived in 1935 and continued to live in the Ashram until his death in 1962. Chadwick had welcomed Annamalai Swami (Bhagavan's former close attendant) to share his room. As it turned out, 1936 was the year when many Westerners arrived to meet Bhagavan, giving this record increased value. Among them were many Theosophical Society members staying in Chennai and visitors from Sri Aurobindo's Ashram in Pondicherry who heard about Bhagavan and made their way to meet him.

In 1936, Bhagavan was fifty-six years old, a healthy and active middle-aged man. The Jungle Hermitage described by Paul Brunton was gradually making way for the stone buildings that can be experienced today. The developing Ashram had its own kitchen where Bhagavan was the chief cook and Annamalai Swami was busy arranging the daily construction work under Bhagavan's supervision and guidance. Bhagavan also drew the plans and made design decisions.

In this current volume we have given Sri Gajapathi's story a larger focus as it has become clear that in addition to his remarkable ability with English literature, he was also a gifted teacher. He came to Bhagavan after a powerful dream, seeing him walking on Arunachala. As he faced Bhagavan in their first meeting, there occurred a deep unconditional surrender. From that moment he always said his devotion was his *sadhana* [practice]. Throughout his six-month stay (of which only three months of his diary have survived) it is evident that he was deeply close to Bhagavan. On the last afternoon of his visit, 31st December 1936, Bhagavan invited him to a rare personal meeting, during which a profound energetic transformation occurred, which I surmise was a moment of Self-realisation.

Destiny played a crucial role in the manuscript's preservation for eighty-eight years. Swami Rajeshwarananda, an Ashram resident and Gajapathi's friend, helped Gajapathi pack up his old house. Finding the notebooks in the pile to be burnt, he encouraged Gajapathi to take them to Bhagavan – which together they did in 1948. Bhagavan was overjoyed and gave them his blessings.

Some months after Bhagavan's passing in 1950, Gajapathi sent a completed manuscript to Swami Rajeshwarananda at the Ashram, with a foreword by Mr Reddy, a close devotee and Prime Minster of Madras State (Preface). It appears at that time the Ashram was short on funds and with only a small group of the closest devotees still residing there. Consequently, the manuscript went unpublished. I first came across it on Amazon, downloading it from there in 2021. I was deeply touched and immediately recognised it as a treasure.

Despite its blessings and historical value, the manuscript faced further challenges. At some point it had been typed and stored on computer discs. It appears that a flood at the Gajapathi's family home, partly destroyed these discs or some of the notebooks. Later, part of the original manuscript was typed up in a modern font. In 2019, it was sent to the Ashram by Athreya, a Bhagavan devotee, together with seventeen pages from the original notebooks, but the Ashram declined to publish the manuscript.

In January 2022, during my 22nd annual Bhagavan Homage Retreat in Tiruvannamalai, I approached the Ramana Ashram authorities about the manuscript. Previously I had written three times to the President, Dr Venkat S. Ramanan, offering our publishing team's support in bringing the manuscript to publication. I never received any reply and it soon became clear that, despite having been given the manuscript three years previously, in 2019, the Ashram authorities had no intention to publish it and even responded with unexpected hostility toward Open Sky Press during our efforts to engage with the President, which was both puzzling and disappointing.

Recently, while working on this volume, it became apparent that in 1950 the Ashram had the complete manuscript from Gajapathi's six-month stay in the Ashram. Unfortunately, no other complete copy exists as the portion covering October to December was later lost in the family flood.

Once again destiny stepped in. The situation with the Ashram's hostility left me with some doubts as to the value of publishing, but then a miraculous turn of events occurred. A visitor to one of my meetings introduced me to Swami Hamsananda, the Founder President of the Athithi Ashram, which provides medical care, food and accommodation to *sadhus*. Swami Hamsananda shared some stories from his life, including how, in his twenties, he spent three years sleeping on the floor of Annamalai Swami's tiny bedroom. Annamalai regaled him with wonderful stories of his life with Bhagavan. Later, Swami Hamsananda became an Ashram resident where he looked after the older residents from Bhagavan's time.

He also worked for several years in the publication department of the Ashram. At our last meeting, he told me the quality of the manuscript was of such value that we should plan to publish the entire manuscript in several volumes. He compared it with *Talks*, a book covering talks given by Bhagavan over the same period as the manuscript. In comparison to *Talks with Sri Ramana Maharshi*, which devotes only thirty pages to the period covered in this manuscript – July to September 1936 – our three selections will offer eight hundred pages of detailed teachings, including unique dialogues with Western seekers.

Talks was recorded by Munagala Venkataramiah from 1935 to 1939. He was also Bhagavan's main translator of English and Tamil. It's noticeable that most of the dialogues that Gajapathi Aiyyer recorded with Western visitors are absent from *Talks*. As Bhagavan's primary translator of English and Tamil, Munagala likely found it challenging to take detailed notes while actively translating, which may explain the absence of many dialogues with Western visitors. It is conceivable that Sri Gajapathi stepped in to fulfill this task, capturing a rich collection of dialogues that might otherwise have been lost.

Throughout the months of working with this manuscript, I have come into a deep empathy with Bhagavan himself, which has been profoundly moving. Often it felt almost like being in his meetings. Gajapathi writes beautifully with profound insight and particular sensitivity. His connection with Bhagavan was deeply felt. Over the course of more than a year of daily involvement with this manuscript, my conviction in the authenticity of Sri Gajapathi Aiyyer's part of the manuscript has only grown stronger. The team working on refining this book expanded to five members, each of whom generously donating their time to this labour of love.

The manuscript has appeared through the huge efforts of a Bhagavan devotee, Athreya, an Indian man living in Chennai. Open Sky Press became involved after we made contact with him. He is pleased that we have taken on the publishing of the manuscript. His mother, Nalini, had typed up the manuscript. As a gesture of his affection and trust, Athreya has given us four pages of the original notebooks as written by Gajapathi, as well as some complete notebooks from the 1930s, possibly transcriptions of the originals.

Working with this manuscript has deepened my connection to Bhagavan in ways I couldn't have imagined. The profound insights of Sri Gajapathi Aiyyer's writings and his intimate relationship with Bhagavan have made this project deeply rewarding. Supported by devotees like Athreya, who shared fragments of the original notebooks, this book represents a labour of love and devotion, ensuring that Bhagavan's teachings reach a wider audience.

Thanks to the dedication of a small, passionate team, we have preserved the authenticity and integrity of this manuscript. Collaborating with individuals like Swami Hamsananda of the Athithi Ashram further validated the manuscript's significance. We believe this manuscript is a treasure, not just for its detailed teachings but also for its authentic portrayal of Bhagavan's daily life, the Ashram adventures and the transformative power of his presence.

John David, Director, Open Sky Press, March 2025

Book Formatting

Using these Fonts and Symbols

The following Fonts are used throughout the Book

The Diarist's font........................ Normal
The questioner's font....................... *Italic*
Bhagavan's font.............................. **Bold**
Stories from Bhagavan.................... ***Bold Italic Indented***
Stories from others....................... Normal Indented
Sanskrit word............................... *Italic*

The following Symbols are used throughout the Book

.... Between Questioners or Happenings

.... End of Day or End of a Chapter/Text

Q: Questioner, B: Bhagavan, G: Gajapathi, C: Chadwick,
K: Kunja Swami, Sar: Sarvadhikari, TKS: T.K. Sundaresa Iyer

Further Notes

ED....................................... Editor's Note
Sanskrit word [meaning].............. In the text and a detailed Glossary
Antiquated English.................... Replaced by modern English
August 10th.............................. Meetings are set out in Date Order

Sri Gajapathi Aiyyer

Diarist of the Aham Sphurana Manuscript

Sri Gajapathi Aiyyer

Narrator, Diarist and Bhagavan Devotee

There has not been discovered any confirmed photo of Sri Gajapathi in the Ashram archive. However, this interesting photo from 1936 was for a long time on display in the Ramana Ashram dining room.

Sri Gajapathi stayed in the Ashram from 5th July to 31st Dec 1936 and could very well be the spectacled, cerebral-looking young man marked as number (1), sitting between his presumed friends Major Chadwick (2) to the right and Annamalai Swami (3) standing to his left. The manager Chinnaswami (4) (Bhagavan's brother).

5th July 1936

Gajapathi: Oh! No. The moment I came here and Bhagavan looked at me, I forgot all about myself. Now I think only of Bhagavan, who is already a Jnani. *So for whom am I to ask* Jnana?

B: The secret of *Jnana* [spiritual knowledge] is *bhakti* [devotion]. Unselfish Love – motiveless, incessant, intransigent Love – is the key that unlocks the Gate of the Heart once and for all.

How Gajapathi Met Bhagavan

Swami Rajeshwarananda was a resident of Ramana Ashram in Tiruvannamalai and the friend who prevented Gajapathi from destroying his diaries, then bringing them to show Bhagavan in December 1948. He received the manuscript from Gajapathi in December 1950, after Bhagavan's Mahasamadhi *[death of a realised saint] and later wrote this following introduction. He is buried at the back of the Ashram, which indicates that he was a close devotee to Bhagavan. ED*

Swami Vivekananda has said of Sri Ramakrishna, that *'a mere glance from him could change a whole life.'* I am no Vivekananda, but I proceed to emphatically assert that merely being in the hallowed presence of the Maharshi could bring about a total transformation for the good in one's life. Many have benefited just from seeing his form in the flesh and blood. Which privilege, alas! is denied to us hereafter and some have left glowing accounts that bear testimony to the unique splendour of this unrivalled Master of the world of Spiritualism. Reading accounts of how he, though apparently disinterested, rechartered the lives of many towards the One True Goal, lifts one's spirits and reaffirms faith in the Master.

One such is the case of Sri Gajapathi Aiyyer. He lost his parents when he was very young, in a tragic incident that left him with a sneering, cynical approach to life, one that questioned the need for system regulation and order in a world so tightly ruled by the iron fist of fate. He was raised by his father's sister's family, one I am in acquaintance with, and attempted to be given a B.Sc. Education in the St. Joseph's College at Trichinopoly, but eventually fell into evil ways on account of bad company. He became an anarchist in his views and began to participate in activities that fall within the region of questionable morality. I mention these details without fear that the reader's opinion of the man would be framed in poor light because the transformations that manifested in him should be seen as being exclusively the miraculous work of Sri Bhagavan. Only if one forms a picture of the man as he was before he met the Maharshi, does he realise the magnitude of change that the Master's influence has managed to bring about.

In the early 1930s, he was afflicted with a severe gastroenterological condition that left him unable to eat anything. What the reason is I do not mention here. The family that he was staying with did not know what to do with him. In those days, Western systems of medicine could not be afforded by such small *agraharam* [traditional South Indian Brahmin village] people, whose only affluence was that they abounded in penury. Indeed, they were largely unknown, and everyone depended upon community-made herbal concoctions and decoctions and powders for everything from toothache to muscular sprains. One day a relative brought some *thiruneer* [sacred ash] from the Tiruvannamalai Annamalaiyar Temple. This was secretly mixed in the liquid intake ingested by the boy, and the same night he had a dream in which a yogi wearing nothing but a ragged *koupeenam* [loin cloth] was doing intense *tapas* [disciplined practice] in a cave on the side of a mountain.

Soon the boy recovered but began to brood more and more on the dream because thinking of the yogi mysteriously brought tears in his eyes. Then someone in the family told him he had recovered only by the grace of Lord Annamalaiyar, because only after consuming the *thiruneer* secretly mixed in his liquid diet for a few days did he begin consuming solid food again. The youth was enraged when he learnt that they had been mixing things in his intake without obtaining his permission beforehand, but when his anger cooled down, he paid heed to his elders' advice to visit the Annamalaiyar Temple and express gratitude for the recovery to *Lord Shiva*. Thus, never having heard of Tiruvannamalai before, he visited there with his aunt's family.

Proclaiming before starting, *'Don't think I will bow before* Shiva. *If* Shiva *Himself personally appears before me and begs me to do obeisance to him, I may oblige. Otherwise, there is no chance... I am coming with you only to admire the architecture of the temple since you say that it is very grand and marvellous...'* Notwithstanding his blasphemous attitude and speech, they started. When the train reached close enough to the Arunachala Hill, the boy was flabbergasted to see the same mountain that he had seen in his dream. After the temple visit, he was very keen to find out if the portion of his dream of the yogi performing penance in a cave on the Hill was also true. He made enquiries as to whether there was any such cave and person. He was told that nowadays the yogi no longer stayed up on the Hill and that his followers had constructed an Ashram for him.

The yogi's name? Sri Ramana Maharshi. The boy, much to the astonishment of the family members, wanted to visit the yogi. They went to Sri Ramana Ashram. What happened next was that the young man, in the middle of his 20s, began to behave like an infant with its mother, and refused outright to leave the presence of the Sage, whose glance seemed to have touched some chord deep within him. He tearfully requested the Sage to give him *diksha* [spiritual initiation] into his Order of Monks. The Sage was not forthcoming with any reply but sat motionless. The boy did not budge either but continually tried to persuade Sri Bhagavan to give him *sannyasa* [monastic life], saying repeatedly, *'Now, you are my only hope...'* Ashramites (residents of the Ashram) told him that there was no Order in the Ashram. He refused to believe it, saying, *'Because I am young you want to dissuade me from taking* sannyasa.*'* Meanwhile, his relatives were totally shocked to see the boy's instantaneous decisive jump to the exact opposite end of the spectrum.

They pleaded with Sri Bhagavan to bless the boy with a well-paying job and a happy married life, at which juncture the boy glared at them angrily through his tear-filled eyes. Sri Bhagavan did not give any reply to this either. Eventually, they permitted the boy to stay for six months, fearing that if they completely refused to yield, he might run away and they might never see him again. Cheap accommodation was found in the town for him. After this stay at Tiruvannamalai, the boy had changed completely. When his relatives came to take him back to Tiruchirappalli, they feared he might want to stay for a still longer duration, but the boy had become silent and withdrawn and left with them without protest or demur. Now, what miraculous operation of ego exorcism did Bhagavan, Our Light and Our Way, perform on this boy?

Madras December 1950

Gajapathi's Love for Bhagavan

Sri Gajapathi Aiyyer's background life story told in his own words. ED

I was born in Tirupattur, near Trichinopoly. At fifteen I lost my parents. I was taken to my father's sister's house in Trichinopoly, near the Rock Fort. I was given a good education and made to enrol in St. Joseph's College, in the B.Sc. Chemistry program. I soon fell into undesirable habits owing to evil *vasanas* [structures of the mind] dormant in me, as I now realise with the benefit of hindsight. As the days passed, I grew worse. One day I collapsed from what I thought was stomach pain. The professional diagnosis was partial cirrhosis of the liver accompanied by intestinal bleeding. I had hidden my vile habits from my conservative family, but through the doctor, they came to know of it. They were deeply shocked and asked me what fault it was in their upbringing that had caused me to go astray.

I had no reply and hung down my head in shame. I became depressed and decided that I wanted to die. To that effect, I threw away the doctor's medicines but pretended that I was taking them to keep my family happy. I grew sick and weak and I was convinced every night that I would never wake up to see the light of day again. One day, by Bhagavan's miracle, the illness abated. The same mysterious miracle found me, a complete non-believer, at Sri Ramana Ashram begging for Bhagavan's *diksha*, on the evening of 5th July 1936. I was told there was no Order there, although I observed several swamis wearing saffron robes present at the place.

I wanted to stay there permanently. My family permitted me to stay for six months and left after finalising some inexpensive lodging for me in the town, some distance away from the Thirumanjana Gopuram (gateway tower) of the Arunachaleshwara Temple (main *Shiva* temple in Tiruvannamalai). They knew I did not mind walking long distances but enjoyed long walks. These six months and thereafter I performed only one *sadhana*, Love for the Master. Which is the same as total relinquishment of my will so as to facilitate His to take over. His eyes have arrested the activities of my soul. I became as a snake facing a snake charmer's flute, unable to think of my personal self (including education, career, employment, possible future and the like). Love for him flooded my soul and I had no idea why. The sum total of the mind and mental faculties became only this love and everything else seemed ridiculously trivial, unsubstantial, unimportant and dream-like. He did not display any *siddhis* [spiritual powers] except this one: he made me fall in love with him.

I must explain that this love was an experience in that it was not anything I did but rather something I felt. It was and is utterly ecstatic in nature. Sometimes, sitting in the Hall looking at the figure on the Sofa, tears would begin to well up in my eyes and I would hastily wipe them away. Why tears? If I knew, reader, I would not hesitate to tell you. I was evidently not alone in this strange experience, for I observed the same thing was happening to a man sitting at the Master's feet, who would keep watching the Maharshi's face intently and then allow silent tears to fall on his lap, moistening his white *vaetti* [cloth wrap for the lower body]. I later learnt that this simple looking man was the celebrated master poet Muruganar, who had written many poems about Sri Bhagavan in Sangathtamizh (pure Tamil language). The love I have for the Master is not sustained by an effort of the will; I have no conscious role in it. When people mean they love someone, they think they like him or her. This is love motivated and sustained at the level of the intellect, through thoughts about the object loved.

I am not talking about this kind of love at all. Here, there are no thoughts, only effortless awareness of being, which surges up to swallow the thought-making faculty whole as soon as it is invoked and thereafter remains by itself shining as Blissful Love. I am perfectly aware that this love is indeed only a prelude to *Brahmajnana* [the state Bhagavan was in], for the Master has said that in *Samadhi* [Union with Reality] there is Perfect Peace and no sensation of experiencing anything. Was this love towards Bhagavan not desirable or advisable, then? I thought so in the beginning, but later came to realise that it was Bhagavan himself. *'The Love that shines in the cavity of the Heart as 'I'-'I' when the turbulent mind is stilled in its source is known as the vision of the* Nijaswarupam *[true form] of the Guru.'*

I would read this later amongst one of the poems shown to me by an Englishman I met in the Ashram, Major Alan Chadwick. This towering, booming Caucasian had served in His Majesty's army during the Great War. Reading Paul Brunton's *A Search in Secret India* had convinced him that Bhagavan was his Guru and straightaway he had sailed over, remaining in the Ashram grounds ever since. (Major Chadwick died Easter Sunday 1962.) Remarkably, he told me one day, *'Bhagavan himself has acknowledged explicitly that the connection existing between him and myself is ancient, that it has carried over across several scores of previous births.'* I pointed out to him not to repeat such statements in the future, at least whilst I was in the vicinity, as I did not wish to hear anything derogatory about Bhagavan. *'Why, what is derogatory about it, young man?'* he asked in some surprise. I responded, *'The Avatar has no bondage, not in the present, past or future. He comes only for the salvation of humanity, in this one birth expressly graciously assumed for the purpose. Suggesting that he was born in the past means implying that our Bhagavan was in bondage in the past. Such a view is not only blasphemous but also absurd.'*

He did not seem pleased by the remark, saying, *'It was the Master Himself who said so; I am not saying it.'* In general, however, interaction with people in the Ashram was exceedingly rare; I preferred then as ever to keep myself to myself, or rather myself to Bhagavan. The Love I felt for Him had no physical or psychic token that one could observe from outside. I did not, for instance, try to touch his feet or plant my head on his feet, as I have observed people doing. I have also not had any trance-like experiences or visions. I cannot say that I tried to cultivate love for Him, but rather say that coming into his presence Love recognised itself to be Love and thus ceased to crave after an object to love. This experience of True Love was its own reciprocation and did not crave recognition from an outside source. Yet, I occasionally fancied that Bhagavan's eyes shone at me whenever he looked at me.

One might wonder coming into a *Brahmajnani's* [person with knowledge of the Eternal Reality] presence why the pupil should not try practising *jnana yoga* [path of self-knowledge] to obtain liberation, instead of adopting the sentimental *bhakti* [unselfish love for God] path. However, where was the volition in me to commence any *sadhana*? *Sadhana* wants to achieve something and progress toward some goal. The more time I spent in Bhagavan's presence, in fact, the more incapable I grew of performing any form of *sadhana*. I could palpably feel my individual sense of volition waning and waning, till the point was reached when I no longer thought about when, how and in what manner I could attain *Brahmajnana* – my supreme priority on the day I first set eyes upon him and was trying to persuade him into giving me *diksha*. Compared to this nectar-like experience of ambrosial Love that has descended on me like the primordial deluge and destroyed the tendency of my mind to seek out happiness from objects of sense pleasure, the question of even my soul's Salvation, that is, the merging of the *jivatman* [individual soul] with the *paramatman* [supreme Self], or *Atmasakshatkaram* [Self-realisation], seemed to have faded into an abyss of total non-importance and irrelevance.

I no longer felt responsible for anything, because I had stopped perceiving needs. The dream body fulfilled its dream requirements by making use of dream objects, that was all. Bhagavan's gracious Love was the only thing that seemed Real. Three or four days after my arrival here I was gripped by a meaningless desire to record the conversations going on in the Hall. I tried to drive the desire away but soon had to oblige, because if I obliged, I was peacefully immersed in the Love current I have mentioned, whereas if I resisted, awareness of the current became dim, and I was plunged headlong into misery.

It may be asked if the Master was himself averse to notes being made. I do not think so. When he finally did see my notebooks (p. 20) he even had a kind word to throw in about it. These rules were framed by the management and he had nothing to say about it. Of course, he had a say in it, but he said nothing. He was really supremely aloof from everything. It was not that he bore a flippant or frivolous attitude towards the world; indeed, he was careful never to hurt but always to help. It was merely that there was no world available to him to see. The world as the world, had for him vanished long ago and now, no matter what was seen, it was only the Seer who was seeing Himself. Left to his own way, he would live in the forests and happily thrive on leaves and roots.

This post of 'Bhagavan' was irksome to him and the Sofa he considered a cage. This impression one was able to arrive at when one studied his behaviour closely. As I walked to the Ashram in the morning from the temple, I would be filled with the joyous anticipation of seeing his blessed face, and as I walked back late into the night, with that of recounting the words he had uttered that day on paper. I slept on an average only two hours per day, but mysteriously it had no adverse impact on my health for my Master saw to that. Thus, when I bid a tearful farewell to Bhagavan on 31st December 1936, my notebooks accompanied me away from Ramana Ashram, as a secret token of His Grace.

13th July 1936

Gajapathi Describing Bhagavan

Whilst compiling this manuscript I can see I have largely ignored the opportunity to question Bhagavan. He watches others raise questions and doubts. He records the conversations. Why does he not himself feel tempted to ask any question of the Sage, except for a handful of occasions? Does he assume his own omniscience? Or perhaps he imagines that Bhagavan might not be able to answer his queries? It is nothing of the kind, gentle reader. Put your anxieties at rest, please.

Many who come to the Ashram are raised on a background of *Vedanta* (the culmination of *Vedic* knowledge, including the *Upanishads*, Brahmasutras, and Bhagavad Gita). They are able to tackle Bhagavan on various theories and hypotheses that they have come across in books. I have no such background.

One of my maternal uncles was, at the time I was a teenager, district library superintendent. I could pick up whatever book I liked, provided I either renewed it or returned it on time, and no money need be expended from my pocket.

Being somewhat of an introverted character in those days, I would thus fill all my spare time, of which I had a lot, in reading everything from Geoffrey Chaucer to Robert Louis Stevenson. My background therefore was in English Literature, so I knew nothing pertaining to the various doctrines relating to theories of creation, et cetera. My appetite for library books chiefly revolved around fiction, especially castaway fiction. Not without some sheepishness I admit that my principal favourite authors at the time were Frances H. Burnett, L. Frank Baum, Lewis Carroll, Charles Kingsley, R.M. Ballantyne, Erskine Childers, Johann David Wyss and A.C. Doyle (for Holmes). That does not mean I restricted myself to this list. I also read Edward Gibbon, J.C. Stobart, Thomas Nashe, Henry James, George Bernard Shaw, E.M. Forster, Nicholas Breton, Francis Bacon, John Donne, Robert Burton, Thomas Hobbes, John Evelyn, Friedrich Schlegel,

Johann Wolfgang von Goethe, Ben Jonson, Thomas Overbury, Thomas Browne, John Aubrey, Giacomo Casanova, Margaret Cavendish, Francis Godwin, John Milton, Ivan Turgenev, Nikolai Gogol, Bram Stoker, Jules Verne, Miguel de Cervantes, H.G. Wells, James Joyce, Edgar A. Poe, Louisa M. Alcott, O. Henry, Guy de Maupassant, Oscar Wilde, Jerome K. Jerome, Walter Scott, Joseph Conrad, Alexandre Dumas, Dickens, D.H. Lawrence, Tolstoy, Anton Chekov, Dostoevsky, Jane Austen, George Eliot, Herman Melville, Victor Hugo, Jonathan Swift, Henry Fielding, Aphra Behn, Frederick D. Maurice, Tobias Smollett, Frances Burney and anything else I could lay hands on and that appealed to my fancy – but it had to be fiction. I had no taste for metaphysics, philosophy, essays, speeches, textbook-style historical accounts or anything of the kind.

It was a chance encounter with these two books that introduced the awakening of some throb of yearning in me, that till today I am at a loss to explain the nature of: *The Pilgrim's Progress* by John Bunyan and *Ramakrishna The Man-Gods* by Romain Rolland. The first I chanced upon whilst at school, and the second, the year before college.

Whilst reading these two main books I would weep without knowing the reason; some strange yearning took possession of my soul and electrified the entirety of my whole. I wanted to fall in love. Not with woman or man, for that would be fleeting, transient business. I wanted to replicate what Ramakrishna had done with *Bhavatharini* [the Divine Mother]. I wanted my love to be accepted by the one who sustained this cosmos by Her will. For then alone would I have the solace of knowing my Love to be immortal. There is not the least sexual tinge to this Love; this clarification becomes necessary because some minds are quick to interpret all love as being of an amorous nature.

Neither is this Love what one harbours towards family members, friends and pet animals; that is boring attachment amounting in some cases to, at the most, affection of a long-standing nature. This Love has passion in it. One feels one's chest is going to explode with it any time. One feels like singing and dancing with the joy of it. Yet what precisely it is about that one is clueless. The mystery of the matter adds to the ardour of the Love.

Till 5th July 1936 I never succeeded in discovering the object of this Love. On that day when my Lovely Master, who is Love Itself, locked his eyes with mine in a tight embrace that lasted for one moment in Eternity but from which there could really be no disentanglement or disaffiliation, I discovered my Love's Love. I discovered Bhagavan. Had I read metaphysics I could ask him questions about how the world had come to be. I had read, by the way, only to kindle this magical Love, which had nothing to ask, expect or anticipate.

Sadhana may be a chore; I have not attempted it. I would not know but this Enchantress called Love, She is a Divine privilege. She does not ask your concentration. She gracefully and effortlessly absorbs it into Herself. What is left? Only She – Love. Since She had never any doubts to ask, I never really had anything to say to Bhagavan at all, because, quixotically, I recognised Her to be the internal Bhagavan shining from within.

The outer Bhagavan was the banner for the Love that my Heart resonated with. And he proved by his perpetual, rock-like presence that the Love was not some delusional madness, that it was corroborated by physical reality, by a legitimate source for its sweet fountain-spring of ambrosial nectar. Although being Divine, it must necessarily transcend all physicality.

Therefore, it was indispensable that he should remain outside, because my Love would otherwise become a vain dream once again, with no possible legitimacy for its sustenance or survival. He was there, that was enough!

I could happily bask in the rays of His Glorious Love! Within, I felt only Bhagavan's Love radiating, and in front of my eyes I found, again, only him. So what should the Bhagavan within have to say to the Bhagavan without? He is everywhere by His Grace – what would He have to say to Himself, tell me, Oh! Revered Reader?

The first reason being Love, the second is awe. Whenever I enter His presence, my own inconspicuousness becomes apparent to me, and I shrink before His majestic grandeur. He is the last person to give Himself any airs. For this precise reason, one feels foolishly redundant saying even 'I' in His presence. If saying 'I' is ruled out, where is the scope to say anything else, tell me, Oh! Revered Reader?

Before meeting the Master, I wanted *Brahmajnana*. I wanted to escape from the wheel of births and deaths. Soon after, I dropped all such foolish ideas. When we have found the Lord Himself, can then anything be asked of Him? The thing supremely worthy to be asked for is verily Him; when He is found, what to ask, what remains to be asked for? Thus, after meeting Him on the first occasion, the idea that I am personally responsible for my Salvation, or for anything at all, gradually faded out and died. Hereafter only He counted, only He mattered. For He alone is my Love. When one does not consider the personal self to be worth a single strand of hair, will he ask anxious questions about its ultimate fate and scope for Salvation, tell me, Oh! Revered Reader? Thus, the above factors are the reasons why I usually never encountered the need to question the Maharshi on anything.

13th August 1936

Bhagavan the Vedic Rishi

I must here make the observation that when Bhagavan reads out Sanskrit verse, it feels and sounds as though *Veda Vyasa* [sage who wrote the *Mahabharata]* himself is doing so. It makes one wonder what a miracle it is that a *Rishi* from the era of *Vedic* India should actually live in our midst today. I ruminate as to how many know that the world actually contains such a rare gem. After the publication of Mr Brunton's book, *A Search in Secret India*, I muse to myself that there must be many around the globe, as evidenced by the fact that almost invariably, since the time of my arrival here, thrice a week a new Caucasian face shows up at the Ashram; and not all come for *Brahmajnana* or to even intellectually acquaint themselves with the doctrine of *Ajata Advaita* [highest philosophy of non-duality, or 'uncreated non-duality'] taught by the Master.

What is the reason for the fascination? The person of the Sage himself! He possesses and exudes an invisible magnetic charm that cannot fail to mesmerise the sensitive heart. I feel fortunate to be captivated by his dizzying aura. I wonder how many like me have already been trapped in his unrelenting net of Grace by his charismatic persona. The idea of beholding a *Vedic Rishi* in the flesh excites the curiosity of people. So far one has read about *Rishis* only in mythological fables. Yet here he is, in the flesh and blood, living amongst us mortals! Anyone who has heard him but once will agree that Bhagavan's divine voice and euphonious melody in giving animated life to the words of poet saints can never be forgotten. His mere presence guarantees peace, but his cadence whilst reading out poetic works brings incomparable solace to restless minds. I am sure that if I had eyes that could peep into the heavens, I would now see the *Devas* [Gods] pausing in their work.

December 1936

Sri Gajapathi Leaving Ramana Ashram to Marry

At the end of 1936, my family had decided on Vaidehi to be my wife; she was a close relative and known to me. A letter arrived at the Ashram addressed to me and I was informed of their decision. My aththai (paternal aunt) had decided that if I were not married at the end of my stay at Ramana Ashram, I would become a *sannyasi* [an ascetic], which idea was abhorrent to her. So, she had written to me saying that in February 1937, I was to get married. It was not a question of asking my opinion; they had already finalised it and I was merely to fall in line.

I showed the letter to Bhagawan. He read it slowly and with great attentiveness. Then Bhagavan folded the letter and handed it back, extending it towards me, the piece of paper held out between his right index and middle fingers, saying: ***'Keep it.'*** I took it back and anxiously asked, *'Should I run away from home to avoid it?'*

The Master did not make a response, but somebody in the Hall had this to say to me: *'When the question of renunciation was being discussed, you yourself, sitting in this very Hall, once said that only cowards run away and that one must, according to Bhagavan's teachings, throw the weight of one's burdens on the Higher Power and carry on with the life of outward action.'* Somebody else now subtly made the observation that the Master himself had run away from home at the age of sixteen.
B: I did not think, *'I am running away.'* That is the difference.

G: So, if I do not think 'I am running away,' *I can run away?*
B: One who does not think, *'If I do not think, can I do as I please?'* has ceased to struggle against the apparent will of the Higher Power and has given up his cares and concerns for good, having long ago stepped aside to make way for the intellect to fall into the dictatorship of the numinous intuition that arises in those who have surrendered without reserve.

The actions of the intellect and body of the *jiva* [individual soul] that has unreservedly surrendered itself to the Almighty are guided by Him; the mind that is lost as a result of such surrender does not remain to concern itself as to their repercussions or moral propriety. He (the *jiva* who has genuinely surrendered himself) is not responsible for what goes on. Some power takes hold of his body and makes him do things. He is not involved.

G: If I surrender to the Higher Power, can I avoid this impending marriage?
B: One who has surrendered with an ulterior motive has not surrendered at all. Is it possible to deceive God?

G: If I marry, I may not have the mental strength to refrain from sexual activities and they might become unavoidable for that reason. Therefore, Self-realisation will become impossible.
B: That is your opinion.

G: So, running away from home is no good?
B: You may take it from me, that it will make your situation much worse.

G: What is the recourse left for me then?
B: *Ananya Sharanagati* [unconditional surrender].

G: If, after that sharanagati, *I get married, entangled in the horrific woes of* samsara *and therefore fail to Realise the Self?*
B: No one remains after *sharanagati* to complain *'I have not Realised the Self,'* or ask, *'Even after* sharanagati, *why am I yet to Realise?'* or to raise any other doubt or complaint. It is a state of perfect *mounatapas* [austerity of silence]. First, learn what *sharanagati* is. It is to merge in the source of the ego.

G: So, it seems that I am to surrender once and for all, and not care about what happens afterwards?
B: Yes. Yes, that is it.

Therefore, I had to get married and there was nothing I could do about it. I initially wondered why I had to go through such hell, while others in the Ashram were happily settled there forever at Bhagavan's feet.

Then I decided Bhagavan's will was in operation and that whatever happened, happened with his knowledge only and therefore there was no reason to feel upset. Obedience to his will is my only priority now; my own personal salvation or deliverance from the wheel of births and deaths does not count anymore.

This conviction is the fruit of my intense spiritual training under his watchful eye; the only *sadhana* was Love, and that meant the same as surrender, the disappearance of the faculty of personal will and meek, unquestioning obedience to the Master's will or God's will.

1948

Saving the Manuscript from Being Burned

In the words of Swami Rajeshwarananda, Sri Gajapathi's friend and supporter. ED

Soon after leaving Ramana Ashram, Gajapathi married and then went to Madras for further studies, in Law. Thereafter, he went abroad and returned only after Independence.

In 1948, Gajapathi Aiyyer shifted to Madras for employment reasons. He was now an ex-Civil Serviceman and a newly established practising advocate. Since he had no plans for offspring, he wanted to be near relatives who were in that city, so that when old age attacked him, he would have someone to draw physical support from. Psychologically I know that Sri Bhagavan has been his pillar of support from the moment the Master's eyes looked onto his for the first time. He had, with my encouragement, decided to move to Madras.

I visited him when he was bundling the contents of his somewhat dilapidated house at Trichinopoly into oblong tin crates, to be shifted to Madras. In one corner was a heap of old yellowed-with-age documents. He said he wanted it burned and asked whether it would be better to do so near the well in the backyard, since the heap was huge and the fire could become unwieldy. The house being of the olden *agraharam* type and made mostly out of wooden beams and rafters, one had to exercise caution. Smilingly recollecting the impetuous pre-Bhagavan Gajapathi from a decade earlier, I agreed, and we both carried the bundles to the backyard.

I noticed a few notebooks that were filled in his scrupulous, tidy writing. They did not seem like account books or case files. So, I asked Gajapathi what they were. He laughed and said, *'Oh! That! You remember the six months I spent in Tiruvannamalai with* Bhagavan? *I made notes of whatever Bhagavan did and said every day during those six months, every night in my lodgings.'* I asked him why he did not want to preserve these memories. *'HE is Here'*, said Gajapathi, thumping the right-hand side of his chest with his fist. I told him that these volumes might not be useful to him anymore, but those at Ramana Ashram, not excluding Bhagavan himself, would relish memoirs pertaining to the Master. *'Oh, no! Please don't tell Bhagavan! It will become a big* abacharam *[offence]. I did not seek his permission before writing these.'*

I told him it was alright, that I had observed Sri Devaraja Mudaliar (a resident of the Ashram) maintaining a similar record. I told him that Bhagavan had only encouraged Mudaliar and not upbraided him, but he was adamant and went on saying, *'If Bhagavan asks me why I have done such an act without asking him first, where will I take and keep my face? It will be considered as* Gurunindhanai *[disrespect towards the Guru], for which there is no atonement in the three worlds. Even God cannot remedy the offence done to the Guru. I will be condemned to Eternal Damnation. Everyone will say, what an* abacharam *he has committed against Bhagavan.'*

I tried to reason with him further, but that only upset him into quietly saying, *'What has prompted you to visit me at this busy hour, I wonder? Why don't you visit me next week at Madras? Vaidehi has already left. She is at her brother's house in Madras. Shall I give you the address?'* Saying so, he reached for the can of kerosene. I deftly caught hold of his wrist, and shouted, *'If the first* abacharam *is writing these diaries secretly, the second is destroying them secretly. A wise man stops with the first.'*

Gajapathi stopped dead. He seemed paralyzed by fear. *'What to do now?'* he asked. He was sitting on the floor with his hands on top of his head. *'I have lost everything.'* I said, *'Let us show it to Bhagavan, and let him judge.'* Eventually he agreed to this proposal.

December 1948

Sri Gajapathi Visiting Bhagavan with His Diaries

In December 1948 Sri Gajapathi Aiyyer and his friend Swami Rajeshwarananda took a trunk containing half a dozen notebooks to Ramana Ashram and it was unpacked in front of Bhagavan.

In Aham Sphurana *p.231 (2022) we published photo examples of pages from these notebooks and had their paper authenticated by Institute of Conservation Sciences, Cologne, as being from the 1930s. ED*

Bhagavan ran through the books patiently. They are hardbound notebooks, all of the same variety, done in beautiful red rexine. The pages are serially numbered from one to three hundred, in black ink. The pages opening onto the left-hand side have their number inscribed at the top left corner and those on the right-hand side at the top right corner. The pages are lined with bluish lines in narrow spacing, and filled with young Gajapathi's meticulous note-making competencies, all written in pencil.

Bhagavan smiled and said, ***'See, how nicely the child has written everything!'***
Swami Rajeshwarananda: Gajapathi feels that he has committed an offence by chronicling your words without having sought out your permission.
B: Does not matter.

Gajapathi: I only wrote for my own recollection; if shown to others, will it not lead to confusion? Bhagavan gives specific advice to individual persons on spiritual matters; if shown to an unrelated person will that person not erroneously think that the advice is also applicable to his own case, and so mislead himself, with unwarranted consequences? Yet Swami Rajeshwarananda wants to make it available for all in the Ashram to inspect.

Swami Rajeshwarananda: Bhagavan's words are more solemn and sacred than the Upanishads *[sacred Hindu scriptures] even. Why opine they could mislead anyone?*

B: Somebody may have the same doubts as that of the entries in these books.

Gajapathi: But Bhagavan gives different responses to the same question to different persons, depending upon individual temperament!
B: If the reply found is not satisfactory, the search continues! The earnest seeker does not make himself content with the receipt of a response felt by him to be unsuitable, or only partially satisfactory. An intellect made subtler and subtler by repeated and prolonged submergence in Being, will automatically reject advice that directs it away from the Heart.

Practising firm permanence in the Shining of the Heart strengthens the faculty of intuition to the extent that it seeks out, time and again, only those words that redirect its course toward the self-resplendent Heart; such discrimination is not a function of the fictitious sense of individual free will; rather, it is automatic and comes by God's Grace to the sincere seeker.

Gajapathi was about to say something, but it was time for the *veda parayanam* [*Vedic* chanting in Ramana Ashram] to begin.
Bhagavan, reaching for his stick, remarked before leaving:
There is a destiny guiding the course of events. One need not fret about anything, imagining oneself to be personally responsible for it.

Plan to Publish the Manuscript

Swami Rajeshwarananda and myself (Gajapathi) wish to make the contents of these notebooks available to a wider audience. Swami Rajeshwarananda has discussed the idea with myself and I agreed to make a combined synopsis out of the notebooks, so that the Masters teachings shining in them may be published as a convenient teaching reference.

Swami Rajeshwarananda suggests that this book should be published first by an Indian publisher, preferably Gita Press. I have no objection. My own views are that Bhagavan's teachings are for the entirety of mankind. Who picks up the book in which corner of the globe for publication, is not very relevant. These precious teachings should survive the test of time, that is my only agenda.

I was asked to suggest a title for the work. I have chosen *Aham Sphurana* because Bhagavan taught us that this state of consciousness is the doorway leading to final Realisation. I am confident that there is going to be no difficulty in finding a publisher for this work, for Bhagavan's words are nectar-like and bring peace to the reader immediately, in the long run turning his mind towards its source, *Parabrahman* [the Supreme Self].

Many classic texts on *Advaita* exist. They describe elaborately the state of the *Sahajajnani* [liberated sage] or *Stithaprajna* [one who is firmly established in wisdom]. It is not of much use to the *sadhaka*, in my opinion, because he craves for practical instructions he can follow, not descriptions of what remains after the final goal has been reached. No one who has reached the final goal would be interested in reading about it because they would BE it. So, both ways, these books are purposeless.

Maybe they kindle people's curiosity about this state, thus starting them on the path to *sadhana*, with the thought, *'Does such a state really exist behind and beyond the waking, dream, and deep sleep states? Can I also not reach this state?'* As far as my limited intellect sees, this can be their only utility. Bhagavan's words, on the other hand, are uniquely beautiful and pure *sadhana* – even reading or listening to them qualifies to be regarded as a form of *sadhana*, let alone putting them into practice, and this is because they lay bare the means to the One Perfect Reality, without the scum of conceptual or intellectual knowledge having to be surmounted first. There is no theory, only practice. There is no intellection, only experience. There is no misery, only ecstasy. There is no mental activity, only awareness. There is nothing, only Bhagavan, whom I regard as the loftiest attainable pinnacle of Divine Love.

Some might ask why, going to a *Jnani* [Self-realised sage] did this man not follow the path of *Jnana Vichara* [contemplation of wisdom] he advocates, but instead chose to worship the Maharshi as a personal God or deity? I have no answer. I was swept away in his deluge of Love the moment his eyes fell on me, and thereafter no one remained to have the desire to engage in *Vichara* or other forms of *sadhana*.

I would like here to place on record my undying gratitude for Swami Rajeshwarananda, through whose unselfish efforts and by whose reason this book will come into existence.

31st December 1948

Gajapathi's Last Talk with Bhagavan

Yesterday the Maharshi said something that upset my composure completely. It was his usual remark on the inevitability of destiny, but for the first time, I heard it from him in an unusually personal sense. Usually, he would endorse the *prarabdha* [inevitable karmic consequences] doctrine when asked, but yesterday it was not a doctrine which was uttered. It reflects ominously in my mind, but he will not explain further. Perhaps I must steel myself for some shock that I shall receive in the near future. Perhaps someone known to me for many years may die, a family member, a friend. Or perhaps something may happen to me. However, when I run these possibilities against my mind, they do not ruffle it. My own death even is only an eventual certainty for a mortal body and in relation thereto I feel not the slightest unease.

Only one horrific, monstrous possibility produces fear in my heart and reduces me into a whimpering, defenceless puppy: loss of my Love. True death is not destruction of the body, but a so-called life which has not experienced this Love, which is not life at all, but death imagining itself to be life. Who is my Love? This towering personification of Divine Wisdom, wearing only a frail body and a *koupeenam* [loin cloth] and in appearance resembling an impoverished peasant, is in fact the wielder of the most powerful weapon on Earth, that of Divine Love. This Divine Love is the primordial essence out of which everything is in fact made from Jehovah to Lucifer. This Divine Love bears one name only, Bhagavan Ramana.

Today in the afternoon I must go back to Madras. In the morning I seek Maharshi's leave. He does something unexpected, and asks the attendant to pick up a sheet of paper and pencil and hand it to him. He neatly folds with the fingernail of his thumb and tears off a breadth wide strip, scribbles something on the little paper piece and hands it to me. It is the words **'மதியம் வா' 'come in the afternoon'**. Nowadays the Ashram has the practice that for some time after the noon meal, Bhagavan must rest. No one is permitted to go inside then. Sri Bhagavan was giving me the warrant to enter at this time. Overjoyed, the uncertainties of the previous day forgotten, I bow low and take a seat in the Hall, happily watching His face.

Gajapathi Leaves Bhagavan Self Realised

This headline is a natural discovery from translating the Tamil Bhagavan spoke in this extraordinary last meeting with Sri Gajapathi where it appears Bhagavan's strong energy field caused Gajapathi a glimpse or permanent Self-realistion. ED

At noon I enter the Jubilee Hall. The attendant seems to be expecting me. Someone else tries to follow me inside but he is promptly stopped. Sri Bhagavan looks at me with a tenderness that I can never describe.
'என்ன?' 'What?' he asks. I look at Him with a pain I do not understand.
I said to him: *'I feel nervous after what Bhagavan told me yesterday.'*
B: What is it that you mean by Bhagavan?

G: *Pardon, but YOU!*
B: He sighs and motions for the attendant to leave the room. The

attendant who also seems moved for some perplexing reason, bows and makes his exit.

That attitude must go. I cannot be lost.

G: *I do not understand.*

B: The discarding of this body (striking himself on the right-hand side of the chest) **is inevitable. The Real Bhagavan**...

But what his next words were I never managed to find out. The next thing I remember was Bhagavan waving his palm in a dismissive gesture towards the door. Bhagavan's voice saying, **'ஒன்றும் இல்லை, ஒன்றும் இல்லை'** ***'there's nothing, there's nothing'***, the disappearance of a few heads that were framed between door and doorway, and the shutting of the door. I imagine I must have screamed or struck the wall with my fist or banged my head against the floor or some such thing. I do not remember what I did. My bare body and *dhoti* [traditional garment worn by men in India] were covered in a huge mass of vomit. I could not lift my head off the floor. My body was paralysed and benumbed.

Bhagavan's voice was gently saying something. The ears heard but the brain did not process the signals. Minutes later the Sage's compassionate face loomed over mine. He was squatting on the floor and cleaning my body with a white rag and water from an earthen pitcher. I was horrified to have him attend upon me, but I could not move. Minutes later, he pressed his head down on my chest, and the body became relaxed, the hard breathing ceased. I sat up and said:

'Had a dream in which Bhagavan was saying... but in the same room surely...?'

B: He motioned for me to stop talking. **You have been wanting to ask me something. You may ask.**

I was at eye level with him, both of us seated cross-legged on the floor. I could not help observing that despite the condition of his legs he had somehow achieved this posture. He repeated what he had said. I hesitated. He said the same thing for the third time. Tears steadily trickling down my cheeks, face contorted with uncontrollable emotion, I managed, unintelligibly I thought, to say the words at last: **'தங்களை**

ஒரு முறை "அப்பா" என்று அழைக்கலாமா?' *'May I call you "Father", just once?'* My body was racked with sobs, twitching like a fish taken out of water.

He stood up, and said, **'வெறும் ஒரு முறை மாத்திரம் அழைத்துவிட்டு திருப்த்தி ஆகி விடப்போகிறாயா என்ன?' 'Are you going to be satisfied after calling just once?'**
I fall headlong at his feet, wash his feet, wash his feet with my tears, clutch tightly with my hands tied around His feet, press my cheek firmly against his feet and shout **'Father, Father, Father, Father, Father, Father!'** Then, again, I remember no more...

I wake up at the Tiruvannamalai railway station. Five persons from the Ashram are supporting me on all sides, standing around me. The *sarvadhikari* [Ashram manager] counts among their number! I am cautiously entrained. A small paper parcel containing some puffed rice mixed with roasted peanuts is thrust at me through the window of the bogie. The train starts and I pass into a blissful slumber...

17th March 1949

Gajapathi's Last Visit

Arrived here before break of dawn today morning for a flying visit; was able to obtain *darshan* of my beloved Master from afar. No chance of approaching him now. Masses of humanity have congregated everywhere. He does not observe me, he is too weak to keep his head erect for continuous lengths of time, it keeps plopping over backwards in a most unpleasant, grotesque manner, yet slumber is not the reason. The next moment he juts it forward again. The eyes are as distant, aloof and bright as ever.

I became filled with grief to see the pathetic condition of his body, but the grief was on the level of the mind only. He has prepared me well at the end of last year; I no longer am able to feel alarm or disquiet at his palpably deteriorating physical condition. His rigorous training had taught me not to identify with body or mind, but to transcend them and abide as the pure Subjective Consciousness of the Self. The ceremony is over, I must leave. My presence is needed at the law firm, a partner died unexpectedly last month. I do not try to bow, or otherwise try to establish contact; there is no need. Will I see him in the flesh again? Hopefully, but really it does not matter.

For Him there is no death, for Love is Immortal.

15th April 1950

Bhagavan's Death

Yesterday a little past 8 pm, a great light which shone upon the world uninterruptedly for over half a century has been snatched from our watchful midst by the cruel arm of fate. The world knows his compassionate form by the name of Bhagavan Sri Ramana, but for me, he will always be the Radiant One of the Cosmos, my father, mother, protector, saviour, friend and *Gurunadhar* [spiritual foundation], the only source from which I can expect mercy to rain down upon me even without necessity for the slightest solicitation from my side. Lord *Shiva* danced his silent dance of bestowal of blissful transcendental grace for more than half a century at Tiruvannamalai. His work accomplished, he has withdrawn himself to his heavenly abode. That very news that I was dreading for weeks on end was finally announced by this radio set I am sitting by the side of now.

Occasionally, I look at it in a resentful manner, as if blaming it for bringing such ill tidings, as if were it not for this timorous, squawky contraption my Master would have continued in his body. I catch myself frequently wondering sadly why the world should continue after He is gone, particularly why I should continue. Bemusedly I recollect the Master, in his usual animated style, relating a story from the old *Advaita* classic, *Vidyaranya's Panchadasi*. Two men went for employment to North India. One of them died. The remaining man met a wayfarer who happened to be from their village and conveyed the news to him, to be delivered to their homes. This man inadvertently interchanged the names of the two youths, with the result that the dead man's parents were rejoicing and the remaining one's parents were writhing in grief.

I look at the radio and tell myself with a sigh that perhaps if I had never known I could forever assume that that angelic form was still shining, as ever, with the radiance of a thousand million suns in the hermitage at the foot of the holy Arunachala Hill. My eyes then fall on the newspaper: *'The passing away of the Maharshi removes from the midst of his fellowmen a figure of the first magnitude in the sphere of Hindu religion and spirituality.'* How long can one hide from the truth? Sooner or later, one has to come to terms with it. The Buddha has said: *'Accept the pain.'* It is not easy and that is why you and I do not become Buddhas. The past few days were a severe ordeal for me, morning and evening. In the morning I would gaze at the newspaper, heart in mouth, hoping against hope that nothing untoward had happened since the evening or night broadcast of the previous day.

At the bar with colleagues I am safe because they have not the least interest in such matters and have not the slightest clue that I am interested. If they were to come to know that I spent six months of my late twenties in a 'jungle hermitage' in the close proximity of a man who wore nothing but a loincloth, which man I always revere as my living God, they would incessantly make fun of me. They are disdainful of all swamis and mystics and according to them, ashrams exist only to serve as safe havens for expression of profligate, unbridled licentiousness and promiscuity.

In the evening, I would find myself dialling the knobs of the radio set with the same sense of panicked urgency, wanting the broadcast to end as quickly as possible so that I might confirm, as soon as I could, that the ominous piece of news that I so deeply dreaded did not find place in it. The inner struggle was always going on. I tried my best to keep away from the newspaper and radio so that I would not know but was invariably successfully tempted every time by an overwhelming sense of thrilled horror at the thought of the Master's death. Somehow, to imagine that divine anthropomorphic form as a cadaver made my brain writhe and contort in revulsion. When I accessed the news, I was doing so as a result of craving for reassurance, surely there would be no such thing. Surely the Master would cure himself for the sake of us, his children. Surely it was inconceivable that HE should die. Yet it should have been obvious. From the very beginning of his reign of grace at Tiruvannamalai, he had discouraged interest in the miraculous phenomena and had upheld the doctrine of fatalism, as evinced by the note he had written out for his mother when she pleaded with him to return to Madurai.

Even so, I did not want to take seriously the possibility of his physical departure. This in spite of the fact that he had called me to him, quite on purpose, at a time when nobody else was in the vicinity and told me the impending physical demise would be inevitable. Christmas Day 1948 was my last but one visit to the Ashram, the last in which I believe his attention was drawn to my presence. It was a long time since I had seen him in the flesh, and I was aghast and pained at his almost deformed physical appearance. I had asked my friends staying there NOT to write to me about the Master's physical condition. For it was only around that SUN that my life was revolving and my mind wanted to close itself to the possibility that that SUN could ever give out and fade away. I did not want to consider the idea that there would or could be a world without a living Ramana Maharshi. I know his entire teaching lay around the idea that the body is not one's true Self, but I could not help loving the form. I childishly thought that by keeping away from facts I could escape from them, but to no avail.

Of course, I pounced upon the newspapers as soon as they were delivered every morning. Of course, I tuned in to radio broadcasts every evening and as the days went by every night as well. It is my experience as a fanatic of the Master that he will only bestow upon the devotee what is spiritually beneficial to the latter's progress toward Self-realisation and not what seems apparently the correct course of events that should unfold according to the devotee's opinion or common custom. A saint's blessings cannot increase mental impurity, he once said, illustrating this point also with a story. Therefore, although as an inevitable corollary of my foolish ideas, I succeeded in causing myself needless misery, Bhagavan's Grace saw me through in the end.

Strangely, when at 11 pm yesterday the news was announced on the radio, I felt relief. I chided myself for not feeling sorrow instead but soon realised that Bhagavan was still in charge here, and if he wanted me to feel relief, I had no business feeling anything else. Thus, my agony of the last few days is at an end.

25th December 1950

Engrossed in Thoughts of the Maharshi

I am engrossed in thoughts of the Maharshi, while at home or work. For all I know, he is still at the Ashram, majestically seated upon the Sofa in his usual Hall. The special Hall with a stone Sofa that was constructed for him adjacent to the Matrubutheshwara shrine seems to be uncharacteristically grand for him. Indeed, I have learnt that he moved into it, not without extreme reluctance. Such is my imagination.

That is why I do not wish to return to Tiruvannamalai. Entering the Ashram but seeing only his grave would be too much for this frail heart to bear.

Today I sent the promised parcel to Swami Rajeshwarananda. It contains the edited transcript of my experiences with the Master – personally and also conversations he had with devotees in the Hall. These were drawn from my notebooks that he and I showed to Bhagavan on this very date, two years ago! (December 1948)

Swami Rajeshwarananda also asked for one of the notebooks to be sent, so that it can be shown to the publisher as proof of authenticity (p. 230 in *Aham Sphurana – A Glimpse of Self Realisation, ED*); this also I have complied with, and the notebook wherein I recorded Bhagavan's description of his own Enlightenment.

I am hoping to lay the published book, based on the file I have sent to the Swami Rajeshwarananda, at Bhagavan's *Samadhi* soon, though making up my mind to go to Ramana Ashram again will not be easy. To travel down that road in Tiruvannamalai knowing that the Ashram's Hall was going to be empty – that is hard to stomach. I only hope the book does not somehow reach my legal colleagues. Even if it does, I shall deny my involvement and say, *'There are any number of Gajapathis, how do you know it is me?'*

I hope Bhagavan is pleased with me and showers his blessings upon me from the Heavenly Realm of the Heart. The text of the journal herein is the commencement of a punctilious record of Bhagavan's gracious conversations with devotees during a portion of the year 1936, as witnessed by Sri Gajapathi Aiyyer, being documentation, which was heretofore unpublished.

Gajapathi Aiyyer, B. Sc., L.L.B., Madras, Dec. 1950

Gajapathi's Legacy

From a family letter found in the original manuscript:

> 'Someone called Gajapathi Aiyyer died in a freak accident, he was only 42 or 45. Love, Vasu'

In December 1950 Gajapathi sent the completed manuscript, signing off with his name. This means he must have died between December 1950 and March 1951, less than a year after Bhagavan – perhaps showing his deep tie to Him.

The Editorial Group from Open Sky Press, all deepest devotees of Bhagavan, have been so very touched by this spiritual treasure. We will remain eternally grateful for Sri Gajapathi's meticulous notetaking, inspired by his Beloved Master. In our humble opinion, his diary presents new and invaluable aspects of Sri Bhagavan Ramana Maharshi's life and teachings.

Two significant discoveries emerged during the editorial work on Vichara. *First, the full six months of Gajapathi's diaries had been compiled into a manuscript by 1950 and was sent to the hands of Swami Rajeshwarananda at the Ramana Ashram – a time when many of the well-known devotees of Bhagavan still lived in the Ashram.*

Secondly, on Gajapathi's afternoon at the Ashram on 31st December 1948, Bhagavan invited him to a private meeting in the Hall. We would surmise that after his intense devotion, Bhagavan's energy field caused an energetic happening, which could be a glimpse of Self-realisation [Aham Sphurana] *or a moment of Self-realisation. ED*

Essential Vichara Teachings

Who Am I?

Bhagavan's Detailed Introduction to Self Enquiry

A Mature German Seeker

Mind Effort Is Necessary when Practising Vichara

Vichara in the Midst of Worldly Activity

Essential Vichara Teachings

All living beings desire to be happy always, without any misery. In everyone, there is observed supreme love for oneself. And happiness alone is the cause of love. In order therefore, to gain that happiness which is one's nature and which is experienced in the state of deep sleep, where there is no mind, one should know oneself. To achieve this, the Path of Knowledge, the enquiry in the form of Who am I? is the principal means.

Bhagavan 1920s

Who Am I?

When other thoughts arise, one should not pursue them, but should enquire: *'To whom do they arise?'* It does not matter how many thoughts arise. As each thought arises, one should enquire with diligence, *'To whom has this thought arisen?'* The answer that would emerge would be, *'To me.'* Thereupon if one enquires Who am I? the mind will go back to its source; and the thought that arose will become quiescent (still). With repeated practice in this manner, the mind will develop the skill to stay in its source.

When the mind stays in the Heart, the 'I' – which is the source of all thoughts – will go, and the Self, which always exists, will shine. Whatever one does, one should do without the egoity 'I'. If one acts in that way, all will appear as of the nature of *Shiva* [God].

Bhagavan to Sivaprakasam Pillai in 1901 on Arunachala. Published as part of Nan Yar, Who Am I? *ED*

9th July 1936

Bhagavan's Detailed Introduction to Self Enquiry

Q: Sri Bhagavan has said to Sri Pillaival, 'Arivae Nan' *[I am Awareness]. That is the answer of a* jnani. *How can it be applicable to an* ajnani *[someone ignorant of the nature of Reality]? When confronted with the question* 'Who are you?' *the* Jnani *answers,* 'I am awareness alone,' *because* Thannunarvu *[Self-consciousness] or* arivu *[knowledge] is his* Nijaswarupam *[innate essence]. Whereas one who is not, in fact, a Realised Soul, would be lying were he to issue such a reply. So, if one were to ask, who is a* jnani, *the answer may be given,* 'He is one with Awareness, or Awareness Itself.'

Whereas in the case of an ajnani, *like me who is in no way legitimately entitled to make the assertion* 'I am Awareness,' *how can the answer* Arivae Nan *– or other similar statements such as* Aham Brahmasmi *[I am Brahman], or* Brahmaivaham, *for* Brahman *is said to be nothing but Pure Awareness – serve to function as a valid response to the question Who am I? Will Bhagavan kindly shed light upon this point for us?*

B: Our mistake is that we intellectualise the *Vichara* method. We think that the Self can be discovered by the intellect. The intellect arises from the Self and subsides into it. The intellect is not competent to discover the Self. When the intellect subsides, the Self from which it emerged, the Self which it eclipsed, shines. One finds that no such thing as the not-Self ever existed and that no such thing as the not-Self could ever be capable of existence.

The one who makes this finding does not survive to think, *'I have found this'*, or *'This discovery of the Self has been made by me.'* Has he disappeared? No, he never appeared, he never existed. The ego is a fictitious foe; look for him and only Reality remains.

Ignorance is synonymous with the principle of intellectualism or egotism, which makes measurement of variety possible, and as a result the fictitious world of name and form is superimposed or foisted upon the Self – the Self which is only pure Bliss and not aware of any misery or want. Mind is only the false notion of its own

separate existence; the ego 'I' is only an erroneous belief. However, no matter how dense the ignorance, it can never completely hide Reality, as even an ignorant man says 'I'. Thus, the Self is within the direct reach of everyone, but it requires the total relinquishment of all beliefs, ideas, prejudices, judgements, thoughts, opinions, and tendencies toward fulfilment of craving for sensory perceptions, inherited from countless numbers of previous lives or births. Everything you collectively refer to as your 'personality' must vanish. Then Reality will be revealed.

The trouble is that we try to attain to the state of *Jnana*, thinking it to be a goal that has got to be reached by us. When objects of the world are desired, the mind makes plans to obtain them and then executes these designs by using the intellect and body as instruments. We think that we can extend the same approach to *jnanasakshatkara* [profound, intuitive experience of the true nature of Reality]. But can more doing (mental activity) result in Revelation of the Real? Any mental activity leads the mind in a direction that is contrariwise to introversion.

All that is needed to Realise is to be still and that means to keep the mind incessantly submerged in its source. The effort needed for Realisation is not one involving movement of mind or blossoming of thought, but rather one which involves permanently restraining the mind in its source. If abandoning that effort also you are able to achieve perfect repose in the Shining of the Heart, then everything has become still and there are no further doubts or cravings.

Being remains as itself without being disturbed by any *vrittis* [structures of the mind]. The *neti* [not this] method will sift away the not-Self, but who or what is to account for the one who believes himself to be the *sadhaka* [seeker] attempting to discover Reality or the true Self? To discover the falsehood of the *sadhaka's* existence, the investigation Who am I? is advocated as being necessary. Who am I? does not refer to intellectually taking up the line of theorisation, *'I wonder who I might be...'*. Completely arresting the movement of thought waves – which veil the direct experience of Reality shining

in the Heart quietly as 'I'-'I', silently merging the mind in its source so as to make it remain one and identical with the Beingness of the Self – is the import of the investigation Who am I?

Its purpose is not to enable one Self to discover another, for there is only one Self, nothing could be more absurd. Its purpose is to totally despoil and weed out the poisonous, malevolent tree of ignorance, leaf, branch, trunk, shoot and root, so that it perishes once and for all in the blissful light of Absolute Awareness, so that it shatters the embodied state of the *sadhaka* once and for all.

That alone which is True Knowledge can rescue you from getting trapped inside the womb. Knowledge of objects or concepts cannot be True Knowledge. That alone is True Knowledge into which the knower, the known, and the faculty of knowing have been rejected without trace. As long as there is a single *vritti* left in the mind, birth is inevitable. Know that birth verily is the cause for sorrow. Birth is not commencement of existence, as the ignorant assume it to be, it is the assumption of limitations. You, who are originally bliss itself, now find that you have duties, commitments, responsibilities, roles, worries, anxieties, and what not!

When people come here asking for a boon that children be born to them, I smile and keep quiet. What else can I do? The ordinary man cannot appreciate this sort of teaching. He takes his human form for granted and on the basis of that assumption frames his aspirations, ambitions and desires. If asked, *'Who is the one who professes that he was born?'* he is unable to make head or tail out of the question, and becomes even more dejected, thinking, *'This Ramana Swami seems to be cursing me in choice vocabulary; looks as though it might be an unlucky day for me today. Yet he pours out in copious quantities his benignity on these ridiculous foreigners. They want to see God, he obliges them. I want my wife to conceive a child; he utters something I cannot make out, possibly a curse... Which request is more reasonable? Who has seen God, et cetera? Why bother about God now? Better think about Him after retirement, since there will not be anything productive to do at that phase of life. Anyway, better leave the place before this Swami utters another curse.'*

To those who are in genuine need of *Mukti* [liberation], *Mukti* is never far away. The fruit of yearningly wanting *Mukti*, of intensely craving or longing for it, is that the need for *Mukti* somehow mysteriously arises, and once the need arises Self-realisation is totally inevitable.

It must be admitted that in this world where people fight like madmen over land, gold, women, money and the like, extremely passionate longing for *Mukti*, which is a quality in a person that alone could possibly lead him to deliverance, is rare and arises only to him who has performed countless sacrifices, penances, austerities and good deeds in the past or during his previous lives. The common man cannot even admit that the bodily framework implies bondage, that one's true nature is not a gross physical form that is seen by a seer who does not know himself, but formless *chittam* [conscious awareness] or *arivu* [wisdom].

***Arivu* is not the exclusive fiefdom of the *Jnani*. It is common to all. However, there is this difference: In the case of the *Jnani*, there is no *chidhabhasa* [universal Self reflected through the mind] or reflected consciousness to mirror the original unfathomable consciousness of the Self. Because not even a single *vasana* [tendency of the mind] remains by aid of which any reflection could be rendered possible. His belief in, and consequently his ideas concerning, the concept of him being an individual person occupying a body limited by space and time have perished forever. In him there is no *ahamvritti* ['I'-thought], and thus no other *vritti* is possible. He is one and the same as the imperishable Impersonal Absolute, the *Parabrahman* [the supreme Brahman] whereas in the case of the *ajnani*, he has deluded himself into believing that he is a creature of the gross flesh, that he is made up of physical matter. He foolishly accepts the futile idea that his sense organs give him information concerning 'objects' that lie 'outside his self'. He lives in a world of interacting subject and objects, his consciousness is the true Self plus light from the Self which is reflected off the *vasanas*, *samskaras* [mental impressions] or *vrittis*.**

Realisation lays bare the Truth not only that there was never any illusion, but also that illusion is impossible, that no such thing

could ever be, the sun cannot know darkness. The practical measure to carry out *Atma Vichara* [Self-enquiry] does not lie in thinking, 'If I am neither body nor mind nor any of the *koshas* [five layers that cover the true self], then what might I be, I wonder?' nor in thinking any other thought, but in absolutely abdicating the worthless realm of thought and thereafter pursuing the following steps:

1. Find the source whence thought emerges
2. Stay there once and for all, permanently

Really the two steps enunciated above will suffice to bring about *Jnanasiddhi* [attainment of perfect spiritual knowledge], however, the quest has to be relentless if it is to succeed. It is not something that is done a few minutes or hours per day. All of your *chittashakti* [creative power of consciousness] or *kundalini shakti* [dormant spiritual energy at the base of the spine] should be channelled in its entirety towards making the mind stay at its source, ensuring that it does not jump out to chase after objects of sensory gratification or sense pleasure. This is to be done all the time, and with the sum total of the mind, during the states of both *jagrat* [waking state] and *swapna* [dreaming state]. Further, the attitude fuelling the effort must not be, *'I must acquire Self-realisation'*, or *'I must merge in* Brahman *[The eternal Reality]'*, or *'I must escape from this dream and discover my true Self'*, or any other attitude. When any inclination of the will, volition, attitude, motive, intention, desire, drives the *sadhana*, it is doomed to failure, because will is part of the mind and the mind cannot get rid of the mind or even find the mind.

Taking the mind's help to kill the mind is like soliciting the assistance of a policeman to catch a thief, who is in fact disguised under the camouflage of that very policeman. Only a power greater than the mind can absorb the mind into Itself and kill it. To invoke this power, which is none other than God or the Absolute Self, steady, continuous, unceasing and completely volitionless investigation is necessary. If that is done, some Higher Power takes over the worldly functions of the body and runs through them with complete

effortlessness and your interference in these worldly affairs, which it is the *prarabdha* [destiny] of the body to attend to, is no longer necessary, warranted, or even possible.

Everyone in the Hall had been keenly listening. The tufted gentleman was seated near the Sofa. He was listening intently to every word, his head, and therefore the tuft, slightly slanted to one side, his mouth agape, perhaps in awe at the fountain of wisdom that had rained down upon him. He said, after a few moments of silence:

Q: It seems I am doomed. I fail to see how an act can be performed without my wanting or at least vaguely intending to do it.
B: Wanting to do an act without or in the absence of there being the want to do it, is also a want. Our goal is not to take one want away and institute another in its place. We have no goals because a goal implies 'want' underlying it and, since wanting remains, the wanter also remains. Ours is the natural state denuded of goals and wants.

Q: How to reach this state?
B: Is this not just what I have been trying to tell you? The state of absence of volition cannot be reached with the aid of yet another piece of volition. *'I must have nil volition'* is also volition. Do you see it or not? It is like saying, *'Don't think of a monkey while taking the medicine.'* It is impossible, a paradoxical idea.

Q: Still, it is not clear. What should I do? The two steps Sri Bhagavan specified, how to deploy them in the absence of volition to do so?
B: Volitionlessly pursue the *sadhana* of *Atma Vichara* after giving up the idea that the *sadhaka* striving towards Self-realisation exists! Again, do not make the mistake of assuming *'I must cultivate the idea or notion or opinion or belief that the* sadhaka *is non-existent'*. When you are asked to abandon all your ideas, that is precisely what you should do. People are so obsessed with and enamoured by mental activity that they imagine that by some special kind of mental activity, such as meditation, for instance, the Self can be

duped into revealing Itself. It is not so. Only complete cessation of mental activity can reveal the Self. Giving up the personal self or the idea of the *sadhaka's* existence, should, again, be volitionless and unconditional; it should not be driven by any motive.

If you feel tempted to ask for a formula for this also, know that there is none. You abandon the personal self not because you expect or anticipate or want Self-realisation in return (in which case you never really abandon it at all – you only absurdly think that you do), but because in that very act of such abandonment, you discover for yourself, practically, as a DIRECT INSIGHT, that no such thing as the personal self ever existed and that no such thing could ever exist. The actual non-existence of the personal self or ego-self acts as the one and only reason why that personal self or ego-self is abandoned (owing to its non-existence being a necessity for Self-realisation).

This discovery that the personal self does not exist is not mental or intellectual. One does not tell oneself, 'The ego-self does not exist.' One looks for the ego-self, and empirically discovers that, together with or including the discoverer, it does not exist. This is not a matter for intellectualisation, but one for direct experience.

Q: Can all have this wonderful experience?
B: Yes.

Q: Can I also have it? Is it available to foolish persons like me?
B: Simply give up the idea that you are so and so, that you have these and these attributes; rather, remain quite effortlessly free from these ideas and all ideas and there you are, only pure Subjective Consciousness of Being remains.

Q: Remaining free from ideas, should I trace the source of thought and try to remain there steadfastly, or is even this effort counter-productive? I am referring to the two-step formula Bhagavan has graciously given me to reach the Stithaprajna *[firmly established in wisdom] state. The effort made in remaining at the source of thought; does it betray the presence of a corresponding volition or a subtle idea but a ruinous one nonetheless?*

B: There is no contradiction. Shaking off the shackles of thought once and for all, one abides naturally in the thought-free state which involves not the least effort, as ideas or *vrittis* which constitute the reason for thoughts to arise have already been relinquished. This thought-free state is the state of pure being-consciousness-existence-sentience, that hitherto served as the substratum for thoughts to arise from and subsist upon. It is thus the source of thought.

The diversification tendency of spilling over into the realm of thought now extinct, consciousness now merely remains pure; that is, as itself and by itself. This tendency is the veil of *avidyamaya* [illusion caused by ignorance] thrown over Reality. Once this veil is sundered, one stays not merely at the source of thought but as it, for that is the only way to reach there and stay there; BEING THERE. The instruction to stay at the root of thought simply means, therefore, to not hinder consciousness staying as, remaining as, or BEING purely or merely or exclusively Itself.

Q: So, this state of consciousness steadily remaining merely as Itself, undisturbed by thought is called the Sahajastithi*?*
B: No. It is called *Aham Sphurana* ['I'-pulsation].

Q: Then what is the Sahajastithi*?*
B: No description is possible. The reflected being-consciousness which is localised in a physical body is destroyed; after this is destroyed, that alone remains which has always been. It is the Absolute Reality. It transcends divisions such as being and non-being, knowledge-ignorance, light-darkness, et cetera. It is THAT WHICH IS. That is all that can be said of it. That is what YAHWEH stands for in the Bible. Although He seems therein to be a personal God, guiding the destiny of the children of Israel, the Talmudic Prophets of Old knew the transcendental aspect, as did the Christ. God told Moses, *'I appeared to Abraham, to Isaac, and to Jacob, as God Almighty, but by My name, Yahweh, I was not known to them.'* On the other hand, the term Yahweh occurs many times in Genesis.

Is there a contradiction? No. Prophets before the time of

Moses had known the personal God Yahweh, but Moses was the first to whom the transcendental, formless aspect was revealed. The earlier prophets knew the name but not its significance. They loved God and cherished his name, but did not understand the meaning or import of the name. The name means 'I am that I am'. God revealed the meaning of the name to Moses, whereas the earlier prophets had only been given the name. The name means that one who is simply subjectively aware, without knowing any object, is absorbed or transformed into God. This is not an intellectual conviction or mental statement. It is the blossoming of the Heart-lotus *[hridayapundarikam]* of love from within.

Q: So, as respects Bhagavan's method of remaining as Subjective Consciousness, I am supposed to witness without entertaining the notion that I am witnessing, is that right?

B: Who is that one who remains as Subjective Consciousness? Is Subjective Consciousness proclaiming that he is going to remain as Subjective Consciousness? You see the absurdity of it. So, your task is not to remain as Subjective Consciousness; your task is to keep yourself out of the way, so that Subjective Consciousness remains merely as Itself without getting impeded by you. As for witnessing, there is nothing to witness. IT IS, simple Being. When ideas create modifications in consciousness, which is the essence or substance of the mind, another idea made of the same substance is used as a tool with which to annihilate all other ideas; finally, this tool is also destroyed. That is why the example of the stick used to stir the burning funeral pyre is furnished.

Q: So, merely observing consciousness with a placid, thought-free mind is not a sadhana *that suffices to destroy the mind and bestow Realisation?*

B: If the aspirant is unremittingly sincere in its pursuit, the practice that you mention will in due course by itself cause sufficient introversion of mind to facilitate the mind to become ready for successfully investigating Who am I? However, it is erroneous to imagine that the two practices are one and the same, or even similar.

Q: But they both aim at ensuring that the sadhaka *remains attending to mere consciousness; how can they be distinct from each other?*
B: The act of attending to pure Subjective Consciousness alone still involves that one who undertakes such *sadhana*. WHO IS HE?

Q: But there is also that one who investigates, Who am I?
B: He is both the subject and object of his investigation. That is why in the end, everybody must come only through this gate before reaching the citadel of the Heart. Who am I? is the only *sadhana* which is such that the one making it is the same as the one in relation to whom it is made. The snake must bite his own tail. Otherwise, he will not die. Neophytes who complain that Who am I? is not working are given the suggestion that they should watch the thought 'I', or that they should remain attending to Subjective Consciousness alone. Still less mature souls are told to repeat 'I'-'I' mentally, together with simultaneously concentrating on the sense of personality associated with 'I', that is to say with the mental concept of 'myself'.

Those who are not able to do even this should do *pranayama* [breath control], *japa* [mantra repetition], *murti dhyana* [meditation on a form or image of a deity], or *hatha yoga*. None of these practices, however, could possibly serve as a substitute for *Vichara*, nor is it meaningful to confuse any of them with *Vichara* or to imagine any of them to be the same as *Vichara*. *Vichara* is the final door. The 'I' attends to himself, not to his Self. The ego attends to the ego and to nothing else; that is *Vichara*. Attending to Subjective Consciousness, while it is a method having its beneficial use, is certainly NOT the same as *Vichara*.

Q: A popular Caucasian devotee of Sri Bhagavan has opined that the sadhana *of* 'holding on to the 'I'-thought until the one who imagines that he is separate from the Self disappears' *is clearly* Vichara *masquerading under a different name. Is that right?*
B: No. The method of holding on to the 'I'-thought is a precursor to *Vichara* and it is not the same.

7th July 1936

A Mature German Seeker

Today a German gentleman, a former missionary schoolteacher who had been serving in East Africa (known as Tanganyika since the Great War), in the town of Bwaga Moyo, has come to the Ashram for a day's visit. How people in such remote places got to hear of Bhagavan, I could not begin to guess, but he soon revealed – as usual with most Westerners – that Brunton's book, *A Search in Secret India*, had piqued his curiosity to see the Sage personally. He was now staying in Pondicherry at Aurobindo's Ashram and could not resist taking a peek at Bhagavan. He already seemed to know something of the line of Bhagavan's teachings, saying he had discussed it with friends at Aurobindo's Ashram. He was a multilingual autodidact and polymath and was familiar with German, English, Arabic and Sanskrit. He had studied *Sanskrit* literature and *Advaitic* works.

Chadwick had shown him Bhagavan's *Arunachala Pancharatnam*, a five-line Sanskrit poem that Bhagavan had composed in the Arya metre while he had been living on the Hill, at the request of a Sanskrit pandit. He found it to be awe-inspiring. He was regularly practising meditation on the *ajnachakra* [third eye chakra] and now wanted to know if it was possible to go further towards Realisation without joining any monastic order.

B: Outer ceremonies are prescribed for those who are prone to the error of placing form over substance; substance alone is material and THAT alone is real.

Q: Since the Jnani's *omniscience is beyond question, will Bhagavan please tell me whether the extrajudicial extermination of the preceding chancellor, the leader of the Brownshirts, and many others, as part of a 'blood-purge' ordered by the present chancellor with the purported objective of bringing about some form of national deviation is not morally abhorrent? After authorising the execution, the chancellor justified the same by referring to himself as the 'yardstick of justice by which to judge the German people' in a speech to the Reichstag.*

I am crestfallen with the developments going on in my country. After the Kaiser's abdication I thought that the time was ripe for the ideas of Marx-Engels to take shape in the German soil but that was not to be. Will Bhagavan not agree that their philosophy is the one best suited to serving as a decisive panacea to society's ills?

B: Your own ills overwhelm you. Yet, you have moved to the sphere of societal ills already! First be at permanent peace with yourself; once that stands achieved, we can talk about how to bring peace to the German Chancellor and Germany.

Q: I am aware that Bhagavan is a solipsist. However, to dismiss all human problems as being imaginary requires a giant leap of faith towards the idealism end of the spectrum.

B: It merely needs disillusionment with materialism.

Q: According to Sri Aurobindo's claims, he has probed beyond the experience of the Vedic Rishis *[ancient seers and sages of India]. What is Sri Bhagavan's opinion? Is it authentic or not?*

B: Aurobindo's talk of bringing down Divine Consciousness from above overlooks the same being already self-effulgent as the Shining of the Heart. Reality simply IS. How can the question of moving it from place to place, et cetera, arise? People keep asking me about Sri Aurobindo's yoga system and if I give my reply according to my capacity, they go away disgruntled saying, *'These* Jnanis *are always contradicting each other.'* What can I do?

Q: What about Sri Aurobindo's claim that one must commence from Self-realisation and then proceed to bring down the Divine to the Earth?

B: Let us first Realise and then discuss, if need be; not now.

Q: What is the ultimate purpose of a man's life?

B: To find an answer to the question of, *'Why am I, apparently, limited to, and therefore by, a body? Could it really be possible that*

***I am nothing more?'* This question finally resolves itself into the question of, *'Who am I, who is apparently bound by this limitation of being or carrying a body?'* This much is certain: one who foolishly takes his bodily existence for granted, who thinks that it is an inevitable finality that he is, in fact, born, will never succeed in the quest no matter what austerities or penance he might perform. Only the Unborn can know the Unborn. The Unborn knows itself only – that is, it knows no birth or death.**

The intellectual understanding that the bodily existence is futile, undesirable, useless and delusory is the very first step towards Realisation. If you accept the existence of limitations, any *sadhana* performed will have precisely only one result – it will make the ego grow stronger and stronger and stronger. One who wants to transcend limitation should cease to imagine himself to be limited – that will do; yes, it indeed is as simple as that. Instead of simply giving up the unreal, people want to do *sadhana* to eradicate it! Is it not funny?!

Q: Is sadhana *not useful?*
B: Only if it is done without assuming the existence of limitations. The only useful *sadhana* is the investigation Who am I? Everything else is just 'release-of-concept-gas' (movement of mental ideas or churning of *vrittis* within the mind), because the existence of limitations is implicitly assumed and accepted. If non-existent limitations are accepted to exist, how can any *sadhana* performed on the basis of that wrong acceptance have any use, and how can such spurious *sadhana* help you transcend those very limitations?

Q: The logic seems to suggest that the Self can be discovered by the mind.
B: The dead mind becomes the Self or discovers itself to be the Self.

Q: I understand Nietzsche talks about the concept of Eternal Recurrence of the same in Thus Spoke Zarathustra. *Does Bhagavan agree with it? Each time the universe is recreated after the cosmic dissolution, does it exactly repeat itself? If that were to be true, both free-will and Self-realisation would be impossible.*

If everything is going to unfold now exactly as it did previously, my incumbent free will is obviously just a myth. If everything is going to unfold in exactly the same manner in the future as now, I am never going to escape from the cycle of births and deaths!
B: All these are only mental concepts. Even now you are not born. Realise it.

Q: The body was born.
B: Are you it?

Q: My understanding is that the body is part of myself, but Bhagavan's teachings tell me that I am Brahman *and therefore immanent everywhere.*
B: Leave *Brahman* alone. Talk about yourself first. Who are you?

Q: I really don't know... I am pure Subjective Consciousness, is it not?
B: Is pure Subjective Consciousness now conversing with me? Is it saying, 'I am *Brahman*', et cetera?

Q: Then what is the answer?
B: The effortless thought-free state is the answer.

Q: How to attain it?
B: There is no question of attaining anything. BE and the very doubt *'How do I merely remain as BE-ing?'* is an assured means to get trapped in the endless labyrinths of thought created by the mind. Why seek out a 'process' to 'achieve' something so fundamental as one's own consciousness of one's existence? Simply BE. It is your very nature.

Q: I am unable to realise it.
B: This is also only a thought. Get rid of all thoughts and all will be well.

Q: I have heard of the Jnana Vichara *technique expounded by Sri Bhagavan. How could asking oneself the question Who am I? lead to transcendence of mind, when asking the question itself is only an activity initiated and sustained on the level of the mind?*

B: The *Vichara* begins with the mind and ends in the Self. Mind turned fully inward discovers itself to be the Self.

Chadwick was asked by Bhagavan to give the man Bhagavan's Who am I? to read. He read it and then asked:
Q: I find it shocking to consider seriously Advaita's *proclamation that the* jagrat *[waking state] state is nothing better than a dream. It amounts to saying that I am now dreaming whereas I believe to the contrary, that whatever I am experiencing through the senses exists independently of my perception thereof.*

How is it that the numerous disciples of yours, or followers or devotees or worshippers or aficionados or whatever it is that one would be justified in calling them, take gladly to the idea that the world, the same world they experience every day, is a dream?
B: You say it is the same world you saw yesterday that you are seeing today. How do you know that? Through memory. Memories are also illusory. They create a deceptive fabric of intellectual continuity where in fact none exists. What actually exists is only Absolute Beingness or Self. Even in dreams you have memories, go to familiar places, et cetera. How is this made possible?

***Jagrat* or *swapna* [state of dreaming], the same mind draws the poisonous veil of objectification or differentiation over the pure Self, hiding it. This veil is called the screen of *avidyamaya*. Instead of asking who cast this veil, it is more useful to ask who sees the veil. Then you will see there was never any veil. This is called Self-realisation. The desire to do *sadhana* to attain it is meaningless and self-defeating because this desire presupposes the existence of someone apart from the Self who is doing *sadhana* to reach the Self.**

Q: The Realisation that you call Sahaja Nirvikalpa Samadhi – *can I get it just by giving up the idea that I am an individual person? Or should I frequently remind myself of my actual Divine Nature?*
B: You may persuade yourself into believing, *'I am not the body but the Self.'* The consequence? Your troubles increase. One set of mental concepts has been substituted for another.

Q: Should I not do any sadhana? *Is all* sadhana *useless then?*
B: You need not do anything except to dwell incessantly and intensely on the inner sense of 'I'. That is good *sadhana*.

Q: Is it not good to remember all the time that I am the Self?
B: And who is the one that is doing the remembering? He is not the Self. He is an arbitrary mental conceptualisation of the mind masquerading as the actual Real Self.

Q: What is the difference between 'dwelling on the I' and 'effortless abidance in thoughtless being'?
B: The former is used as the stepping stone to obtain the latter.

Q: Different spiritual teachers recommend different sadhanas. *Which to follow?*
B: *Sadhana* is the means to regain the Self. However, the idea *'I am doing* sadhana' renders the *sadhana* totally pointless and useless. *Sadhana* becomes natural if attraction to worldly pleasures stands removed. Desire for worldly pleasures will put you in shock when you realise the world is only a dream.

Q: I still find it impossible to believe this solid world could only be a mere dream.
B: (smiling) **Two different categories of spiritual aspirants or *sadhakas* exist. One is the *Kritopasaka* [one who has practised worship] and the other is the *Akritopasaka* [one who has not practised worship]. The former is born of aeons of serious and steadfast spiritual practice directed along the correct channel (that of making the mind turn selfwards or sourcewards), born with the intellectual conviction that the cosmos he sees around him is the merest of illusions and that expending one's mental faculties upon it would be the ruin of one's inherent nature of abiding peace and unshakable happiness.**

The latter is shocked and unsettled when informed that there is no difference, for all practical purposes, between the *jagrat*

and *swapna* states. The firm intellectual conviction that the perceived cosmos is seen, owing to delusion, as being constituted by multiple disparate entities – while the truth is that it is vested in the same Substratum, *Adhishtanam* [fundamental underlying reality], or *Sadhvasthu* [the one true existence] as the Seer – is born only as a result of arduous spiritual practice which is possible only if the *Satguru's* abundant Grace is available as a catalyst. This Grace descends unto him alone who perpetually bathes his heart in the effulgent glow of unselfish and non-reciprocation-expecting Love of God, humanity, or any other single minded ideal of pure, ecstatic devotion or *Parabhakti* [supreme devotion]. This intellectual conviction (as to the world's objective unreality) is the seed of *Jnana* that grows into the tree that chokes the poisonous weed of egotism or *ahamkara* [I am the doer idea] at its root. It destroys it once and for all, such seed having been planted long ago in the fathomless, dark misty depths of the mind by way of the Supremely merciful glance of Grace of the infinitely compassionate *Satguru*.

Q: So, the widely held perception that without a Guru, even Atmajignasa *[enquiry into the nature of the Self], let alone* Atmasakshatkaram *[direct experience of the Self], is totally impossible, is…?* (He left his words trailing in the air, for the Sage to rhythmically conclude.)
B: Unequivocally and absolutely correct.

Q: What about the fate of one who never comes across this sort of Guru *personage in his lifetime? One of such immense spiritual eminence as Sri Bhagavan is, after all, hardly possible to be found or encountered again in, say, the busy streets of London, Linz, or Leningrad... they seem to be a great rarity, yet they are asserted to be altogether indispensable if one wants to achieve victory on the spiritual path.*

God seems to have conspired specifically and heavily against those who aspire to His state. Leaving alone the effort required to be made, even the teacher whose help is anything but avoidable seems to be greatly difficult to locate.

The Maharshi remained silent; someone in the Hall remarked, *'To precisely sort out this difficulty, Sri Bhagavan, the Avatar of the Age, has been sent down to us by God, so that, yet living amongst us, he may illumine our way to the divine Supreme Truth.'*
Someone else chimed in, *'Sri Bhagavan is a* Jnanasiddha *[someone who embodies perfect knowledge], the Impersonal Absolute, not a mere Avatar. An Avatar is a manifestation of one of God's excellencies; the* Jnani *is God Himself. Sri Bhagavan has himself reminded us of this on many occasions. Is that not so, Bhagavan?'* Bhagavan only remained silent and serene. If he had heard – no doubt he had – he betrayed no indication of it. The original questioner seemed slightly deflated at Bhagavan's silence; not to be discouraged, he began again.

Q: *Yes, some say Aurobindo is the Avatar of the age, while others say it is Meher Baba. Still others say it was the late Sai Baba. Yet others maintain that* Sri Krishna *was the last Avatar in the anthropomorphic form before Kalki Avatar arrived at the time of cosmic dissolution. For others, it is Buddha, Ramakrishna or Confucius. Will Bhagavan tell us in what way His experience of consciousness is superior to that of these, since, allegedly, they seem to be mere Avatars, and not* Jnanis*? And really who is the Avatar corresponding to this era in mankind's history, a particularly tumultuous one?*

Germany has announced her intention to rearm herself, an indication of the belligerent attitude of the National Socialist Government. Surely an Avatar is necessary from age to age to look after the world to ensure that mankind's evil-doing collectively remains lesser than his acts of benignity? Jnanis *do not act in the world, except to ensure the merest existence of the physical body – is that not so? So, where is the Avatar who is going to look after our poor mortal selves, and also the world?*
B: The experience of genuine *Nirvikalpa Samadhi* [state of being temporarily absorbed in the absolute] naturally precludes 'others'. Thus, there is nothing apart from the Self of Him who has irrevocably lost his little self in It. Because there is no second, no other, nothing foreign or alien to or apart from the One Immutable Absolute Self, so the question of comparison simply never arises. All True Masters are ONE, not because they identify themselves with something in

common, but because commonly the faculty of identification (of one thing with another) does not exist in any of them.

As for Avatars, each one sees according to his own mental convictions and predispositions – to establish the finality of one's own viewpoint amidst others will result only in fruitless skirmishes. You may continue to believe in whatever pleases your own fancy, but expecting corroboration from others for your worldview of the universe will serve only to increase your sense of mental unrest and agitate the mind further.

Q: So, the idea of the Avatarapurusha *[divine incarnation], God-manifest, who comes down from age to age* [sambhavami yuge yuge], *is just... a fallacy, only as good as a fairy-tale? Do not the Holy books of the various faiths speak of these blessed beings, whom we might worship, since manifestation makes available a form to worship. That with which we might elevate ourselves to the zenith of spiritual perfection and purity, puissance and divinity? Jesus, Mahomet, Zoroaster, Buddha, what about them? Specifically, does not* Krishna *say,* paritranaya sadhunam *[for the protection of the righteous], et cetera? How can these considerations be ignored?*

B: Your mental predilections and proclivities foist upon you the erroneous idea that there is a God outside your Self and that He needs to send down messengers to guide you and show you the way to reach Him. If you keep on journeying, you will never reach.

Therefore, I say, enough searching, call off the search, give up the idea that there is a goal and be yourself. Nothing more. The great Masters, each in his own tongue, but each from the same Heart, attempted to give you this message only, BE YOUR SELF. The Masters you mentioned and others, each doubtless had and has and continues to have always, his specific, special or unique role in man's spiritual evolution, but the zenith spoken of by you will certainly not be reached by discussing the question, *'How can all of these* Mahanubhavars *[those with great experience of the Absolute] be right? On what points do they contradict themselves? Is it not our imminent task-on-hand to clear up these apparent contradictions and seeming mutual inconsistencies? Will that not endow us with special spiritual merit?'*

Men waste entire lifetimes quite fruitlessly like this. This effort, if harnessed fully to keeping one's *lakshyam* [aim] fixed entirely on Self or Reality, would have resulted in *Mukti* [emancipation] long ago. Instead, countless lives have been frittered away on account of these wrong and foolish ideas about reaching Truth by using the *buddhi* or the reasoning faculty, when, in fact, precisely collapse of that faculty results in the revelation of Self or Reality. What a pity.

Q: It is still not clear. The avatarapurush, *is he just a mental concept like the* gandharvas *[celestial beings known for their musical and artistic abilities],* rakshasas *[supernatural, often demonic beings],* bhuthas *[friendly to mischievous spirits], et cetera? Has not this tangible world witnessed the advent of many such great men, Bhagavan himself not excluded?*
B: The trouble arises when we use their teachings to satisfy our intellectual palate and appetite. To the unwise, it does not occur to try and practise, instead using it as a subject of discussion at gatherings of philosophers and metaphysicists. Therefore, I say unto the earnest aspirant, do not try to write essays on it. Do not try to present articles of great erudition on it. Do not try to gain followers for your newly discovered maxim or device of apotheosis or precept of ancient wisdom. Do not conceptualise it mentally and then, getting trapped in those very concepts, moan and complain that you 'see no progress'.

Do not go on discussing or talking about it. Do not tell your self, 'First I shall obtain intellectual mastery over the technique and subsequently shall begin the application thereof.' Instead – plunge into the practice HERE and NOW; stick to the teachings of any one *Mahanubhavar*, and all will come right in the end. Masters are there only to show you the way. Man fogs the fulfilment of their purpose by merely theorising or intellectualising about their respective lives, advents and teachings, such as asking, 'Is this one or that one a *Siddha-purusha* [perfected being], *Muktapurusha* [liberated being], or an *Avatarapurusha*?' Of course, these are your mental concepts only. In fact, the Master, being not at all different from the formless Absolute seated in the tabernacle of the Sacred Heart of Man, is really synonymous with your own True Self and that being so, why seek him anywhere else?

Q: For myself I am now convinced, but I am worried about the hopeless spiritual condition of the world, which seems to be enveloped in profuse darkness. When will all the people of the world wake up to the fact that they are living in the ghastly darkness of ignorance and understand that the world around them is a dream so that they can obtain genuine illumination? What about those unfortunate ignorant millions of the world who have never met a genuine Satguru *[True Guru] in their life? Supposing their* prarabdha karma *[accumulated past karma responsible for current life experiences] dictates that they spend the entirety of their lives being relentlessly tossed around in the evil sea of* avidyamaya, *as a result of the Guru's acquaintance never coming to transpire. What then?*

For how many lifetimes more will their ordeal of ignorance have to last, and when at last would such unfortunate ones meet their Guru, so that through Him their redemption could be vouchsafed for certain? Such unfortunate persons, never having had the extreme good fortune of meeting Bhagavan during his blessed sojourn on this Earth, which, owing to his stay here has become itself a sanctified land, must need count themselves exceedingly unlucky – what, therefore, would Bhagavan have them do? What can they do? What will be their fate?

B: The fate of each one depends upon his merit. Take care of yourself and others can take care of themselves.

This answer was evidently not to the questioner's liking. He seemed to toy with the idea of placing forth additional arguments before Bhagavan as to why mercy ought not to be showered in profusion upon the 'ignorant' masses of the world until Chadwick pacified him with the following:

'Bhagavan has said that when longing for God or intensity of meditation has reached a feverish intensity pitch, the Guru automatically manifests before the devotee.'

Even then, the man seemed about to say something when the Hall's attention was riveted by Bhagavan's voice suddenly reading from Scripture the words of a Jewish carpenter, no less a genius in the realm of Spirit, the heartthrob of many a lonely, man-forsaken soul yearning for Divine acceptance:

'Ask, ye shall receive; Seek, ye shall find; knock, it shall be opened unto thee.'

When Bhagavan said, ***'it shall be opened'***, the man was thrown into a sort of paroxysmic joy and he was unable to contain himself – he rushed forward toward Bhagavan, screaming, *'Saviour! Thou hast handed me the key to the Kingdom of Heaven, the Nirvana I have been seeking always! Nirvana! Saviour! Saviour! Mountain Saviour! Jesus Mountain! Here! Fancy!'* His further blathering words were arrested by a catatonic fit which suddenly seized him. Bhagavan's attendants slowly eased their grip on his shoulders and shirt-collar – for, afraid he might attack the sage, they had spontaneously come forward and caught hold of him, to prevent his advance toward the Master, whom they revered and adored as their living God.

Slowly he sank low on the ground and sat with his hands clasped around his knees like a small, morose, gloomy child. Presently he would murmur a few inaudible words, and then relapse into silence. Someone fetched him water, which he ravishingly gulped down and then said something incomprehensible. An hour or so later he seemed to have regained normalcy, though the attendants' uneasy, nervous eyes were still riveted on him. He made to move toward Bhagavan and the attendants immediately jerked forward. Bhagavan said to them, ***'Let it come, leave it!'*** yet, like djinns (supernatural beings) that zealously and jealously guard treasure, they stood, alert, about him, lest the Master should have to suffer some untoward bodily ill on account of some freakish mishap. The man now looked eager to communicate his gratitude, which was writ so largely and openly upon his sensitive face. In a low tone, he said something to the Master, leaning over. Bhagavan smiled, showed the other his palm in benediction, and the latter bent low in reverential farewell, departing the next instant from the Hall.

This is how a chance encounter with Bhagavan brought drastic transformations in the lives of those fortunate enough to discover 'the jungle hermitage'. The encounter may last only a few hours, but the transformations might last for life. That was the last I saw of the German from the town of Bwaga Moyo. Now people in the Hall wanted to discuss him. Someone mentioned that a man, having this same name, had written an essay on the teachings of Keshab Chandra Sen (19th century Indian social reformer and religious leader), which he had encountered in some magazine; he wondered if it could be the same man; then, turning to Bhagavan, he asked:

Q: This fortunate man who left now – did Bhagavan just give him an experience of the Sahajastithi*?*
B: His mind began to subside in the Heart, and the bliss was objectified as the object of his long contemplation or meditation, manifesting externally as a stupefying vision of mesmerising charm. If the bliss is understood to be not apart from one's Self, one will stop attempting meditation and simply resolve oneself into THAT WHICH IS.

Q: All I want to know is whether what he experienced – can it be called the Sahaja Samadhi *of the* Jnani*, which He is always immersed in?*
B: No. While ideas still remain in latent form, *Mukti* is totally impossible. However, a mind that has once tasted the nectar of bliss of the *Atmaswarupa* [the true form of the Self] will repeatedly try, even involuntarily, to regain it; such efforts will become more frantic and intense as the individual's desire for his beloved chosen Master waxes more and more in his Heart due to the operation of God's Compassionate Divine Grace. Eventually, the love reaches such a level of crazed longing that the *jivatman*, recognising its total helplessness to reach the state of Supreme Union aspired for, surrenders totally to the Higher Power, saying with outright candidness, *'I do not count anymore. I do not want to be, nay, already I am not. Only you are. Only you matter, because only you exist.'* When this stage is reached God effortlessly absorbs the devotee in Himself. The fact remains, however, that there is nothing to be gained or attained, even now you are in *Sahaja* [union with the divine], only you think

otherwise. Get rid of thought and all will be well. Thinking *'I am the Self'* is a meaningless diversion of mental energy, because when the option of forever remaining as pure Subjective Consciousness that is ever volitionlessly free from disturbance caused by the mischief of thought is always available, which fool would instead prefer to think that he is the Self?

It is like the story of the king who forgot all about his royal throne and started wandering all over the streets of his own empire, screaming at the top of his voice, *'I am king! I am king! I am king!'* like a madcap, instead of calmly walking over to his palace, entering it, and occupying his rightful throne. When he thus roams around on the streets, does he obtain any respect or affectionate treatment? No. People throw stones at him in contempt, saying, *'Admit you are a penniless pauper and we will give you tasty food, decent clothes and other help. Stop pretending to be the king. It annoys us, for we bear much affection toward our most high Royal Excellency. If you were really the king, and have indeed actually lost your way to your Natural Residence, would you not simply proceed to your throne and occupy it, instead of wasting your energy on the roadside meaninglessly shouting,* "I am king"? *Would our king, the veritable embodiment of dignity and decency, ever behave like this? Stop your nefarious activities immediately. Shaming the king's name is a serious offence.'*

This of course only enrages the deranged king further, and he gets into fist fights with his own beloved citizens. Eventually he is arrested for misbehaviour and public rioting and brought to the Royal Court for Trial. Meanwhile everyone is puzzled upon seeing the throne empty. They wonder where His Majesty might be, for his punctuality was the stuff of legend (as were his numerous other good qualities). They say to themselves, *'A madcap who has tried to insult the king on the streets must be urgently executed, and at this crucial moment, where has His Majesty gone – how can the judgement be delivered in His absence?'* When the king sees his familiar courtroom, his mental faculties are restored to their normal state and through gentle explanation he makes the Royal Court understand the actual situation.

They are horror-struck once their disbelief has subsided. They at once beg his pardon for having bound him in chains. He in turn begs them to forgive him for having let them down by having permitted his mental faculties to become so deranged and distorted as to reduce him to a wandering lunatic on the streets, a disturbing contrast to his usual radiant figure on the throne. Then he moves over to occupy his usual seat at the head of the Royal Assembly. No sooner than he touches the throne does he awake into (relative) reality, the whole incident of him wandering on the streets as a madcap never happened. He had simply fallen asleep on a busy day at the Throne and had been dreaming of this entire unpleasant sequence of events. The truth was that he never stirred from his throne but had been sitting on it all along whilst the dream had been playing on in his mind.

Everyone was moved by Bhagavan's narration, because he had personally acted out each of the parts. One could see the pain and indignation on his face. His own citizens were laughing and jeering at him in response to him putting forth his rightful claim of entitlement to kingship. One could see the joy; he was restored to his palace at last and none of this ridiculous madcap business would cause him any trouble in the future. One could see the incredulous wonder and astonishment as he awoke from the dream and opened his eyes to the real world (real in the relativistic sense). There never had been any madcap business. He had never moved from the throne from the time he had occupied it on the morning of that day!

Q: The illustration fails to address the question of why the dream should have taken place at all. I wondered how Bhagavan was going to tackle the question. Dreams generally happened afterward if some difficult to digest exotic delicacy was served at dinner, but somehow it seemed unlikely that the Sage would furnish that particular response... and he did not.

B: On account of attachments, desires and other *vrittis* prevailing in the mind the world seems real as an objective entity. In fact, if the world appears it is just the Self. It requires something apart from the

dream, the perceiving subject, that is, to tell that a dream, or anything at all, is being experienced. On enquiring if such a subject exists, we find that it does not, but that what exists is only the substratum in which the apparent subject and apparent object seemed hitherto to be vested. There is no subject and object but only the *Adhishtanam* [substratum] of the Heart, as, in fact, was always the case. Only all this long we were not paying attention to the Truth.

If you try to find ignorance, you will not succeed, because no such thing exists; it is a non-existent thing that is giving us so much trouble. All eventually return to the palace of the Self. Only when the *simhasanam* [royal throne] is touched can the king wake up from his terrifying dream, not otherwise. Some roam around for years in the streets as madcaps before they permit themselves to be captured and returned to the palace. A few mentally succumb to the first blow received from an upset citizen, and think, *'It seems that it might be difficult to continue to cope here with blows raining left and right; it would be better to surrender to the authorities and be done with it, no matter what the consequence'*, immediately acting accordingly. It has to be noted that without the troublemaker's consent, he cannot be marched to the Royal Palace. For raining down any number of blows no consent need be obtained; that is how this dream universe works. Also note, in one instance, a two-minute dream of the king may run for even sixty years in the dream world, whereas a six-hour dream of his may run for 1/144th of a second in the dream world. Time is a function of the faculty of the imagination. It cannot possess the property of Being, which is Absolute Nature.

Bhagavan then told the epic story of King Lavana which occurs in the Yoga Vasishta. A Sage visits the king's court, and a long story concludes with the Sage explaining the teaching in Bhagavan's words:

One who understands the illusory power of the mind will never again be content with sense pleasures; he will long for the Supreme Bliss of the Self. *'Come on, wake up, Lavana!'* King Lavana saluted the Sage with reverence and returned to his palace. He pondered well

over One who wants to transcend limitation should cease to imagine himself to be limited – that will do; yes, it indeed is as simple as that. Instead of simply giving up the unreal, people want to do *sadhana* to eradicate it! Is it not funny?!

He pondered well over the facts mentioned by his Guru and soon realised the Supreme state of *Brahman* through the method of *Atma Vichara*.

At Sri Ramana Ashram, the incredible, incomparable Bhagavan Ramana Maharshi crashed into the sofa, sweating. The Hall was spellbound. The Sage had, true to his habit, play-acted the performances of every one of the story's characters. For some moments the Hall remained in stunned silence. Having popped in for some purpose and seeing Bhagavan narrate a story, even the *sarvadhikari* [ashram manager] had remained glued to the floor. Then a volley of questions exploded like gunfire. It was I who took the lead.

G: I am of the opinion that the true identity of the sorcerer is that it was Vasishta himself, who gave Lavana that experience to enlighten him. What does Bhagavan say to this?
B: (laughing) **I am also of the same opinion...**

G: I would like Bhagavan to give me the same experience. I shall not be frightened. I am prepared to do anything to obtain Brahmajnana *[knowledge of Brahman].*
B: If you must desire, desire for Reality, not illusion.

20th July 1936

Mind Effort Is Necessary when Practising Vichara

Q: When can it be legitimately asserted that the investigation Who am I? has begun to bring about a beneficial result?

B: At present there is a 'you' who is endeavouring to practise *Vichara*. The attenuation and eventually extermination of that 'you' is the goal of *Vichara*. If you interminably hold on to the practice of keeping the mind incessantly merged in the Beingness of the Self, there will come a stage when, rather than the mind asking Who am I?, the entirety of the mind stands transformed into the investigation Who am I? There would then remain no possible scope for the mind to occupy itself with any other concern. It is at this stage that the mind begins to sink into the Heart. Effortless and volitionless inherence of mind in the thought-free and torpor-free state is the indication that *Vichara* has been carried out properly.

Q: But sadhana *involves the need for effort. Should I not make an effort to constantly remain in the state of pure Subjective Consciousness?*

B: Pure Subjective Consciousness remains as Itself and by Itself always. What is that entity known as 'you' which makes the assertion that it ought to remain as pure Subjective Consciousness? There can be no investigation into pure Subjective Consciousness because It is simply Being and nothing but that. *'What is that apparent second entity besides pure Subjective Consciousness which wishes to abide as pure Subjective Consciousness'* is the question. As for making an effort, yes, effort is necessary until the mind has learnt to remain spontaneously merged in pure Subjective Consciousness.

Carry on with your effort until the need for effort stands completely exhausted. So long as there remains one who can make an effort, that is how long effort is necessary. Destruction of the one making the effort is the goal of the effort. When effortless and volitionless submergence in the Shining of the Heart has become

the natural state of the mind, it is discovered that effort and volition have dropped away of their own accord. Also, it is essential to abandon the spurious idea that it is you who are responsible for your emancipation.

Q: Who then is responsible?

B: There is no need for us to burden ourselves with the mental concept that there is an 'I', or that there is something needed to be done so as to get rid of this 'I', and that there ought to be somebody to take responsibility for the successful execution of the task of exterminating the 'I'. Remain free from all mental concepts, because so long as they remain, Realisation is impossible. *Sadhana* ideally neither ought to proceed out of a framework of concepts nor ought to arise as a result of belief in a collection of ideas.

Investigate Who am I? for the sake of *Atmajignasa* [enquiring about the Absolute Truth] and not because you believe it will fetch you something called Realisation. Your mental ideas, whether those appertaining to what you are imagining to be Realisation or others, are a definite obstacle to Realisation. Break away from them and remain free of them.

Q: But how?

B: By refusing to pay any attention to them. It is by holding onto 'you' that the ego arises and gives birth to thoughts, ideas, and fantasies. Hold onto yourself and the ego will not arise.

20th July 1936

Vichara in the Midst of Worldly Activity

Q: Can meditation or Vichara *be carried on in the midst of worldly activity?*
B: The feeling *'I am working'* is the hindrance. Enquire, *'Who works?'* Remember to ask yourself Who am I? every time such false notions of doership trouble you. Then no work can bind you; it will all go on automatically. Make no effort either to work or to renounce work. Your effort is the bondage. Simply perpetually remain as you ARE, mind merged in its source so as to be indistinguishable from the Beingness of the Self. And do not bother about the question of whether the body ought to work or idle away.

If you remain non-attached (neither attached nor detached for both are volitional), the body's *prarabdha* will effortlessly carry it through whatever activities are meant for it in this life. You remain surrendered to the Self, everything else disappears. No more questions, doubts, or misgivings arise. This is the way for unshakable *shanti* [peace].

Q: Back at home, they have introduced the following new prayer in my local church after the Vesper service: 'My Lord give me the courage to change what requires to be altered, the serenity to accept what cannot be helped and the insight to be able to tell the one from the other.' *Is this not what Bhagavan calls the surrender of the responsibility for one's life to God?*
B: What you describe is a baby step towards unconditional surrender, which is quite unequivocally absolute and does not ask this or that. Letting go of everything is called surrender. The one whose mind has totally surrendered would have nothing to ask. He may simply think *'I let go'* once and thereafter he abides as the eternally silent one whose ego remains perpetually merged in its source.

The prayer you describe is a partial surrender. If the strength of the *sadhaka's vairagya* [a spiritual practitioner's detachment] be maintained, throughout all hours of waking and dream, at an all-

consuming level of intensity, then partial surrender leads to absolute surrender. Absolute surrender is the goal of all spiritual practice.

Q: For one who has completely surrendered, is Vichara *unnecessary?*
B: Having surrendered without the slightest reserve, who should be left to make the *Vichara?*

Q: Is it true that by coming around this Hill repeatedly, Realisation can be gained in a relatively short span of time?
B: Provided you unconditionally surrender yourself to the Hill.

Q: Does Bhagavan have any parting instruction for me?
B: Only the usual.

Q: Which is?
B: To perpetually abide in the state in which the ego is merged in its source.

Bhagavan Teaching Dialogues

In Diary Date Order

Summer 1936

July - September

Diary Date Order – Summer 1936
5th July 1936

Vairagya, Vichara and Grace

Q: Is it true that for complete beginners, meditation on an object is easier than attempting to practise Vichara *[Self-enquiry]?*
B: Yes. As the aspirant gains one-pointedness *[ekagrata]* of mind, then he can commence with *Vichara.*

Q: Should sadhakas *[seekers] then be discouraged from taking up* Vichara *whilst yet being beginners?*
B: Let us leave each one to take up that method or path which appeals the most to him. All other methods, if persevered with long enough, eventually lead up only to *Vichara. Vichara* begins to have significant effect after the aspirant is able to plainly distinguish between the inward-turned and outward-turned mind, and hastens to avoid the latter and inhere in the former as soon as he has observed that his mind is wandering.

Q: How shall I get vairagya *[renunciation]?*
B: A correct understanding of the actual nature of happiness will lead you to it. Now you seek happiness but think that happiness flows into you from the outside world, or that your mind absorbs happiness from the external, objective world. But what is the truth? Far from causing happiness, the appearance of manifestation is the cause for all our wretchedness. The pleasure that is got by interaction of the mind with objects of sensory perception also has the obverse side of pain. The desire for happiness is right but you have been deluded by *avidyamaya* [illusion caused by ignorance] into imagining associated pain and transient pleasures to be real happiness.

Sensory perceptions yield short lived pleasure which moreover causes pain in its wake. Pain and pleasure alternate with one another

in the world. To ascertain the difference between fleeting, momentary and pain-associated happiness with the Supreme Happiness of the Self and confine oneself wisely to exclusively the latter is known as *vairagya*. Knowing that pursuit of sensory fascinations leads only to pain, why do you go in that direction? It is owing to the pull of the old habits of the mind. After these *vasanas* [mental habits] wear off, you will have abiding peace. The habits cannot suddenly be shaken off in one day. They will go only by prolonged *abhyasa* [practice] and steady *vairagya*.

Q: What is the role of the Guru in making the mind steady?
B: The Guru will only suggest that you surrender yourself unconditionally. He will not give you anything new which you have not got already.

Q: The mind is peaceful for a while, but after some time, again, the old mischievous tendencies assume control over the mind and lead it astray. I don't know what to do.
B: By continuous practice you will succeed in retaining the mind in its source. The state of submergence of mind in its source is its natural state. If you want to regain the natural state, a tremendous fight is inevitable.

Q: What is the one thing which I should know properly so as to gain the upper hand in this fight?
B: That you should never trust anything being deposited into the field of your consciousness that may pull you away from the path that leads into further and further introversion of mind.

Q: So, visions are not necessarily a sign of spiritual progress?
B: Do not be deceived by visions. Even if I appear before you, do not believe it. Only continuously attend to the task of keeping the mind incessantly submerged in the Shining of the Heart. This is the only thing you need to do; remain permanently submerged in the Shining of the Heart.

Q: Guru's Grace or God's Grace is required for it. Please bless me with your Grace.

B: Introversion of mind and Grace are the same thing. The natural Self-luminosity *[Sahaja Swayam Prakasha]* of the soul is the Grace of God or the Grace of Guru. Why go searching outside for Grace? Is it not fruitless to do so? Is there anything outside you?

Q: So, Grace is something I can acquire as a result of my own efforts?

B: Effort allows you to obtain Grace, not deserve it.

Q: What are the indications that a person is a chosen recipient of the Grace of God or Self?

B: There is no need to bother with conceptualisations of Grace, such as the one that you mentioned. Grace is said to descend upon the introverted mind because introversion of mind and Grace are the same thing. Grace is essentially the same as the Self.

Q: I am not able to come here as often as I would like to. My work commitments prevent it.

B: You regard the physical body as real and hence all your troubles, whereas there are no limitations in the Self. Time and space are operative on the physical plane. Since we think that we are physical, we are enslaved by time and space. Realisation means not imagining that you are this and that, not thinking that you are conditioned by so and so circumstances. Are you in the world or is the world in you? In deep sleep did the world come and announce itself to you? Nevertheless, did you not exist in deep sleep? Are you different from the one that existed in deep sleep? Why then bother about time and space, which are merely concepts conjured up by the effervescent mind? Know that what you are in sleep is your true nature. That sleep continues even now, hold on to the state of sleepless sleep and see if these questions arise.

Q: How to sleep without sleeping?

B: By always retaining the mind in its source and never allowing it to

stray outwards. By practice, the state will gradually become spontaneous. That perfectly spontaneous state of continuous, volitionless and effortless thoughtlessness is the coveted state of sleepless sleep. That is the object of our efforts. It will come only by long practice.

Q: How to remind myself that I am not the body?
B: Compare the present state with deep sleep. Were you with a body in sleep? Did you not exist all the same? The same 'I' which slept is now also present. Hold on to Him. The experience of bodilessness that was in deep sleep is also now. Even now you are bodiless. Only rein in the malefic force that asserts contrariwise thought.

Q: How shall I get Nirvikalpa Samadhi *[state of being temporarily absorbed in the Absolute]?*
B: What is *Nirvikalpa Samadhi?* It is to remain permanently submerged in the Shining of the Heart. In sleep, swoon, death, and so on we merge into the Heart unconsciously. In *Samadhi* [union with reality] we merge into the Heart consciously. Why remain apart from the source? Who is that one who wishes to remain apart from his source? Is his existence not mere pretension? The idea of your existence as an individual being is called *moola avarana* [covering the Truth]. The idea is false, because as soon as he is steadily called upon to investigate himself and announce his existence the ego flies away. Then only Reality is left. This process is known as Realising the Self. But there is nothing to be newly gained. The one who dissipates the clouds does not create sky.

Sadhana Is Needed

Q: I have listened to lectures on Advaita *and read much* Advaitic *Scriptures. Yet there is no Realisation for me.*
B: A man devoured an entire library's worth of books on swimming

but was afraid to even scratch the surface of the water with his toe. Yet he wanted to win an Olympic gold medal at the next swimming event.

Q: I understand that Bhagavan is trying to exhort me to commit myself to sadhana *[practice]. Now please tell me what* sadhana *is and what its aims are.*
B: *Sadhana* means to make effort to turn the mind inwards. The aim of *sadhana* is to achieve a perpetual state of mind in which there is effortlessly and volitionlessly maintained thought-free and lethargy-free Subjective Consciousness. The consequence of *sadhana* is that it eventually brings about Realisation of the Real.

Q: How long shall I perform sadhana*? And which* sadhana *is the best?*
B: *Sadhana* is needed until the one who could perform it has completely disappeared. The *sadhana* chosen depends on the temperament of the individual concerned. The most direct way is to investigate Who am I? Those who are fit for it *[pakvis]* can plunge themselves into practising the *Vichara* as soon as they hear about it. Others, who do not find the *Vichara marga* [path of Self-enquiry] so appealing, may need to first qualify themselves with other practices, such as *murti dhyana* [meditation on a form of God], *pranayama* [controlling the breath], *hatha yoga* [physical yoga techniques], *mantra japa* [repetition of a mantra]. Once the mind has thus attained a certain degree of ripeness *[pakkuvam]*, it will automatically feel the pull of *Vichara*.

Q: How long will it take for me, by performing sadhana*, to become a* Jnani *[Self-realised sage] like Sri Bhagavan?*
B: Remain free from the idea that there is something called Realisation which you yet have to attain. This idea is also an obstacle that needs to be given up before Realisation can be had. Perfect freedom from ideas, for ideas are nothing but thoughts that emerge from arbitrary mental conceptualisations, is necessary to have been obtained before that denuded state of mind can be gained which is essential for securing Realisation.

Q: If I go on practising Vichara, *will thoughts stop at one point in time?*
B: Yes, that is the aim. Ceaseless practice is essential until one remains, without the least effort or volition, in that natural and primal state of mind which is wholly free from thought and intention.

6th July 1936

Vasanas – The Obstacles to the Final State

Major Chadwick was an English army officer who lived in the ashram from 1935 until his death in 1962 and was a close devotee of Bhagavan. ED

Chadwick: Practice means encountering every thought with the counter-thought, 'To whom has this thought arisen?' Am I correct?
B: Asking Who am I? should return the mind to its primordial nature of Naked Beingness. That is its purpose and goal.

C: Beingness or subjective awareness uncontaminated by thought is also a component of mind. It remains after asking Who am I? Thus, when Bhagavan propounds that asking the question leads to destruction of mind, I am puzzled by the statement.
B: Beingness is not a component of the mind; it is its substratum. When that uncontaminated awareness remains so permanently, having once and for all lost all volition to spill itself over into the realm of thought, it is also destroyed, but you have no role in that final destruction, nor do you have any power to bring it about. It is left entirely to the Beyond.

C: After that final destruction, what is left?
B: The Beyond. It is known as *Parabrahman* [the supreme Self]. It cannot be described. The mind cannot imagine it. Yet it is your true Self.

C: So, our final aim is only this Parabrahman. *Attaining it is called Self-realisation. Am I correct?*
B: There is no attaining it. If the reflected consciousness is cleared away, only the original consciousness remains. Destruction of the reflecting phenomenon, namely the delusive ego-mind, is the goal, or rather reveals the Goal. That is Self-realisation.

C: Once attained, can Self-realisation be lost?
B: The nomenclature used should be clear. Even a glimpse of *Brahman* [the eternal reality] by the mind in the realm of subjective awareness, can be called Self-realisation. Does it lead to freedom from rebirth or embodiment? No. A man cannot become a high officer merely by visiting one, making note of his educational qualifications and mimicking his attire. The exceedingly rare state of *Sahajajnanastithi* [established or dwelling in *Brahman*] is available only to one who has no *vrittis* [structures of the mind] left in the mind. Desires, attachments, opinions, preferences, traits of personality, et cetera, are all examples of *vrittis*.

They cause pure Subjective Consciousness to spill over into the deceptive realm of thought, and trap one in the vicious cycle of births and deaths, that is, of embodiment. In those whose bondage is strong, *vrittis* are found to have impregnated themselves so strongly and deeply that they manifest as *vishaya vasanas* [desire after sense objects]. *Vishaya vasanas* are difficult to eradicate because they carry a pretentious, duplicitous sense of legitimacy about them. For instance, if a man is starving, try to go and tell him it is all in his imagination. You will likely be placing yourself at the receiving end of a few well aimed blows.

C: (laughs) But then surely...the basic requirements of bodily-sustenance, food, water, clothes, a modest roof over one's head...surely these can be considered reasonable?

B: Do not think that they are your requirements. They are the body's.

C: I am not the body, yet it is my duty to take reasonable care of the body. Am I correct? Not all have the Herculean spiritual strength to throw themselves into an abandoned underground cellar filled with centipedes and rats and focus on the Self only!

B: There is no need to fall into any cellar. If the 'body am I' idea is given up and one surrenders oneself unconditionally to the mercy of the Higher Power, then responsibility for the body's maintenance is automatically thrown on the Higher Power and He carries on from there. You should not think, *'I have the duty of taking care of the body.'* You have entrusted yourself to him, leave everything including the body to him. He manages everything supremely well. His ways are mysterious but in the end the job is done.

C: I have heard Bhagavan saying that the total destruction of all vasanas *is possible only in the final* Sahajastithi *[natural state]; I have also heard him say that without such destruction being effected the said state cannot be gained. It sounds paradoxical.*

B: It is paradoxical on the spurious, apparently real level of the ego only. The ego is a self-contained illusion, when it goes away you find that it never existed.

C: I do not understand.

B: If Zeno's paradox of the racecourse were to be true, we should find it impossible to move from one place to another. Yet so far as the paradox is concerned, it appears sincerely true when studied or considered in isolated intellectual light. Is our day-to-day life experience compatible with the inference that is to be drawn from the paradox? Do we not find motion possible? Likewise, when pondered over using the intellect, the question of Self-realisation is a vexatious paradox; if the intellect is bypassed or transcended only the realm of Being remains. Therein no questions arise and only silence reigns.

C: Vasanas *are a decisive obstacle to Self-realisation; yet repeated and continuous practice of* Vichara *roots out the* vasanas *and liberation is ultimately gained. So far it is clear. Can Bhagavan please tell me how the* vasanas *arose out of what was originally pure Subjective Consciousness?*
B: The idea that *vasanas* are at present irrevocably riveted together with consciousness and that removing them through *sadhana* involves splitting these two ordinarily intertwined components of mind, is an incorrect understanding. *Vasanas* are seed-like impressions that direct consciousness along the narrow, finite channel known as the intellect. *Vasanas* are infinitesimal, insentient, imaginary accretions that appear to have gathered atop the fathomless Self and prevent it from shining. They are neither real nor natural.

Only Being is Real. You may dive into or submerge yourself in the Shining of the Heart and forget about annihilating the *vasanas*. Abiding in that state in which mind has permanently been rendered one and identical with the Beingness of the Self, one need not worry about the fact that the mind is yet to die a conclusive death. Let *granthinasam* [destruction of the knot] happen when it is destined to happen. You remain attending to ensuring absence of promiscuity of thought, and that is enough. When thoughts about *vasanas* perturb you, see whose *vasanas* they are.

C: The Self is the Almighty; such tiny vasanas *are able to obscure it!*
B: The obscuration is self-notional only. There is no ignorance in fact. Yet whilst *vasanas* remain the final state will never be gained.

12th July 1936

Pure Subjective Consciousness

Q: What does the practice of Vichara *feel like whilst one is actually engaged in it?*
B: Go on seeing, *'What is this "me"?'* But doing it intellectually is not the right way.

Q: All mental activity does involve the intellect.
B: Yes. This is cessation of mental activity. Realisation is not 'you' attaining to some exalted state. Realisation is the irreversible death of 'you'.

Q: You mean death of the ego; for I am the Self and cannot die.
B: It is precisely this wretched misunderstanding that causes so many *sadhakas* to go astray.

Q: I don't understand.
B: You are the ego until the ego has been destroyed. What is the use of intellectually denying the existence of the ego while still remaining as it? Why falsely arrogate yourself to the status of being the Heart? Is it the Heart who is talking to me now?

Q: Am I not the Self?
B: Whose Self are you?

Q: I am the Self of myself.
B: Is there, or is there not, in you an intermediary entity subsisting on thought forms?

Q: Yes. Thoughts come. But they are not apart from the Self, that is what I tell myself.
B: No, that is not the way.

Q: What am I doing wrong? Please tell me.
B: You are still operating on the plane of the intellect.

Q: Tell me how I can get past it.
B: 'I' cannot get past it. 'I' is 'It'.

Q: So, I should learn to overcome myself?
B: No. Learn to subside into the actual Self.

Q: But how?
B: Resign yourself to pure Subjective Consciousness.

Q: Effort is needed to remain in that state. There is the one that makes the effort. His presence is unavoidable.
B: Yes, the *ahamvritti* ['I'-thought] can only be further and further attenuated, but can never be completely destroyed by effort, because the one making that effort still remains. However, when a certain critical radius of introversion is reached, the Heart reaches over and pulls you inside, finishing the job. In order for this to happen, however, the *ahamvritti* should be reduced into a single, infinitesimal point bereft of dimension.

The *ahamvritti* can finally wander into this point-like form only by means of deploying a *sadhana* in which the one making the effort is the same as that in relation to which the effort is made.

There is only one such *sadhana*: Who am I? 'I' is not merely a thought, it is a deeply entrenched idea, which thus requires a deep incision to uproot. Therefore, the wisest thing for one to do is to catch hold of this foundational thought, the 'I'-thought, and examine it. What is this 'me'? Giving thereby no chance to other thoughts to distract one. There lies the true value of the *Vichara* and its efficacy in getting rid of the mind.

There Must Be a Burning Fascination with 'I'

Q: I try to follow Bhagavan's Vichara *method. I do not succeed in Realising. Why?*
B: Why do you practise *Vichara*?

Q: Because I want to Realise.
B: That is the mistake.

Q: I don't understand.
B: There must be a burning curiosity about or fascination with the 'I', including with its source, per se. If investigation of the 'I' is carried out with some other motive, it will never work.

Q: How can I acquire this fascination?
B: It comes automatically once a certain degree of spiritual maturity is reached.

Q: How is this maturity to be attained?
B: Various ways are available. But whatever previous development there may be, earnest *Vichara* escalates it.

Q: *That is arguing in a circle. I am strong enough for the quest if I am mature and it is the quest that makes me mature.*
B: The mind does have this sort of difficulty. It wants a fixed theory to satisfy itself with. But actually, no theory is necessary for the earnest *sadhaka* [one who engages in spiritual practice] who toils with unintermittent determination to erase the mind.

Q: Is it necessary to be free from even the desire or resolve to Realise?
B: Yes. But that would be one of the last desires or *sankalpas* [desires] to be expelled.

Q: When my health takes a turn for the worse, as it does occasionally, I feel fear. What should I do during those occasions? Should I tell myself that I am not the body but the Self, and that there is thus no need to worry because the Self is deathless, or should I investigate to whom the fear has arisen? Which approach is more in conformity with Sri Bhagavan's teachings?
B: The latter.

Q: Does the act of visiting sacred places of pilgrimage also contribute to introversion of mind?
B: Yes.

14th July 1936

Tantric Sex and 1/128th of a Second of No Mind

Q: It cannot be denied that it is sexual desire that causes man to engage in coitus, even when reproduction is not the motive. Yet the desire is dormant in man. He is not to be blamed for his body's biological urges. Yet if the desire is not eradicated there can be no hope of Liberation.

Why has God created such urges and cravings in man? Do they not raise a barrier between man and God and prevent the former from attaining the latter? Does God want to make it difficult for people to attain Him? If so, what sort of ridiculous God is He.

Also, can I please have Bhagavan's opinion on the ancient Hindu practice of Tantric sex? Is it genuine? Is there any benefit in it?
B: The urges you mentioned are *vasanas*. *Vasanas* are beginningless but one can put an end to them by engaging in steady, continuous *Vichara*. *Vichara* can only be into the not-Self. The Self needs no *Vichara*. There is no need for one Self to discover another. There are not two selves. What is not-Self, has no Being and is therefore of no relevance. People call the investigation into one's faculty of 'I'-ness

Atma Vichara [Self-enquiry], whereas it would be more accurate to refer to it by the name of *ahamkara Vichara* [enquiry into the nature of the ego]. Instead of asking where the *vasanas* have begun from, ask yourself to whom the *vasanas* give trouble and if the practice is prolonged and unintermittent you will discover that there has been really no trouble nor any *vasana.*

You ask about the biological sexual urge. That is impregnated in the ego-mind-body complex to facilitate reproduction, according to nature's design. If the act did not involve pleasure, man would likely ask '*Why should I give birth to children?*' and there may be no impetus to propagate the species. Thus, the act must involve some sort of paroxysm of joy. If it is intellectual pleasure, only those with highly developed intellects would be able to bring forth children. But nature does not want it to be so. So, the pleasure must be something more fundamental, something that produces an infinitesimally tiny reflection of man's true nature of unlimited bliss.

What is the highest joy man can know? It is the state of no-mind. Daily he experiences it in sleep. Only the yogi has experience of it in waking; for the *Jnani* [the Self-realised sage] there can be no question of experiencing anything. So, nature has seen fit to introduce this bliss of no-mind in the coital act, so that even the most dull-witted ones are not left out of the chance to bring forth progeny onto the earth. All would be tempted towards it, as it contains the inherent bliss of one's own Self. Though heavily veiled by *upadhis* [limitations] to avoid the possibility of the act itself being deployed as *sadhana.*

A moment before the commencement of the spasms that bring about the emission of the seminal fluid, for precisely 1/128th of a second, the mind is removed. It is like a plate being exposed with a very quick shutter speed. The impression of the bliss tasted, leaves behind a strong craving for more such bliss in the mind. This is how men end up addicted to the act. There are schools among the Tantra *sastra* [sacred scriptures] proponents who opine the Self can be discovered by concentrating the mind on the bliss rather than on the act, at the time of performing such acts. They say that if the

concentration is strong enough, the Self will be revealed. To this end they emphasise the need for 'more and more practice' (laughs). I have also heard that there was once an esoteric society in Peloponnese that promoted the same view.

16th July 1936

From Vichara, Aham Sphurana Flashes Forth

Q: What are the indicators based on which I shall be enabled to find out for myself whether I am doing Vichara *correctly or not?*
B: If *Vichara* has resulted in a state of mind wherein it abides as identical with pure Subjective Consciousness, then you have done it correctly. However, it is not easy for the beginner to tell whether his mind is presently abiding as identical with pure Subjective Consciousness, because the torpid mental state of *manolayam* [state where mind structures are hazily projected] is often mistakenly regarded as being the tabula rasa (Latin: clean slate) mental state of pure Subjective Consciousness.

When mind abides as identical with pure Subjective Consciousness, it unmistakeably scintillates 'I'-'I'. Thus, the definitive answer to your question is that *Vichara* has been done correctly when doing it has resulted in the *Aham Sphurana* flashing forth.

Q: And how to recognise the Aham Sphurana *when it 'flashes forth'?*
B: There is no possibility of mistaking it when the experience actually occurs. Whatever description is given is not only useless but also counter-productive, because if a description of the experience of *Aham Sphurana* is given, the mind twists and contorts the present banal experience of outward protruding, copiousness craving mental

impulses into one that seems to perfectly match with the description given; because it wants to avoid getting destroyed.

So, even if you have heard a description of the experience of the *Aham Sphurana* being furnished in this Hall, please make no effort to recollect it. When the *Aham Sphurana* actually flashes forth, you will know it alright. Cognition of the *Aham Sphurana* is not based on intellectual corroboration. It is a direct experience of the Self, inferior only to the *Sahajastithi* [natural state] of the *Jnani*.

Q: Is the Aham Sphurana *something that is felt only by ripe souls?*
B: Yes.

Q: What are the others to do then?
B: (smiling) **Ripen themselves!**

Q: How?
B: *Vichara abhyasa* is the way.

Q: I would now like to ask a slightly different, but related, question. Please tell me how I can find out how much progress I am making with respect to the Vichara abhyasa.
B: The length of time for which you are able to keep the mind in a state wherein it abides as identical with pure Subjective Consciousness is the yardstick by which you can find out how efficaciously you are practising *Vichara*. However, more pragmatically, it is the degree of the absence of both mental boisterousness, imagining this and that, and mental lethargy, falling into a pleasant state of mental relaxation in which thoughts are absent but sleep is poking its head just around the corner, for example the mental sensation experienced immediately after a post afternoon meal in which one's favourite items of delicacy have been consumed, especially when there is not much work anticipated for the remainder of that day, is the means to measure progress. However, the desire to progress is an obstacle so get rid of it. Ask yourself who it is that wants to measure progress.

An Unhappy Major Chadwick

Chadwick: (unhappily) I have been staying here for months. I see no improvement in me. If anything, my condition seems to be taking a turn for the worse. The viscosity of my thoughts is on the wax. I am consistently using Bhagavan's Vichara *method. Yet there is no diminution in the strength of the army of thought that I am attacked by day after day.*

I am desperate to Realise in this lifetime. Or, if I am born again, Bhagavan must also agree to be born again to help me Realise in the next life. Without Bhagavan what can I do?

Someone from the back of the Hall called out, *'He is a* Jivanmukta *[liberated soul]. Where is the possibility of further birth for Him? Is not the suggestion absurd?'*

Chadwick merely ignored him.

B: Give up the idea that you are striving for Realisation.

C: (aghast) What?! Bhagavan would have me abandon the quest? Has he decided I am unworthy to Realise?

B: Did you pay attention to what was said to you? You were not asked to abandon the quest. You were asked to abandon the spurious idea that there is a 'you' which is trying to merge with a 'super you'.

C: Yes, the jivatman *[individual soul] into the* Paramatman *[Supreme Self].*

B: Oh! Wonderful! Very good! So, you have also picked up these terms. Only the other day I explained: one who asserts or believes in the existence of the *jivatman* – will he ever Realise?

C: If there is no jivatman *who is the* sadhaka?

B: Exactly.

C: (gloomily) I understand nothing.

B: Throw away the belief in the existence of the personal self. It is only on that erroneous basis that you are now asking questions.

C: But I must remain to perform sadhana!
B: What is the objective of *sadhana?*

C: Destruction of the ego.
B: No, transcendence of the idea of its existence.

C: So, if I just free myself from the idea that I exist as an individual person, the Who am I? method is not needed?
B: First discard that erroneous idea. In having discarded that idea, do not bring in any other idea in its place, such as *Aham Brahmasmi* [I am *Brahman*], I am being consciousness, et cetera. Remain free from all ideas, that is from all mental identification. Let the mind remain in the state of pure Subjective Consciousness free from all objectification or identification.

Then, as and when thoughts arise, tackle them with the counter-thought, 'To whom has this thought arisen?' This arrests the further development of the thought. Then return the mind to its native state of pure Subjective Consciousness. This is the way.

C: Will repetition of 'I am not the ego, but I am the Absolute Self' help to weaken the grip of the ego?
B: No. It is a mental activity. It strengthens the ego and makes it more noisy. Hear these verses (Bhagavan reads out Tamil verses from a notebook): ***Oh mind! Thou hast already suffered, thinking 'I am a* jiva *[soul]'. Do not fall into worse delusion by believing 'I am* Brahman*'.***

In the Transcendental State there is no one answering to the name of 'I'. Man behaves recklessly, even while believing 'I am this very little body.' If he begins to imagine 'I am the Supreme One', will anything remain that he will consider wrong to do?

C: For Realisation, is it enough if I read Bhagavan's works or should I read the ancient Hindu Advaita *texts also, such as Adi Shankara (Famous 8th Century teacher of* Advaita Vedanta), *Nishchal Das (19th century Indian sage), and so on?*
B: (reading out from another page of the notebook) ***When mirage***

water serves to quench thirst and painted fire to cook meals, then deliverance can be had by mere book knowledge.

Just as a dull-witted woman may believe that the festivities of marriage constitute conjugal bliss, so also the foolish man that has not won the experience of Truth imagines book knowledge has brought him that experience.

C: Should I not acquire a good grounding in the basic concepts?
B: The pamphlets made available here will do. Read them repeatedly if you feel like doing any reading. Dig deeper, not wider.

18 July 1936

Bhagavan's Lecture on Shankara

An elderly pandit arrived at the ashram. He handed a slender notebook containing verses written in Sanskrit to the Master. Apparently, he desired to hear from Bhagavan a lecture on *Shankara's Aparokshanuboothi*. When he arrived, the Master was very gracious with him, asking him where he was coming from, et cetera. When he disclosed his desire to hear the aforesaid lecture, Bhagavan kept quiet.

He was told that the Master was not in the habit of giving lectures. If he required any specific clarifications, he could ask. But the pandit was woefully adamant, saying he was an old man and this may be considered the last desire in his life since next month he was going to Benares to die.

He pleaded and begged Bhagavan. Since the latter had already shown him some kindness, the pandit seemed to think he had a right to cajole the Master into giving in to his whims. Then he burst into tears and tried to catch hold of Bhagavan's feet; this the attendants would not allow. So, seizing hold of the sofa, he began banging his head against it, beseeching shrilly, *'Bhagavane! Bhagavane!'* Eventually Bhagavan was forced to relent. It was late in the night when Bhagavan finished the lecture. Except for the usual adjournments to the dining hall and his wonted walk on the Hill, Bhagavan had not stirred from the sofa today, nor had he attended to any other task.

The pandit had keenly listened to every word uttered. At the conclusion, he seemed profoundly moved, and wept, saying, *'Today my life's purpose has reached its consummation; the culmination of all the* punya *[good actions] done by me in this and all previous births has been successfully harvested by me today.'* Bhagavan merely looked on in his austere, pensive manner. When the Master was talking his face would be scintillant with exuberance and vivacity and one felt his incalculable Love pouring out into one; when his attention was not directed towards anyone in particular the look of utter detachment on that same face would often entice, if not spontaneously elicit, a feeling of unutterable awe and indescribable adulation from the onlooker. There were times when a palpable deluge of *Jnana* radiation seemed to fulminate out of the gaunt figure so unostentatiously and unpretentiously seated on the sofa. Perhaps it was always there, and one's mind was alert or sensitive enough to attend to it only on certain occasions favourable to the purpose.

I heard reports of people coming with notebooks filled with questions, sitting for two minutes in his presence, the notebook and all else would be forgotten. Recollecting it later they would laugh at the notebook and tear up the sheets containing the questions they had earlier felt like asking. Whilst he was explaining Shankaracharya's work, I opine I could obtain a tiny glimpse into Bhagavan's own inner state, without any voluntary effort on my part, and it has thrilled me to the core. For the rest of my life, never shall I forget that serene poise, that nonchalant manner of countenance, or that unique combination of indifference and compassion, all arising from an unfathomable inner calm, whilst handling people.

The pandit, once he had finished with his tears, fell prostrate on the floor and stayed so for a quarter of an hour, his hands stretched out before him with palms joined in salutation. The only movement in his body was that his head was speedily half-rotating from side to side, he was pressing his left and right ears against the floor alternately. At length he got up, bent his torso over till it was parallel to the ground, pressed palms still clutched in front of his chest and mumbled a few incoherent, teary words. Bhagavan looked at him and smiled brightly. The man reluctantly retreated towards the doors, unable to tear his eyes away from Bhagavan until he was well through them.

20th July 1936

Mouna Is the Beauty of Eternal Eloquence

Q: What is this mouna?
B: *Mouna* is not keeping the mouth shut. It is the beauty of eternal eloquence.

Q: I do not understand.
B: That which transcends speech and thought is *mouna*.

Q: How to achieve it? I find Vichara *to be too abstract for me.*
B: Hold some *vritti* firmly and trace it back to the source of thought. Pursued constantly, the result of such introversion is that silence of mind eventually becomes volitionless and effortless. Only when practice of *mouna* becomes the natural state of mind will the thinking mind be transformed into a mind that is wholly identical with pure Subjective Consciousness. The only route to Realisation of the Self lies in permanent, volitionless and effortless abidance in and as the Beingness of the Self.

Absence of mental activity is the natural silence of *Jnana*. On the other hand, forced subjugation of the mind is meditation. *Vichara* is more beneficial than *dhyana* [meditation]. *Dhyana* quietens the mind or puts it to sleep, whereas *Vichara* does not rest until the mind is conclusively dead. After *manonasam* [destruction of the mind], *mouna* alone resounds triumphantly in the Heart. So, *mouna* is really eternal speech.

Q: How will worldly activities go on if one gives up all thoughts?
B: When women who are climbing uphill carry water pots on their heads and chat with their companions all along the way, they remain very careful. Their thoughts are focused only upon the loads on their heads. The conversation is mere banter. Similarly, when an earnest *sadhaka* engages in worldly activities, these do not disturb him because his mind abides as one and identical with the Beingness of the Self.

Q: Since the mind of the Jnani *is already dead, who is performing his worldly actions?*
B: He is not doing anything. Some power functions through him. Thus, his actions can never go wrong. There does not remain anything in him that can trouble itself about the body's actions or omissions.

Q: It is alright for the Realised Soul. What of myself? My actions frequently lead to disastrous consequences. Once I attain Jnana, *will I be free from the pain of worrying over whether I have done the right thing in relation to a given set of circumstances or sequence of events?*
B: Reach the state and then see for yourself. Why indulge in idle speculation?

Ripe Souls Attain Jnana

Q: It is said that the Jnani *breathes* Jnana *into others through the power of his silence, that words are not necessary for him. How does the* Jnani *enlighten his disciples? He does not lecture them with homilies. Does he use telepathic communication, then?*

B: His bodily presence creates a natural 'force field' of mental quietness in the vicinity. Science has made the observation that if an adequate length of insulated copper wire is repeatedly wound around an iron truncheon and then electricity is passed through the wire, iron filings placed near the truncheon are attracted to it. There is no modus operandi visible to the naked eye by means of which the magnetised iron is able to influence the iron filings, yet in fact it happens.

Likewise, the invisible waves of *Jnana* radiating off the mindless one, spontaneously effect those around him, whether they are aware of it or not. Sensitive minds become aware of it. Just like iron filings are quietly sucked towards the magnetised iron bar, the *Jnani's* silent influence introverts the mind and facilitates its submergence or absorption in the Beingness of the Self. Once the initial right experience has been gained in vicinity of the *Jnani's* presence, thereafter, as a result of incessant practice, the *sadhaka* understands that the state of extroversion is a departure from the natural state and that effortlessly and volitionlessly maintained thought-free and lethargy-free Subjective Consciousness is the natural state.

The *Jnani* does not plan that such and such person should on such and such day obtain from him such and such spiritual experience. Just like water spontaneously flows from higher to lower levels, the minds of those around the *Jnani* experience the benefit of his presence. Ripe souls attain *Jnana*, middling souls or dilettantes on the path feel tempted to try out *Vichara*, and the layperson feels for the first time in his life that he should set apart time exclusively for contemplation of God. The *Jnani* does not purposely bring about all these transformations any more than the sun is emitting sunshine with the motive of making the flowers on the earth bloom.

By learning from the *Jnani,* through feeling contact, that the denuded state of mind, in which there remains nothing to asseverate 'I', is the correct state for the mind to remain plunged into all the time, the *sadhaka* eventually makes the *manonivritti* [mind turned inwards] state his natural state. It is only then that he reaches the formless realm of Indestructible Peace. Note that all this is from the *sadhaka's* point of view only. The *Jnani* cannot be aware of any 'others' to help, nor is he necessarily even aware that he is bringing about all this; it all merely happens by the Power of the Presence.

Q: I feel no such magnetic effect in Bhagavan's presence. What fault have I committed?
B: I have already said that it requires sensitivity of mind. Nevertheless, your inability to feel its palpability does not impair or diminish its effectiveness. You may not feel the potency of the *Jnani's* silent influence. Yet, it is there and it is helping you, notwithstanding that your opinion may be contrary.

The Natural State of Mind

Q: How long should Jnana Vichara *[contemplation of wisdom] be practised?*
B: Until the natural state of effortless and volitionless thoughtlessness is regained. Consider this ancient story from Thracia:

> ***Once upon a time, a hungry fox seeing some bread and meat left behind by shepherds in the hollow of an aged oak tree, stealthily crept into the hole and obtained for himself a hearty meal. When he finished eating his stomach was so full that he was not able to get out. He began to groan and lament his fate. Another fox passing by heard his cries and coming up enquired the cause of***

> ***his complaining. On learning what had happened, he said unto him,* 'Ah! you will have to remain there my friend until you become such as you were when you crept in and then you will easily get out.'**

So, without regaining the primal state of mind, escape from the infernal abyss known as *samsara* [cycle of birth and death caused by *karma*] is not possible.

Q: What is this natural state of the mind?
B: Pure Subjective Consciousness sustained effortlessly and volitionlessly.

Q: How can I not make an effort to do something and yet do it? It sounds quixotic and ridiculous.
B: You are so used to doing, that your true nature of restful non-doing has become alien to you. Since your departure from the natural state has plunged you into an ocean of unending activity, you have become quite alienated from your natural state of blissful inactivity. So, you are framing the absurd question, *'What can I do to regain the natural state?'* It is like asking, *'In order for the maximum amount of light to be facilitated to spill forth from this lantern, in what position shall I hold my hand in front of the lens?'* If you simply take your hand away, the light shines clear and bright. So, let go of the ego and the Self is revealed. But people will not understand this. They want formulas, concepts, methods. In short, they want something they can 'do'.

Whenever they have wanted something in their lives, they have done something to obtain it and probably succeeded. So, they think Enlightenment can also be won this way. Many charlatans also cater to the psychological requirements of such gullible people, prescribing mental exercises for them that plunge their minds into a state of deliberately sustained bliss. Thus, the poor victims think they have successfully Enlightened themselves! (laughs) **But no! No amount of doing or meditating can reveal the Self. The loftiest, most**

useful, and most legitimate advice that can be given to an aspirant for Realisation is simply *'Summa Iru'* [be still]. But people want a formula by means of which this can be achieved. Therefore, *Jnana Vichara* is prescribed.

One who is desperate enough in his wanting to Realise will not waste time in gossip, he will abruptly abandon everything contained within his mind. Thus, only the denuded mind remains, which too is eventually devoured by the Self. Do not be attached to the body and do not aim at satisfaction of the never-ending requirements of the personal self. These are transient, illusory appearances in the one real THAT. Whatever is born will certainly die. What is perishable is bound to perish. Why entrust your attachment to something that is doomed to disappear one day? *Samsara* is like a glowing red iron rod that one holds in one's hand, wearing the glove of *avidyamaya* [illusion caused by ignorance]. The evil power of *avidyamaya* never allows the full might of the misery of *samsara* to impress itself upon your mind; nor is the pain withheld altogether. If you were to actually feel the full heat of the iron rod you would instantly drop it and *avidyamaya* would be cheated out of her fun. So, the pain is given to you in manageable doses, so that you think foolishly, *'Oh! This life is a mixture of happiness and sorrow.'* Such an attitude allows the yearning for more experience of *samsara* to be still present in you.

One who longs for God with all his heart is helped by God as the glove is forcibly ripped apart. So, one who is a devout *bhakta* [devotee of God] may sometimes have to face stupendous tragedies that may make people remark, *'This is how God rewards his most sincere worshippers.'* This sarcastic statement is actually true in the literal sense. Whilst the glove is still on, you can never be persuaded into dropping the red iron rod. Once it is gone, discarding the furiously hot rod is inevitable because now, unlike before, the pain is too enormous to manage. Totally letting go of all the mind's contents is the only *sadhana* that is effective for Realisation; not destroying the mind. Mind, being fictitious, cannot be destroyed any more, than it is possible to kill a rope that one sees as a snake.

When we talk of destroyed mind, it is only a reference to a state wherein the illusion of world perception is permanently absent. How are you going to destroy what never was and what cannot be? If you want Realisation, all you need to do is this: LET GO OF EVERYTHING. That is, empty your mind. In fact, all who have Realised have done only this in the end, having given up all *sadhana* to be useless skulduggery.

Q: Is sadhana *not necessary to Realise?*
B: The only genuine *sadhana* is to give up all *sadhana*. The aim of all practices is only to give up all practices.

30th July 1936

Aham Sphurana Is the Intermediate Stage

Q: I remember Bhagavan once telling me that there exists somewhere in the human body an orifice as small as a pinpoint from which consciousness always streams out into the body. Is it open or shut?
B: It is always shut for it is the knot of unawareness which seemingly ties the body to consciousness. When the mind disappears in the temporary *Kevala Nirvikalpa* [temporary experience of non-dual awareness] it opens but then shuts again. In *Sahaja* [natural state] it remains always open.

Q: How is it during the experience of 'I'-'I' consciousness?
B: The 'I'-'I' consciousness or *Aham Sphurana* is the intermediate stage. Its function is that it serves as the key which severs the knot permanently. This knot between consciousness and the seemingly physical world is known as the *chidhjadagranthi* [knot

of ignorance]. So long as it remains tied, thus long ignorance lasts. So long as even an iota of the idea remains that one is this or that, that is, so long as the faculty of identification is still alive, so long as the mind identifies itself with the personality, or so long as the mind continues to believe in the veracity of its own contents, the mind will not die and thus the knot cannot be severed.

So long as *vishaya vasanas* [desire for objects] remain latent in the mind, permanent destruction of the mind cannot be achieved by any means. The *sadhaka's* aim must be to drain away the *vasanas* from the Heart. To this end, *Vichara* is the most effective method. It strikes at the root of the venomous tree of ignorance.

Q: Does the enquiry Who am I? lead to any spot in the body?
B: Self-consciousness is in relation to the individual himself and therefore has to be experienced in his being, with a place in the body as the centre of experience. This centre resembles the dynamo of a machine, which gives rise to all sorts of electrical energy discharges. It not only sustains life in the body and the activities of all its parts and organs, conscious and unconscious but is also the link between the physical and the subtle planes on both of which the individual functions.

Also, like the dynamo, it vibrates physically and can be felt by the still mind that pays attention to it. The state in which the denuded mind remains paying attention to this vibration alone is referred to as *Spandabhraja Samadhi* [absorption in the radiant, shining vibration that underlies existence] or *ahamsphoorthi* [awakening of the 'I'-consciousness]. In English, we call it 'I'-scintillation.

Q: If the mind is paying attention to something, as opposed to remaining submerged in its source, can we still call that state Samadhi?
B: The *ahamsphoorthi* or *Aham Sphurana* does not manifest except when the mind is submerged in its source. The mind paying attention to the vibration of 'I'-'I' that occurs in what is genuinely the state of *Aham Sphurana* does not involve duality.

Q: How can that be?
B: Because the mind is paying attention only to its own source, thereby remaining temporarily merged within it. The vibration 'I'-'I' does not constitute an object of contemplation, but rather the perfect introversion of the subject, at least for the time being until the *vasanas* begin to be active in him again.

Q: So, the state of Aham Sphurana *is impermanent?*
B: Initially it may be sporadic. Make it permanent by steadfast practice of *Vichara*. When the mind stands permanently dissolved in the source of pure Subjective Consciousness it is Realisation. In Realisation there is no feeling anything but only Absolute Awareness.

Q: How to reach that centre from where the 'I'-'I' consciousness arises? Is it by simply investigating Who am I?
B: Yes, it will take you inward of its own accord. You must do it with a tranquil mind. The *nivritti* state of mind is an essential prerequisite. That means that the objective outlook or the 'I am the body' idea should be given up. This enjoinment should not be understood to mean that one must think, *'I am not the body but the Immortal Self.'* When you are asked to give up thought, understand that it cannot be done by thinking, *'I must not think thought.'* A tabula rasa (clean slate) is not the same as a slate on which the words 'tabula rasa' have been inscribed.

Q: How will the 'I'-'I' consciousness manifest itself when the Heart is reached? Will I recognise it?
B: Certainly, as pure Subjective Consciousness, free from all thought. It is pristine unbroken awareness of the Beingness of the Self; there is no mistaking it when it remains uncontaminated by thought or by the faculty of intellection.

Q: Is the vibratory movement of this centre felt simultaneously with the experience of pure Subjective Consciousness?
B: Yes. But the *Sphurana* can be felt in a subtle way even when

inherence in the Shining of the Heart has sufficiently stabilised and deepened so as for Absolute Awareness to be very near or during a sudden great fright or shock when the mind comes to a standstill. It draws attention to itself, so that the seeker's mind, rendered sensitive by the absence of perturbation or agitation, may become aware of it. Gravitate towards it and finally plunge into it, the Self.

Q: Is the 'I'-'I' consciousness the same as Self-realisation?
B: No. It is merely a prelude to it. Only when it has led to the *Sahajastithi* of *Jnana* can it be Self-realisation or Emancipation.

Q: Having attained this 'I'-'I' consciousness, how does one proceed therefrom to the state of perfect Realisation?
B: The current makes you drown in it of its own accord. The only thing necessary is to stop fighting it and surrender to it.

2nd August 1936

Waves of Silence Whisking your Mind Away

Q: When sitting in front of a Jnani, *what is the proper mental temperament to be adopted?*
B: People try to purposely silence the mind. They only succeed in making the mind more and more rebellious. If you ignore the mind and its promptings whilst in the presence of one who is awake to Reality, the waves of silence emanating from Him will automatically engulf and whisk away your mind for at least some time. Then you will know what it is to remain in the state of mind in which there is effortlessly and volitionlessly maintained thought-free and languor-free Subjective Consciousness.

Even after tasting such intoxicating bliss the mind repeatedly tries to regain it. So, whilst in the physical proximity of the *Jnani* do not try to fight with the mind and do not attempt to silence it or make it return to its source. Rather pose no obstruction to the Higher Power from silently reabsorbing your mind from the inside. What *sadhana* of millennials of years of arduous *tapas* [austerity] may fail to reveal is revealed in a trice in the presence of the mindless One. Again, when the *Jnani* speaks, do not make the capital mistake of intellectualising his words.

Do not try to do anything with the words. Do not make an effort to implement what in your opinion the words are trying to say. Keep quiet. The words are not meant for the mind or faculty of intellection at all. They are seeds of *Jnana* that are planted by the Guru deep, deep down. If you keep periodically digging up a seed to check whether the same has sprouted or not, it will never sprout. Do not permit the intellect to spoil for yourself the benevolent effect of the Guru's outstretched helping hand of Compassionate Divine Grace. He who would try to 'do' something with the Guru's priceless *jnanopadesam* [imparting of spiritual knowledge] is, as a matter of fact, flinging it into the nearest heap of garbage.

Q: Should I then not practise Vichara *according to Sri Bhagavan's instructions?*

B: Certainly, you may do so. Only it should be done not because Bhagavan has asked you to do it but because you yourself feel the curiosity to explore the 'I'. Bhagavan does not recommend anybody to do this or that. He says what he knows, and different people find different statements of his to be suitable or appealing to themselves based on the contents of the accumulated mass of latent mental proclivities of each one. The fundamental question is, why should somebody tell you what to do? You are in sleep and that is a fact.

The same one that slept is now apparently awake and asking questions and raising doubts, whereas the sleeping one was silent. Why has this transition come over? To whom has it come over? Thus, simply by studying the alternating states of mind, one can plainly see that the mind and its contents are fully illusory. So, remain

without arising as the mind. Instead of doing this why should we adopt and practise a *sadhana* because somebody has asked us to or recommended it to us? Is there any need to ask suggestions from others as to how to get ruined by one's own Self?

Q: Myself.
B: What is your Self?

Q: The mind functioning within the body.
B: What is mind?

Q: The habit of thinking.
B: What is thinking?

Q: Emergence of thoughts.
B: What is a thought?

Q: Thoughts may be memories, desires, resentment, envy, anger, other emotions or feelings, or preferences towards certain things, aversions towards certain others, and indifference towards the rest.
B: You are relating your system of classification of thoughts. The import of the question was, what is a thought made of?

Q: Neural connections in the brain perhaps? I do not know.
B: All thoughts are made of pure Subjective Consciousness of Being, which localised sense of being in turn derives its light from the real Self. Therefore, the absolute Self, reflected light of Consciousness, the notion of 'I', the tendency to objectify, and the faculty of intellect manifest as mind, thoughts, and emotions. They encompass memories, personality, and the *jivatman's* belief in its own distinct existence as the perceiver of an external world. All these issues must be stormed and destroyed before the Self can be Realised. The order must necessarily be from bottom upwards. So, the *sadhaka* must first abandon the erroneous belief that the world is an objectively real entity in itself. This system of classification is for the purpose

of explanatory exposition only. In truth, the ego is one only and looking for it, even this is never found. The quest for the Self leads to the quest for its undertaker, namely the ego. The quest for the ego results in Realisation of the Self.

Q: So, it is ahamkara Vichara *[enquiry into the nature of the ego] not* Atma Vichara *[Self-enquiry]!*
B: Quite so.

The Silent Language of the Heart

Q: I speak, read and write eighteen languages fluently. How many languages does Bhagavan know?
B: Are you conversant in my one and only language?

Q: Yes. I know Tamil very well. I have written a commentary on the Panniru Thirumurai *(a sacred Tamil text), for which, recently, I have been awarded with an 'honorary Philosophiae Magister decoration' from the Annamalai University.*
B: My language is the silent language of the Heart, it can neither be spoken nor be written.

Chadwick (having just entered the Hall and heard the last few words): *Bhagavan has long ago received his decoration straight from Lord Annamalai (form of* Shiva) *Himself, he does not need any universities.*

Q: Who is this white palm tree? Did I solicit any needless silly remarks from him? Anyhow, I fail to understand how silence can be a medium of communication between two or more individuals. What is the use or purpose of language? It is to transmit thoughts from one mind to another through speech or writing. If Bhagavan speaks a language that cannot accommodate itself to these modes of transmission, of what use then, is that language? It will be like a dog that can neither ferociously bark nor cheerfully wag its tail, an instrument devoid of possibility for meaningful application.

C: A dog that has lost both its voice and its tail can still love its master.

Q: What cannot be communicated, but the existence of which can be understood only by inference, serves no purpose.

C: Does Love need purpose?

Q: Anything and everything requires purpose.
B: You find yourself in this body; has it never occurred to raise the question of what might be the purpose of the bodily existence?

Q: The body has a natural cause; it is born because the parents procreate.
B: Are you one with the body?

Q: Am I the Atman *[non-personal Self]? Then why do I have a body?*
B: Does the body proclaim itself to be itself? Does the body say that it has a body?

Q: No.
B: Does the *Atman* say that it has a body?

Q: I have never seen the Atman *I do not know what it is.* Vedanta *is not my field of expertise.*
B: Never mind *Vedanta*. Who says that he finds himself in a body owing to the fact that his parents procreated? Does the body say it or does the *Atman* say it?

Q: As far as I know, neither.
B: Who says it, then?

Q: I.
B: What do you mean by 'I'?

Q: I am shocked to discover that to this elementary question, I am able to find no answer.
B: When you have found the answer to it, then you will know the universal language of humanity, which is Love.

Q: What is the answer then?
B: The permanent disappearance of the questioner.

Q: I am baffled.
B: Come around the Hill today evening. It will be clear.

5th August 1936
How to Win Guru's Grace

Q: Since I am already practising tantra sadhana, *is it advisable for me to simultaneously practice* Atma Vichara, *regard having been had to the fact that I harbour an intense desire to Realise within this lifetime?*
B: What has your Guru asked you to do?

Q: He said that the tantra sadhana *may be stopped when it has ceased to hold any fascination for me.*
B: Then why not fall in line with this advice?

Q: I shall do so. Is Atma Vichara *to be practised at fixed hours in the morning and evening?*
B: Always in all states except *sushupti* [deep sleep].

Q: What is the difference between jagrat, swapna*, and* sushupti, *which are experienced by* ajnanis, *and the transcendental state of* Sayujya *[oneness with God], which is experienced by* Jnanis?
B: There is nothing available for the *Jnani* to experience. He is in *Turiyatita* [most subtle state of consciousness]. As for the *ajnani*, *sushupti* is simple unawareness and does not allow for attention to be directed towards the source, namely *Sat* [Truth], whereas, in the states of *jagrat* and *swapna*, *Sat* can be consciously apprehended and inhered in.

Q: Is there any difference between jagrat *and* swapna?
B: No.

Q: Each dream is a different dream. Last week I came to this Hall and it was the same Hall and the same Bhagavan. So, there is the additional feature of continuity in the jagrat *state. Am I correct?*
B: No.

Q: Why not?
B: Within this dream, you are talking of continuity. Therefore, it is merely dream continuity. In dreams also, we have so many memories.

Q: But since my childhood, I have been exposed to the same people, environment, and world. These were not all created in an instant, as in dreams, but over a period of time. Am I correct?
B: No.

Q: Why not?
B: Memories of objects, objects present, and the perceiving subject; all these are created instantaneously, from moment to moment. Thus, there is no such thing as the past or future.

Q: What a strange view of the world!
B: We have strayed so far away from the Real that fiction has become natural, whereas Truth has become alien. So, when reminded of the

Truth, people become uncomfortable and refuse to accept it. Given the choice between what is right and what is easy, the lesser man opts for the latter always. Unmitigated brutality on the mental plane is necessary in order to make the ego subside. Every time he rises, forsaking his source, he must be invariably crushed and sent back into the Beingness of the Self again. The administration of such harsh treatment needs limitless *vairagya* on the aspirant's part, which develops only with the availability of Guru's Grace.

It is like the strategy followed by a mongoose to eat a snake that has opted for a termite hill as its place of dwelling. Every time the snake raises his head from one of the holes in the termite mound, he observes the mongoose hungrily waiting outside and he drops back into the hole again. Eventually one of these two things happens: the snake becomes extraordinarily desirous of food for his belly, rushes desperately out of the mound in search of prey, and is pounced upon by the mongoose. Has his neck bitten into and is killed instantly, for he has not the strength in his starved condition, to put up any efficacious fight with the mongoose and then is devoured. Or he is too scared to leave the mound and dies in it out of starvation and the mongoose sniffs at the entrance to the mound, easily discovers the fact of a dead snake lying inside, pulls the cadaver out with his claws and devours it.

Q: What is the key to the allegory?
B: We need a mongoose who will patiently wait until either outcome is brought about. The mongoose is *Guruvarutkatakshaam* [the grace-filled glance of the Guru]. It arrives as an unsolicited divine gift from God unto pious souls.

Q: The ego is the snake. Am I correct?
B: Yes.

Q: How to win Guru's Grace?
B: Only by introverting the mind more and more.

13th August 1936
Dance of the Nadis

Q: (perhaps an Indian scholar) *What is the purpose of having taken birth in the vehicle of a human body?*
B: Spiritualisation of the mind; its dissolution in the substratum underlying it.

Q: What does that mean?
B: It is the mind which is the sixth organ or third eye of man. This organ is not one which aids sensory perception. To open this eye is the goal of man's birth into this body.

Q: What is the name of this organ?
B: *Hridayapundarikam* [Heart-lotus].

Q: Is it another name for the sahasraram *[crown chakra]?*
B: No.

Q: Where is it located in the body?
Bhagavan asked the attendant to extract from the bookcase a new, slender volume titled *Sri Ramana Gita* (a devotional and philosophical text dedicated to Sri Ramana Maharshi), which seemed to be an Ashram publication. He asked the questioner to peruse certain specific segments thereof. After some time, further questions were asked.

These *shlokas* [sanskrit verses] say:
• The locus from which thoughts of embodied beings originate is said to be the Heart.
• This Heart is located on the right-hand side of the chest; from there light pounces through the *sushumna* [central energy channel in the body] to the *sahasraram*.

• Through giving up the habit of showing compassion towards the body, and discarding the intellectual conviction *'I am the body'*, one should in a single direction investigate, *'In what manner should the* nadis *[energy channels] be made to dance in order so that one might endow oneself with the discriminative faculty that enables discernment of the real from the unreal?'*
• This dance of the *nadis* should ideally separate the *Atman* from the *nadis*. Then, by means of confining the *Atman* to the *amrita nadi* [subtle energy channel through which the consciousness of the Self flows between the spiritual Heart and the crown of the head] alone, we can make it shine.

Q: Even after reading these verses, I am still clueless. I do not understand how to open the Heart's eye.
B: Only by the investigation Who am I?

Q: Am I to give myself to understand that Bhagavan's Vichara *method is a foolproof means to open the Heart's eye?*
B: Yes. *Vichara* makes the mind completely still. The mind then becomes a photographic silver plate completely exposed to the sun; no matter how long you expose such a plate to mercuric vapour, no image is possible of being obtained. A mind which continuously inheres in the Beingness of the Self loses the ability to form sensory impressions. It is then awake to the Self alone and asleep to the world of sense perceptions. Such a one may be surrounded by countless fascinating objects day and night, yet really, he sees or registers nothing.

Sri Krishna Paramatma [Lord Krishna in his supreme, transcendental form] is said to have fathered 161,080 children, but when the dead infant born to _Uttatra_ [son of King Virata of Matsya Kingdom from the _Mahabharata_] was to be revived by the touch of an _akhandabrahmachari_ [lifelong celibate], none, not even _Shuka_ [highly revered _Vedantic_ sage], dared to touch the child. The _Paramatman_ [supreme soul] calmly walked over to the body of the lifeless infant and touched it. The effect of _Ashwatthama's_ [prominent figure in the _Mahabharata_] mighty _brahmashironamaka_

astra **[devastating divine weapon], which is said to have the ruinous capability to annihilate the fourteen worlds without leaving behind the slightest residue, became useless. Such is the power of the** ***Jnani's*** **incessant, involuntary** ***mounatapas.***

Q: If loss of the ability to form sensory impressions is Jnana, *then sleeping persons are* Jnanis.
B: Sleep is simple stillness. On the other hand, in the case of one who practises ***jagrat-sushupti*** **[experiencing the peacefulness of deep sleep in the waking state], the senses are kept alert but inactive. The mind is awake to the Realisation of its own self-conscious existence but motionless. How can a** ***Jnani*** **make effort to Self-realisation if already realised?**

Q: One whose mind is in this motionless state is a Jnani. *Am I correct?*
B: No.

Q: Why not?
B: Even the subtle mind must be dissolved and lost in ***Kaivalya*** **[true consciousness, nature of the Self]. If the mind is not altogether destroyed, rebirth is inevitable.**

Q: Is the Heart-eye always open in the Jnani*?*
B: Yes. In the ***Jnani,*** **the** ***granthi*** **[knot] obscuring the Revelation of the Heart-eye has been sundered once and for all.**

Q: Can this eye be opened and closed at will?
B: The ***Jnani*** **has no option to close it.**

Q: What is the power wielded by one who knows how to open this eye?
B: He has discovered the elixir of immortality.

Q: By investigating Who am I? can I also develop the ability to open my third eye?
B: Yes.

Q: I feel pain above the navel whilst doing Vichara. *It is real, physical pain. What is the reason and what is the remedy?*
B: Mental introversion is said to cause agitation of the *nadis*. That could be the reason. There is no end to the number of places in the body where pain may be felt. You might do what is needed to make the pain subside if its cause is physical, but pay no mental attention to it. Keep on adamantly pursuing the *Vichara*, no matter what happens. Everything will come aright in the end. The mind is like a pubescent child spoilt by excessive pampering. Pay even the slightest attention to him and soon you will not be able to do any other work. Ignore him completely and he will manage himself successfully somehow.

14th August 1936

Bhagavan's 'Concept Gas' Analogy

Gajapathi: Since Bhagavan's jivatman *has irretrievably merged into Lord Arunachala Shiva, may we take it that when he says something, it is in fact a pronouncement being made by* Shiva *Himself?*
B: If you believe it to be so, so indeed it is. But will any sensible person equate himself with Lord Arunachala and go about proclaiming that he is himself the Lord? Lord Arunachala is the only remaining form and name which evokes the emotion of love from this otherwise petty, useless life.

In Loving to the point of exhausting myself, I have lost myself in my Lord for good, so that my Master alone IS; I am not...

A noble expression of such unfathomable immenseness of

ecstasy is writ on his face as he utters these words that I forget to breathe. In an instant the thought occurs to me that at the moment of death, I may forget my name and my identity, but I shall never be able to succeed in forgetting this face, this beautiful face that is bathed in light from the Deep Beyond; this frightening, terrible face, that is contorted with all the fury of divine, mad Love; this insane face, that indicates the existence of a seductive, fatally charming dimension of depth to the mind of man, one it has hitherto been loath to explore, but upon having beheld this wondrous sight is tempted to plunge head-first into, throwing caution and sanity to the wind as he had done...
After some time, I addressed the Master thus:

G: If I were to relate what Sri Bhagavan has just said to me to an audience consisting of dilettante followers of his teachings, most of them may refuse to believe that he spoke such words; it is universally believed that Sri Bhagavan is a staunch exponent of the Jnanamarga.
B: (turning to face me with a kind smile) **There is no infidelity in the *Jnani's* words when he says that he still sees his Guru as the Guru, and neither is there infidelity in his words when he says that all of cosmic manifestation is the Self. When the *Jnani* abides in his natural state of Self, his subjective state of experience of Absolute Truth is known as *paramarthikasathyam* [the Ultimate Truth that transcends duality]. This actual Truth of the Self cannot be communicated but can be known only by first-hand experience.**

In using intellectual and linguistic contrivances to explain to 'others' this Truth, it must be adapted to the temperament of the listener, or else the words serve no purpose and turn out to be fruitless. The *Vedantist* is told that the Self is all and that there exists nothing but the Self, but *bhakta* is told to worship a God and the *Jnani* confesses that he still mentally worships the Guru. How are we to reconcile these apparently conflicting ideas? The explanation is that within the framework of duality, it would be meaningless to deny the existence of duality. The *Jnani* is not bound by duality but respects worldly conventions of dualistic outlook notwithstanding that he does not stand to gain or lose anything by doing so.

The *Jnani's* behaviour is always a mirror of the events and circumstances in the midst of which he finds himself. The problem of seeming inconsistencies arises to those surrounding the *Jnani* and watching his behaviour who are afflicted with the malady of being prone to excessive thinking. As far as the rational man is concerned, what he hears should be logically coherent and consistent. He wants a theory or basis which he may rely upon or out of which he may function. One thus far used to working from inside of intellection or structure exclusively, cannot all at once accept 'ex nihilo nihil fit' (Latin: nothing comes from nothing). On the one hand, since knowledge, not-Reality, or creation, is simply impossible, anything may happen or not happen or both at once in the relativistic world of space and time, which is merely an illusory appearance that is not different from the mind projecting it.

On the other hand, Truth cannot be expressed because in that state there is none present alongside Him to witness or experience it, that he might form a description of it. So, everything is a gigantic lie, even the words you are hearing now. J. Krishnamurti has said, *'The description of the thing is not the thing.'* But the understanding that everything understood is false does not come easily and generally can be attained only as a result of prolonged *abhyasa*. If such things are communicated unto the common man, he will only gloomily shake his head and walk away from you, saying, *'But how can the* Advaitic *teachings themselves be untruthful?'*

The teachings point out that everything is unreal, but they do not mention what it is that is real. The implication is that the Real cannot be described. If all conceptual understanding is abandoned, including the idea that conceptual understanding is futile and ought to be abandoned, what is left over is the Real. For the mature aspirant *[pakvi]*, Bhagavan's teachings are not suggesting that the seeker should do anything, but only that all doing be abandoned. When Bhagavan is silent, he is being Truthful. Everything he utters is only a lie, even these words.

The Caucasians who visit here occasionally leave behind publications on metaphysics. From them, I have been able to describe

a few adjectives that can be used to explain the unreal nature of the objectively perceived cosmos: The world is said to be a *'perception-contingent, interminable phantasmagoric flux'* and in such a world, which is NOT, anything could appear or disappear. Thus, what you presently hear and see need not tally with ideas you have formulated and pickled away safely inside your brain. Neither objects of sensory perception nor arbitrary mental conceptualisations remain in the *Jnani's* field of view. Inwardly, yes, the *Jnani* Loves. His Love is non-dual Love. It is the Self Itself.

G: So, the Self can be attained not only by Jnana Vichara, *but by unselfish Love also?*
B: Yes. The Enlightened *Muni* [sage] was not born into *Jnana*. He was attracted towards the presence of a *Mahatma* and having attached himself to him, obsessively loved his *Jnanaguru* to the point where he melted into his Love. Then again melted as that Love into his *Jnanaguru*, so that only the *Jnanaguru*, who is Love beyond the reach of imagination, remains.

Know that the *Jnanasiddha* alone knows the true meaning of Love. If you covet this Love, oh child, give up everything and turn within. Give yourself up to the unknown, for He is the unknowable. You cannot reach Him. Surrender quietly to Him, and, becoming prey unto Him, be DEVOURED by Him. This is wisdom and this is *shanti*.

G: The idea 'ex nihilo nihil fit' is used by the Greeks in the sense that the principle of causation must be correct. They say that effect can come only from cause.
B: I meant it in the opposite sense, the literal sense.

Chadwick: (entering the Hall and bowing) Has he begun to discuss Greek philosophy again, Bhagavan?
B: (smiling) **If we don't pamper his mind, who will?**

G: If told, 'everything is an illusion', *people may find it disturbing...*

B: Which is why they are told, *'Find your Self'* or *'Know Thyself'* leaving them to make the discovery by themselves that there is no world to see, but only the Self. Actually, saying *'everything is being zero'* or *'there is not anything'* is more meaningful. Strictly speaking, *'Know Thyself'* is absurd. How can there be an entity apart from the Self that knows the Self? There cannot be any such entity. Similarly, the Self cannot have anything to know, just as it cannot be known by anything. People may say, *'Bhagavan teaches that the Self is Self-aware or that the Self knows Itself.'* It is not correct. Knowledge implies *vritti.* There are no *vrittis* in the Self. It is Purity or Completeness Itself. The Self does not need to know itself, because it is knowledge itself.

It cannot know itself or anything else, because it is in motionless timeless realisation of actionless reality, which is itself; therefore, it is ignorance itself. Yet the Self transcends knowledge and ignorance. Nothing can know the Self, because there is nothing besides it; therefore, there is no such thing as not-Self. That day on which man awakens into the living realisation of the fact that knowledge of the not-Self or ignorance of the Self is impossible, is the day on which he awakens into his true, imperishable nature of immortality. This teaching alone is verily the nectareous ambrosia which rouses man from the sleep of his illusory mortality.

Chadwick's eyes were moist with joy by the time Bhagavan had finished enunciating these words.

G: While the teaching sounds simple, practising the state of effortless and volitionless thoughtlessness does not seem to be so easy.

B: The biggest tragedy is that people, instead of giving up everything, think that by doing some practice they are going to go somewhere or attain something. If everything is thrown away, only *Jnana* remains. Supposing you want to make space inside a room, how do you go about it? Hurl away the useless objects taking up space in the room, it is as simple as that. There is no question of importing space from elsewhere. If all ideas or *vrittis* [mental modifications

or conceptualisations] are thrown away or given up, only the Self remains. If you are able to realise the truth that what you are giving up is indubitably more obnoxious than the waste material in your intestines and what you gain is indubitably worthier than your life in this ephemeral body, you will be able to give up everything in your mind in one, neat, simple stroke. To such a one *Jnana* comes in a trice, then what awaits is only the Kingdom of Heaven from which there is no return possible.

Chadwick: We are unable to develop the conviction that the world is worthless or mirage-like, that is the problem.
B: There is no need for any new convictions to be cultivated. Give up even your existing convictions.

C: The conviction that the world is unreal can be used to combat the conviction that the world is real.
B: (laughing) **Oh! Is that so? Have you heard the story of the monkey that kept chasing its own tail?**

C: No.
B: Possibly the story will be told only after the conclusion has come to pass; you see, the story is yet to conclude. The monkey started at the beginning of *Satya Yugam* [golden age]. Still, he is going on.

C: He must be a very energetic monkey. Bhagavan must have fed him peanuts with his own hands. (All three of us laugh.)
G: What is the analogy?
B: That will be the perverse fate of one who endeavours to counteract concepts with concepts. The fetid odour of *concept gas* can be eliminated only by diverting the gas away from the mind room. Instead, some want to release into their own originally odour-free, pristine and blemishless mental environment more and more poisonous, odious *concept gases* thinking, *'Aha! This* concept gas *will fight all the previous ones!'* If this should keep on happening, as it does indeed in the case of many unfortunate beings on this Earth,

what will the result be? (laughs) **Will not everyone suffocate unto death? What has caused the absurd mentality which prompts man to go on releasing one foul-smelling *concept gas* after another? HE HAS FORGOTTEN THE BLISS OF HIS ORIGINAL ODOUR-FREE ENVIRONMENT!**

He thinks being surrounded by the miasmic fumes of his own *concept gas* is his natural state. When it has all become patently and obviously unmanageable, he goes to a charlatan, who says unto him: *'Sir! Be certain that your anxieties end today. What I have with me is the most precious* concept gas *in the world, released by the Self-realised sages of the Himalayas. Here I have captured it in this brownish-coloured bottle. You are indeed fortunate that you have met with me today, Sir, have not the least doubt about it. Forthwith take this invaluable gas into your room and release the same. Then you will come back and thank me till your mouth aches.'* Delighted, the man rushes back into his bad-smelling room and with tremendous eagerness does as told. What is the result? He ends up burning his nostrils. He thinks his delicate nostrils are to blame and thus harbours no ambition to pick any quarrel with the charlatan. What does he do next? Goes to another charlatan.

This time the gas has been released by the sages of the Vidhya Hills. And then another, perhaps this time the Podhigai Hills. And so on, and so forth. Finally, he decides these foreign gases are only making his room smellier and, abjectly resigning himself to his miserable fate of having to put up with his putrid mental environment, gives up hunting for newer and newer exotic harmless *concept gas* to release. Then a friend of his chances to meet him and asks why he should look so despondent, whereupon the man confesses unto him his malodorous problem. *'Oh! Is this all?'*, says the other, *'Don't worry. I know just the thing to set you aright. In the Arunachala Hill, there is one* Koupeenadhari-Swami *[loincloth monk].* The next moment the vexed man catches hold of his friend by the scruff of the neck and shouts wrathfully into the alarmed man's face, *'I shall have no more of it, I tell you. It is all a grand fraud; I realised the fact just some time prior. ALL GAS STINKS.'*

'Pray, do not enrage yourself, my good man,' **says the calm friend, shaking himself free from the first man's irate grip.**

'This Swami will neither demand any money from you nor will he give you any gas to release.' 'Then what is he a Swami for?' 'He never announced himself as a Swami. People understand him to be this or that depending upon their individual temperaments of mind. I am sure you will benefit by visiting him.' **The man reluctantly makes the trip, telling himself,** ***'At any rate I don't have anything to fear from the possibility of disappointment, since this time I have no expectations. What is probably going to happen is this; he will try to sell me a bottle of his gas, and I shall refuse to buy it and come away peacefully, after telling him, 'Thank you very much for the kind offer, Sir, but you see, my nostrils have been assaulted with enough gas for this one lifetime. If he tries to persuade me into making a purchase, I shall slap him and run away from the place.'***

When he puts his difficulty before the *Koupeenadhari-Swami*, he expects to as usual be handed a bottle of *concept gas* and demanded money, but the Swami, being no gas releaser, merely decorously says, *'Open the windows.'* The man is stunned. *'Can it really be that simple?'* he wonders. For a time, the man is reluctant to give up the rancid odours to which he has been for a long time now acclimatised. Then he begins to yearn for the odour-free state. Finally, he abandons altogether his penchant for *concept gas* and throws the windows open as per the advice of the *Koupeenadhari-Swami* of the Arunachala Hill. Then sweet fresh air, which he has not experienced in his living memory, bursts into the room, and he dances for ecstatic joy. He remembers all his various exploits with the different charlatans he had encountered and enjoys a hearty laugh at his own expense...

Chadwick is unable to contain himself. He has already collapsed against the wall of the Hall in laughter at hearing Bhagavan's 'gas analogy'. His spasmodic fits, which are yet to abate, are now observed with a curious eye by early inmates and visitors trickling into the Hall.

'Shoo! Shoo!' **says Bhagavan, smiling and putting a finger to his lips.**

Chadwick with difficulty manages to straighten himself up. He wipes away the tears trickling down his cheeks and tries to look serious.
G: Concept gas stands for vrittis, *the bottles stand for instructions on* sadhana, *releasing them in one's room means trying to practise any mental activity as* sadhana, *and opening the windows is* summayirutthal. *Am I correct?*

C: Hey, boy! Isn't it obvious?
G: I still want to make sure. So, I am corroborating my understanding with Bhagavan.
B: Supposing you want to make space inside a room, how do you go about it? Hurl away the useless objects taking up space in the room, it is as simple as that. There is no question of importing space from elsewhere. If all ideas or *vrittis* [mental modifications or conceptualisations] are thrown away or given up, only the Self remains.

G: What does Bhagavan *say?*
B: Yes. Also, the reluctance to abandon one's age-old mental predilections is exclusively the handiwork of – But at that moment the Brahmins enter the Hall. It is time for the chanting of the *Vedas*. For now, the conversation is at an end.

A French Visitor

A curious, altogether ridiculous personality has arrived at the Ashram dressed in a three-piece suit, a beaver hat, and an ascot cravat. In this weather, his skin ought to catch fire; I wonder how it still seems to be intact. He carries an ebony cane mounted with a miniature bronze roaring lion's head. He is attracting curious glances everywhere.

Apparently the *sarvadhikari* had fallen down in a fit of fright upon first seeing the man and his cane. Thinking he must be polite to his hosts, he takes off his hat whenever he meets anyone in the Ashram, with the result that people here have come to the conclusion that some madman has been let loose upon them. Thinking they are going to be attacked, everyone runs away from him as soon as he is spotted.

His head is abnormally large and looks like a gigantic ostrich egg. The rest of his body is malnourished and thin. He sports a completely bald head and a pencil moustache. A comical goatee adds the finishing touches to the eccentricity of his appearance. Bizarrely, his protuberant eyes look hilariously tragic – they convey the impression of a man who is unable to take himself seriously, but has always longed to. He entered the Hall and bowed low to Bhagavan, hat clasped in hand tucked against tummy, monocle dangling in the air and all. Bhagavan seemed to survey him with quiet interest. He introduced himself, with Chadwick acting as his interpreter. His name is Monsieur Pierre Géant but he is known as 'L'affolé néant' (the distraught void) by his friends. He comes all the way from the Lebanese Republic (which was formerly part of the Ottoman Empire).

He was always interested in mysticism and the prospect of experiencing a personal union with God Almighty. In 1896 he had arrived at a turning point in his life: he met Swami Vivekananda in England. Vivekananda had recommended to him to study his Guru's life, as well as *Vedanta*. Then the Distraught One had engrossed himself in Sri Ramakrishna and *Vedanta* for years. Sri Ramakrishna's experiences thrilled him to the core and he wanted them replicated in his own case. Just when he was feeling hopelessly dejected and agitated that Ramakrishna was in the flesh no more, Paul Brunton's book was read out to him, quite casually, by an English-speaking friend, and the 'Maharishee' therein interested him profusely. So, he had come straightaway in a steamer, the next available one.

He had questions for Bhagavan.

Q: Is your teaching the same as Sri Ramakrishna's?
B: All Realised Souls are in the same state and therefore only the manner (vocabulary) of expression varies and so there can be no other difference in the teaching.

Q: If 'I am God' is the Truth, does it not amount to arrogance?
B: It does not mean you, as you incumbently imagine yourself to be, are God. It means God is the Real 'I'.

Q: There is a self which coexists with the personality and attaches itself to the body. This is known as the mind. Then there is the Parabrahman *mentioned in the* Vedanta. *This is known as the Impersonal Essence of man. Which is my True Self? Can I have more than one Self?*
B: The mind is a phantom. In the Impersonal Essence, the mind is nowhere to be found.

Q: How to reach it?
B: There is nobody there to reach it. Thus, there is no reaching it. Subside and let the Light shine forth. Subside as the mind and you shine as the Self.

Q: Practically, what is the method for it?
B: The investigation, Who am I?

Q: But this investigation also is made with mind only.
B: It commences no doubt in the mind. It ends in no mind.

Bhagavan asked Chadwick to read out Who am I? to him in French. This was done and the creature listened carefully, cocking his huge head against a meagre shoulder so that his left ear should be better exposed to the sounds emanating from Chadwick's lips. Presently he extracted a small ear trumpet from the folds of his laborious clothes and grooved the ear-piece into his left ear. The bell of the contraption was positioned to face Chadwick's direction. Bhagavan looked at the surprised faces in the Hall and laughed. Presently:
Q: What is the authority for saying that the world is a dream? Where is the proof, I mean?
B: Did you exist in sleep?

Q: Yes.

B: Do you exist now?

Q: Yes.
B: Then what is the difference (in the two states)?

Q: I am not aware of my body and world (in sleep).
B: Being aware of the body and world is called dreaming. Remain unaware of them now also. That verily is *Jnana* or Reality. This alone is the state of true wakefulness.

Q: But how can we call this world a dream?
B: Why not?

Q: There are so many people on the Earth. If it is a dream, whose dream might it be?
B: Yours.

Q: But why pick me out specifically? For instance, it may even be the dream of the amiable Monsieur Chadwick here.
B: Only you are there.

Q: What about you, then, sir?
B: No, I am not here or there. I AM. There is no here or there or anywhere. I AM THAT I AM.

Q: I comprehend not.
B: Evidence produced by the sensory organs is merely mental in nature. All knowledge of diversity is fictitious mental information. The Source of your Being is Real. There is nothing else.

Q: I want proof.
B: If proof is given to you, how will you be able to believe it?

Q: I comprehend not.
B: The proof given to you, if any, is also going to be mere mental information only.

Q: What can be believed, then, as true?
B: Whatever is believed is false only. Truth is in Being only.

Q: How to attain this Being?
B: By giving up the idea that there could be anything to be attained and all other ideas.

Q: Practically, how can I go about it?
B: Investigate, Who am I?

Q: Will repetition of sacred syllables not be helpful? Do not the sacred chants of your religion hold some sort of latent spiritual power? By unlocking this power or energy can we not reach the state of Enlightenment?
B: You have been appraised of the direct method.

Q: The others are by-lanes or diversions?
B: Yes.

Q: Should food restrictions be followed by a seeker after Enlightenment? Can I eat pork and veal?
B: Try to thrive on grain and fruit.

Q: Can the investigation of Who am I? be done in your presence only? If I do it at, say, Nantes, would I able to succeed in Enlightening myself? Is your physical presence needed in order to bring about a successful outcome to the practice?
B: It is introversion of mind that matters, not geographical loca-tion. If the mind is kept steadily poised in introversion, such questions cannot arise even. Locate yourself neither in Nantes nor in Tiru-vannamalai nor anywhere else, but rather locate yourself in the source of the mind.

Q: Is worship of, or even belief in, a personal God permissible?
B: Yes.

Q: Does it not thwart one's progress towards Enlightenment?

B: When you become ripe enough, you will no longer feel that it is you who are praying.

Q: Is philanthropy a distraction or ought one try to help the suffering world?
B: It varies according to the temperament of the individual's psyche.

Q: I see. What about my case?
B: When you see suffering, what thought first crosses your mind?

Q: 'I wish God had created a world in which there was no suffering.'
B: Those destined to help think: *'Let me see what I can do here...'*

Q: Is there any need to officially renounce my affirmed affiliation into the La Rochelle Temple?
B: No.

Q: Occasionally I become frightened when my health takes a turn for the worse. How to remain free from such fears?
B: You already know that for this perishable body made of the elements, destruction is certain one day. Why crib over the inevitable?

Q: But how do I keep fear at bay?
B: By not identifying yourself with the body or mind.

Q: But how to get rid of such erroneous identification?
B: Only by relentless pursuit of the investigation, Who am I?
Then the Distraught One proudly produced a gift for Bhagavan, a small tin box which rattled. Bhagavan opened it and smiled.

Q: (beaming happily) They are roasted seeds belonging to the St. Ignatius fruit. Fruits produced by the tree Strychnos ignatius! Very difficult to obtain ever since the War, sir! Specially procured for your consumption, if I may be permitted to say so, sir!

This chapter was also published in Aham Sphurana. *ED*

16th August 1936

The Scintillation 'I'-'I' Is Aham Sphurana

Q: (perhaps an Indian scholar) *In* Talks with Ramana Maharshi*, it is said as follows,* 'Realisation of *Jnana* is always a *vritti*. There is a distinction between *vritti Jnana* [temporarily merged in the absolute] or Realisation, and *Swarupa* [essential nature], the Real. *Swarupa* is *Jnana* itself, it is consciousness. *Swarupa* is *Sat Chit* [Absolute Existence Consciousness] which is omnipresent. It is always there, self-attained. When you realise it, the Realisation is called *vritti Jnana*. It is only with reference to your existence, that you talk of Realisation or *Jnana*.

Therefore, when we talk of *Jnana,* we always mean *vritti Jnana* and not the *Swarupa Jnana* [Realisation of one's True Nature]; for *Swarupa* itself is *Jnana* Consciousness always.' *I find this passage completely baffling. Would Bhagavan please explain it to me?*

B: When the mind ceases to take any interest in the objective world and remains volitionlessly and effortlessly inhered in its nativistic, primeval state of pure Beingness, it is *vrittijnanam* [temporarily merged in the Absolute]. One may be said to have reached the state of *vrittijnanam* only if and when his mind remains so not as the result of any motive or objective but because of the fact that now it does not know anything else. The mind, which was earlier consciousness obscured by a labyrinthine network of *vrittis*, is now reduced into simple consciousness of Being to which effort or objective is altogether alien. Then there is no question of straining oneself to remain still. Stillness is now the natural state.

This is *manonivritti* [mind turned inwards] or *vrittijnanam*. In this state, there is nothing available to deflect one's attention away from subjective awareness. The mind remains transfixed at the point of its origin. The light of 'I'-'I' can be clearly felt to be shining. The experience of the scintillation 'I'-'I' is called *Aham Sphurana*. Since this state is not brought about by means of expenditure of any mental effort, but rather on account of reduction of the mind, some books say that it is a transcendental state.

Q: Is that the state of the Jnani*?*

B: No. When even the rarefied mind is destroyed in the Beyond, it is the *Sahajastithi* of the *Jnani.* But you need not worry about all this. It is unnecessary. It is enough to lose the ego. Thereafter everything is automatic.

Q: Does steady practice of Vichara *make the aspirant see the world as a dream or does it make the world seem as if it were a dream?*

B: There are those who, resultant of having assiduously accessed and paid meticulous attention to books or discourses on *Vedanta*, or having made themselves acclimatised to the teachings explicated in this Hall by coming and sitting here often, intellectually believe the world to be a dream, or that it could be a dream. These aspirants have yet a long way to traverse. There is another category of aspirants who see the world not as world but as dream. Intellectually imagining the world to be a dream or mentally conceiving of the world as being a dream is not the same as actually experiencing the world as a dream.

In the mature aspirant, the *jagrat* and *swapna* states are indistinguishable from each other. He is perfectly aware that he is dreaming. The degree of fluidity, fungibility, mutability and impermanence that the world takes when you experience it as nothing but a dream is not something that you can be made to understand through usage of conceptual explanations. Generally, only after prolonged and sustained practice of mental introversion is this state gained.

Q: Does the Jnani *also see the world as a dream?*

B: No. In his case, there cannot be any world to see. Himself is all that exists.

Q: How can I tell whether I have deluded or conned myself into thinking that I have attained Jnana, *or whether I have actually attained* Jnana*?*

B: The *Jnani* does not care whether he is a *Jnani* or not; in his case, therefore, this question cannot arise and neither can any other.

Q: So, if doubts or perturbations arise, it cannot be Jnana. *Am I right?*
B: Yes.

Q: Receiving upadesha *[instruction] from the Guru is necessary before one commences* sadhana. *Am I correct?*
B: *Upadesha* means to return something to its original position. Return the mind to the Beingness of the Self.

Q: Will Bhagavan give me hastha diksha *[initiation through touch, by the Guru] so that I can be assured of his Divine Grace?*
B: There are three types of initiation *dhrik* [gaze], *sparsa* [touch], and *kurma* [subtle energy].

Q: Which one is followed at this Ashram by Sri Bhagavan?
B: The third one.

Q: Which one carries maximum efficaciousness?
B: The third one.

Q: Will it suffice for obtaining Shaktipada *[transmission of spiritual energy]?*
B: Yes.

18th August 1936

Summa Iru, Remain Naturally Without Thinking

Q: I also want to Realise the Self and become a Jnani *like Sri Bhagavan. What should I do?*
B: Do not do anything. Step aside and permit the light to shine.

Q: I do not understand what I should do to Realise the Self.
B: *Summa Iru.* It means, 'Remain naturally without thinking.'

Q: As distinct from suppression or control of thought?
B: Yes.

Q: In my case effort is needed to remain without thinking.
B: Yes, that is the problem.

Q: How am I to reach the state wherein I am able to effortlessly remain in the state of absence of thoughts?
B: Only by pursuing the investigation, Who am I?

Q: How long to investigate?
B: Until investigation is no longer possible.

Q: If I am able to effortlessly remain in the state wherein there are no thoughts, can I also become a Jnani*?*
B: Undoubtedly.

Q: God's Grace is said to be necessary for it.
B: Yes.

Q: How to win God's Grace?
B: Only by relentlessly pursuing the investigation, Who am I?

Q: Is not everything predetermined?
B: That argument is not meant to be used to justify anticipation of failure.

Q: So long as the idea or belief 'The world is real' *is sustained within the mind,* Vichara *will yield no benefit. Am I correct?*
B: Yes. But the *Vichara* itself will progressively facilitate you to see the truth that anything perceived is merely the handiwork of the faculty of imagination.

Q: Is it belief in the objective reality of the world that is preventing me from Realising?
B: Not only that idea, all arbitrary mental conceptualisations *[vrittis]* must be eradicated from the mind before there can be any possibility of Realisation.

Q: Why so?
B: *Vrittis* act as water in a cauldron which reflects the sun as an image upon its surface. Thoroughly empty the cauldron. That is the *nivritti* state of mind. When the cauldron has been toppled and broken into pieces, chance of reflection any further is permanently ruined. This is the *Sahajastithi* of the *Jnani*.

Bhagavan then turned to the attendant and asked him to pick out a certain volume of the Bengali work *Sri Ramakrishna Kathamrita*. But that gentleman could not succeed in identifying the same from the bookcase. Bhagavan himself retrieved the volume and gave it to someone to read out for the Hall, in Tamil:

> **One attains the state of *Brahmajnana* [knowledge of *Brahman*] when the mind has been destroyed. When the mind disappears and the ego has scarpered without leaving behind the least residue, that which was arrogantly proclaiming itself to be 'I' is discovered to have always been non-existent. It is possible to reach this state through the paths of *bhakti* [devotion] or *Jnana*. The *Jnana-anveshaka* [seeker of knowledge] considers the world as a mere dream or hallucination. Once perception of the world has ceased, only the 'I'-Consciousness remains.**
>
> **Imagine that there are ten cauldrons filled with water. They all reflect the sun. Now, totally how many suns do you see?**
> Devotee: Ten reflected suns and the one true sun.

Sri Ramakrishna: Imagine now that one of these cauldrons shatters into pieces. Now how many suns do you see?
Devotee: Nine reflected suns and the one true sun.
Sri Ramakrishna: Well, supposing that nine cauldrons are broken, how many suns would you see?
Devotee: One reflected image of the sun and the one true sun.
Sri Ramakrishna: What remains after the last cauldron is broken?
Devotee: The one true sun.
Sri Ramakrishna: No. No words can possibly describe what remains. It is what really IS. When there is no reflected sun, how can you tell that there is the real sun? In the state of *Samadhi*, the 'I' vanishes. What a man experiences then cannot be expressed through ideas when he comes down to a lower plane.

Q: Is Bhagavan now talking to us from a lower plane, then?
B: Sri Ramakrishna is describing *Nirvikalpa Samadhi* [temporarily absorbed in the Absolute]. In the *Sahajastithi* there is no lower plane or higher plane.

Q: The example befuddles me. The sun is never obscured by its reflection on any number of surfaces. Reflections of the sun do not affect the sun itself in any way.
B: Exactly.

Q: But the Self is obscured by the ego.
B: Did the Self complain of being obscured by the ego?

Q: So, bondage is a fact only from the ego's point of view.
B: Quite so.

Q: In that case how did the ego arise?
B: Whose ego?

Q: Mine. But who am I?
B: Find out.

19th August 1936

Bhagavan Does Not Know Who He Is

Q: Bhagavan exhorts all to investigate Who am I? Does he know who he is?
B: No, he does not. Loss of the *vipareetajnana* [false understanding] of 'I' is the goal.

Q: I comprehend not.
B: Realisation is nothing to be gained afresh. The Self is already here and now but overshadowed by illusory ignorance. When such ignorance tries to find out its own nature, it vanishes and the Self alone is left to shine eternally as the residue. To the Realised One there never was any ignorance. So, investigating Who am I? does not lead to acquisition of any knowledge appertaining to who you really are. It destroys the existing wrong notion of who you are, that you are currently harbouring within the mind.

When the *Vichara* has completed this destruction in its entirety, what is left is the Self. There is no such thing as the Self knowing itself. Knowledge is a *vritti*. The Self is free from *vrittis*, 'Know Thyself' therefore, is meaningless. *'Get rid of thyself'* would be more relevant, or *'abandon thyself once and for all'*. Mental activity cannot bring about peace. Abandon the mind for good, and what is left is peace only and peace eternal; peace from which there is no return possible.

Q: It is quite tempting. But how to do it?
B: Only by the investigation, Who am I?

From left (1) Annamalai Swami, (2) Chadwick, (3) Chinnaswami. In the back Dr Mees (4). Around 1936

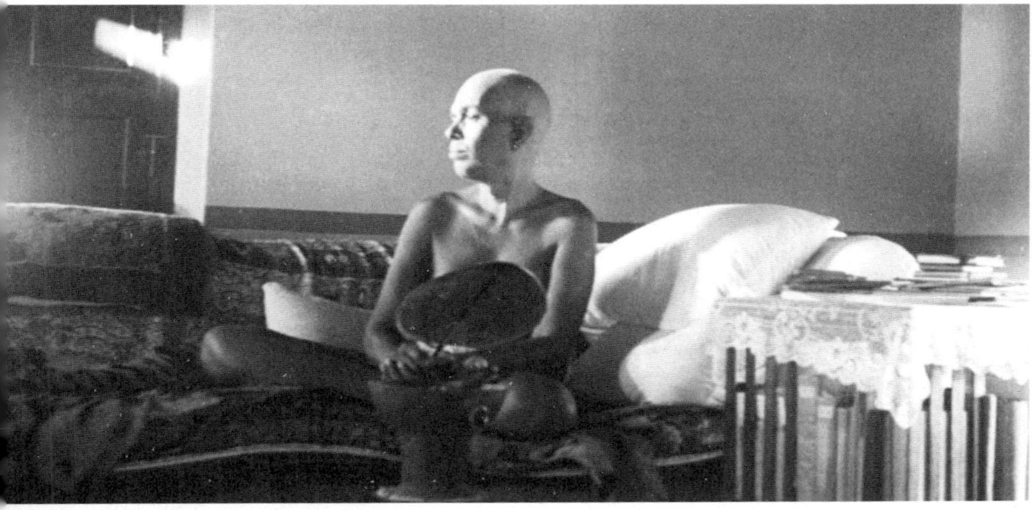

Major Alan W. Chadwick
was a British Army officer who became one of Sri Ramana Maharshi's closest Western disciples, coming in 1935 and staying at Ramana Ashram until his death in 1962.
(below) Bhagavan with **Paramahansa Yogananda** in 1935

Guy Hague (1), Eleanor Pauline Noye (2), Swami Lakshman Joo (3)

21st August 1936

It Is Decidedly Advantageous to Practise Both

Q: I have heard Bhagavan saying that in order so as to Realise the Immortal Self, one must either investigate the question of Who am I? or unconditionally surrender oneself to the Higher Power. My question is: Are Who am I? and surrender mutually exclusive or can they be practised together?
B: Yes, certainly it is decidedly advantageous to practise both at once. Speaking with regard to functionality, aside from the terminology, there is no actual difference or distinction between these two approaches: the one leads to the other and the other to the one.

Keep the Mind Poised in Alert Stillness

Q: How to remain in the natural state or nivritti *state without wanting to remain therein?*
B: Remaining in the *nivritti* state without wanting to remain therein, and without making effort to remain therein, is the only way to *Jnana*; it is certainly possible, even easy, for one whose *vairagya* has reached a climactic pitch.

Q: How to cultivate vairagya, *then?*
B: Only by investigating Who am I? relentlessly or by trying to unconditionally surrender relentlessly.

Q: Is the Vichara *done by means of focusing our concentration or faculty of attention upon the right side of the chest?*
B: There is no nexus between these two practices. The one is different from the other and the other is different from the one.

Q: Which one leads to Jnana*?*
B: *Vichara.*

Q: What about the practice of focusing our concentration or faculty of attention upon the right side of the chest? Is it useless?
B: Why do you say that it is useless? It leads to concentration of mind. For those who lack the wherewithal to engage in *Vichara* or surrender themselves totally, practices such as *japa*, *pranayama*, concentrating on the right side of the chest, gazing at the light emitted by a lamp in an otherwise dark room, *hatha yoga*, *kundalini yoga* [physical practice that focuses on the awakening of kundalini energy], and so on and so forth are suggested. For the one who can investigate or surrender, these are not necessary.

Q: When visitors come into Bhagavan's physical proximity, what should they do to derive from his potent, sacred presence, maximum spiritual benefit?
B: They should not do anything.

Q: I comprehend not.
B: *'Keep the mind poised in alert stillness'* is the import underlying the utterance, *'Do not do anything.'*

Q: How is that done?
B: Again, only by means of *Vichara.*

Q: Ultimately, the thing called 'I', does it exist or not?
B: Why are you asking me? Find out.

Q: Why does Bhagavan not wish to share his discovery with me?
B: Each one must discover the Truth for himself. The lotus of the Heart must bloom from within. Realisation cannot be shared; the *Jnani's* proximity can act as a catalyst, nothing more. If *Jnana* were something outside you, it could be handed over to you on a golden platter.

Q: Bhagavan forcibly liberated his mother, I have heard. To a Jnani *all are equal. The compassion shown by you to your mother, please show it to me also.*
B: I am not withholding anything from you. Those who are ready get It, even if they want It not.

Q: I am trying to surrender but how do I go about it?
B: To surrender is to abandon the absurd idea that there is a 'you' which is capable of 'doing'.

Q: Practically what am I to do?
B: Kill the ego by completely handing over responsibility for your life to the Lord, by realising your arrant helplessness in anything and everything, by feeling all the time, *'Not I, but Thou, O my Lord!'*, by giving up all sense of 'I' and 'mine', and by completely leaving it to the Lord to do what and as he likes with you. Surrender can never be regarded as genuine so long as the *sadhaka* wants this or that from the Lord.

True surrender is Love of God for the sake of such Love and for nothing else, not even for the sake of Emancipation. Allow the feeling, *'I am helpless by myself, whereas God is utterly omnipotent; other than throwing myself completely upon Him, there is no means of safety available to me,'* to become an unshakable conviction. Thus, gradually develop the stance of mind that God alone exists and the ego does not matter. This stratagem also leads to the same goal of *manonivritti* [freedom of mind structures].

26th August 1936

An Incident Between Bhagavan and His Brother

Bhagavan's Grace was unwavering, but without the *sarvadhikari's* (Bhagavan's brother) grace, you could not set foot inside the Ashram. But yet, here he stood now, in Bhagavan's placid presence, quaking from tip to toe like a dry linen smock waiting to be collected away from a washing line jiggled about by the rough wind. He said skittishly: *'Bhagavan must pardon me. I do not understand what Bhagavan is trying to tell me.'*

B: Did you not ask Pillai to cycle and buy some rat poison from the town?

Sar: But the rats are marauding all the rice and other jute bags filled with foodstuffs, ruining the contents!

B: So? Is murder the solution?

Sar: But after all, they are mere rats.

B: Oh! Is that so? In that case, 'this' (loudly striking his own chest with open palm) **is also a rat. Ask Pillai to buy double the quantity. One portion may be given to the four-legged rats; another may be given to this hefty two-legged rat.**

Why are you blinking? After all, you are planning on doing away with them because you consider them pests. According to you, they are eating foodstuffs but not doing any productive work in the Ashram and the punishment is the death penalty inflicted by means of administration of poison. Good. But why are you showing partiality in applying the logic? 'This' is the biggest pest in the Ashram. The four-legged rats, poor things, swallow a few morsels to fill their tiny bellies and go away. This two-legged rat swallows entire mouthfuls three times a day. Does he do any work for the Ashram in return? No.

So, let your penalty remain as it is, only, let its jurisdiction

cover this giant two-legged rat also. (turning to face me) **Who are we to question the propriety of decisions taken by the Sovereign? We are after all nude beggars who ought not to be permitted a say in anything. What do we know? Of course, the Sovereign is right. I have only one last wish** (turning to the shocked *sarvadhikari* again). **Will you please grant it? Please ensure** (again loudly striking his own chest with open palm) **this one is plucked out first. I do not want to see anybody being killed.**

Bhagavan leant back on the Sofa and turned his face away from us. He had become emotional and his chest was heaving. He was perspiring. The *sarvadhikari* had become a statue. My cheeks were drenched in silent tears. Suddenly the *sarvadhikari* burst into a loud wail and a cascade of tears. He caught hold of the Master's feet and pressed his head on them. Those sleeping at the back of the Hall woke up in alarm and looked about them with panic. The *sarvadhikari* was banging his head against the wall, cursing himself. *'Oh, headless body! Oh, great sinner! Oh, demon! You have done like this!'* Now all rushed from the back of the hall and seized the *sarvadhikari* by the shoulders; they tried to calm him down. But he continued to squirm and thrash about until Bhagavan looked into his eyes again. The Master said kindly:

B: It is alright. On 1st September you are planning to make vellachcheedai (traditional sweet), are you not? Enhance the quantity. I will myself ask Pillai not to buy poison but rat booby-traps. Therein we will place the vellachcheedais. For the rats, fry it in ground nut oil. They will feel tempted by the smell and fall for it. Then we can ask Pillai to release them in the forest behind *simha-theertham*. It is a location too far for them to return from.

The *sarvadhikari's* sobs were yet to abate. Sri Bhagavan then added in a gracious cadence of voice, **'Have you understood?'** The *sarvadhikari* bent down, wiped his eyes and blew his nose on his wet dhoti, prostrated full length on the ground, pressed either ear alternately upon the floor several times successively, got up, stooped down with folded palms and closed eyes in front of the Master and left, still sniffing every now and then. Everyone in the Hall was looking dumbfounded. Some bent down and asked me in a low voice what had happened. I was about to respond when Bhagavan, for a single second, directly turned and looked into my eyes. I fell silent.

28th August 1936

It Really Is That Simple, BE

Q: What is the secret of attainment of the Kingdom of God? Is it only Vichara*?*
B: Those who are unable to understand the method of investigation Who am I? or those who find it unappealing, may take up the practice of *chittaikagratha* [one-pointed mind], single-mindedness, which is holding on to one thought to the exclusion of every and any other until that one thought also disappears in the Beingness of the Self.

How did *King Shishupala* (cousin of *Lord Krishna*) obtain Salvation? By hating *Sri Krishna* from the very core of his heart. Therefore, be it love or hate, a single idea must be held fast until that also collapses and dissolves into the Beingness of the Self. Then only the *nivritti* state of mind is left. The Truth cannot be had by means of nourishing the intellect with the fodder of objective knowledge. Knowledge of diversity is only ignorance. Words can only point to the Truth.

Understanding them does not mean you have gained True Wisdom. Words or concepts obscure the Truth further and further; they create confusion where none need exist. Hui-Neng (sixth patriarch of Zen Buddhism) has said: *'Truth and words have nothing to do with each other. If Truth is the sun burning in the sky, words are like the finger pointing at it. The finger itself can never reach the sun. All it can do is to point to its location. Some are deluded into thinking that the finger is the sun. If you want to see the sun, first*

tear your eyes away from the finger. The sun of Truth is not anywhere apart from you. You are verily It. If you will Realise It, you must throw away everything you yet know. Within our impure mind, the pure one is to be found. The true import of meditation is to realise inwardly the calmness of the essence of the mind. My friend, the grand secret is inside you, look within, and wake up!'

If Reality were something external to or apart from you, it could be handed over to you on a platter. This IS you. Only, relinquish imagination and BE as you ARE. We are not trying to attain the Self. There are not two Selves, one to attain the other or the other the one. All that is necessary to do is to give up the not-Self; this done, the Self alone remains. Will anyone call this difficult? Acquiring can be difficult, for it requires effort. But you are asked only to give up, that is, to cease all effort or imagination and simply BE the Real. Realisation is simply the art of letting go of everything that the mind contains.

To KNOW *'I am God'* is wisdom, not to THINK *'I am God'*. To know is to remain subjectively aware without the involvement of effort or volition. With incessant practice, this becomes the natural state. When the possibility for volition or effort has completely died away, then you will be swallowed by the Self automatically. The thing to do is to NEVER FORGET BEING. Remembering Being is not thinking about Being; it is Being Itself. Thought is one thing, and Realisation quite another. 'I am' is wisdom, not thinking that you are. Stop living in the self-imposed misery of Self-denial, face Reality. Therefore, simply give up all pretence of being this or that, and merely BE. BE, that is all. It really is that simple. BE.

Q: Bhagavan mentioned that Shishupala *(character in the Indian epic* Mahabharata*) attained Salvation by hating God. How can anyone hate God?*
B: Oh! Many do.

Q: But how can hate lead to Salvation?
B: Why not? For decade after decade, *Shishupala* nurtured in his heart a fierce hatred of *Sri Krishna*. There was no other thought

in his mind other than his hatred for *Sri Krishna*. The hatred was so vitriolic and strong that it eradicated all other thoughts. So, all the time *Shishupala* would be thinking about *Krishna* and *Krishna* only. Other thoughts had become impossible. This hatred broke out or found an expression in *Yudhishthira's Rajasuya yajna [Vedic* royal ritual in the *Mahabharata]*. So, *Shishupala* became fortunate enough to be killed by the hands of *Sri Krishna*, a blessed privilege even the desireless *Bhishma* coveted but could not obtain.

Q: Which is the best method of killing the ego?
B: It varies upon the temperament. Those whose minds are structured to think in terms of logic opt for *Vichara*. Those who prefer to worship God, surrender unconditionally to Him. The best thing to do is to take up both and deliver a double-whamming attack upon the *ahamkara* [ego]. Do we not walk on two legs? Once God or Self sees that you are making an earnest effort, he will guide you from within, of his own accord. *Bhima* (central character in the *Mahabharata)* was fighting with *Jarasandha* (prominent antagonist in the *Mahabharata)* for a long time, and *Sri Krishna* was passively watching. Just when it became apparent to one and all that *Bhima* was going to lose, *Sri Krishna* told him the secret of destroying *Jarasandha* and *Bhima* won.

Q: Why not tell him at the outset?
B: Because then he would become complacent and certainly lose on account of carelessness. God lets us struggle for a while. That is because the attitude of helplessness must germinate in you. You must realise that you are completely helpless and therefore completely dependent upon the Almighty even to raise your little finger. Only then will the ego, which arrogantly says 'I', subside.

Have you heard about the history of Swami Vivekananda? When his father was supporting his family, he laughed at whatever Sri Ramakrishna told him. When his father suddenly died and suffering swept him away like a gigantic deluge, he recognised his helplessness and his proud spirit found solace in humility only. It

was then, not before, that he surrendered unconditionally to his Guru, who saw his ripeness and opened his eye to True Wisdom. If the ego still has a choice, rest assured, it will never subside.

The ego MUST be browbeaten into surrendering. There is no doubt that God will eventually show you the light. But first, he will make you surrender. If that surrender can be brought about only through suffering, so be it! Somehow or the other we must cross to the shore. Struggle madly to strike the Light and see if you do not make it. The common man thinks, *'Come what may, I can take care of it.'* It is not until he begins to actually feel, *'No, I cannot do anything at all. If God, in His limitless Mercy and divine Compassion, does it through me, it would happen; otherwise, it would not. Either way, I am not involved; my helplessness in anything and everything is unequivocally absolute'*, that he is ready to receive the teaching of *Ajata Advaita*, not before.

Trying to be humble is a sham, an exercise in self-deception. Actual humility lies only in total helplessness and complete surrender. Did not *Sri Krishna* make *Kuselar* (childhood friend and devotee of *Lord Krishna*) sit on his own throne and wash his feet with tears of affection and joy? What did *Kuselar* bring to *Sri Krishna*? Three handfuls of broken *attukulu* [puffed rice]. It seems paltry. To *Krishna* it meant the world and more. I am the bondslave of my devotee's Love, says he. Yet the only thing people seem to want to do is to pour their money into donation boxes. Who is interested in your money? Have you grown big enough to enrich Him? *Poosalar* and *Katavargoen* (ardent devotees of *Lord Shiva*) both constructed temples; but which temple was God more interested in consecrating? So, to unconditionally Love God is the most exalted state possible; it is to know the Self.

Q: Bhakti *presupposes duality and* Vichara's *objective is Realisation of the final state of non-duality. How can these two be practised at the same time?*
B: For those whose *sadhana* rests on a foundation of conceptual theory or firmament of intellectual contrivance, Realisation is indeed impossible. Mental doctrines are not the way to Realisation.

Q: But the faculty of logic is needed for Vichara!
B: The reasoning *'I am not what I was hitherto imagining myself to be',* is only the preliminary phase of *Vichara* and this, as pointed out by you, involves logical or intellectual analysis. However, the actual point of *Vichara* is to achieve a perpetual state of mind in which there is effortlessly and volitionlessly maintained thought-free and languor-free Subjective Consciousness. This state certainly does not involve the functioning of the thinking faculty, whether called by the name mind, intellect, faculty of reasoning and logic, or any other name.

Q: But how can bhakti *be reconciled with* Vichara? *The* Ajata Advaita *doctrine refuses to sanction the existence of God. So, how can practitioners of* Vichara, *who have accepted this doctrine, entertain or harbour feelings of* bhakti? *Since God does not exist, what is the point of* bhakti? *Is it not silly?*
B: Only those who have attained the rare state of *Sahajajnanastithi* can truthfully say *'God does not exist.'* For the others, he does exist after all. His reality is on a par with yours. His existence will continue until yours is destroyed.

29th August 1936

Firm Assurance from the Master

Q: For the past five years, I am trying to Realise the Self by using Bhagavan's Who am I? method. But there is no progress because my ego is sabotaging all my sincere efforts.
B: Never mind. Go on with your *abhyasa*. Let the ego do his worst. You do your best. And Bhagavan will take care of the rest.
The man's eyes shone with tears of joy at this firm assurance from the Master.

Why Are Jnanis so Rare in the World?

Q: Why are Jnanis *so rare in the world?*
B: On the other hand, all are verily *Jnanis*. The common man is one whose *Jnana* is covered up with *upadhis* [limitations]. A few, finding them irksome, manage to shake off the *upadhis*. This is the one and only difference.

Q: What is the way to get rid of suffering?
B: Get rid of the sufferer, that is the only way. Only so long as there is a sufferer can there be suffering. When there is no sufferer, suffering is impossible.

Q: I know that Bhagavan mentions Who am I? often, as the most efficacious means for man to Realise his Immortal Nature. But I have also heard him talk of the method of self-surrender. What is the difference between these two methods?
B: Surrender or Realisation is the fruit of *Vichara*. Ripe minds readily give up everything in a single stroke as soon as they are exposed to the truth of *Ajata Advaita* (that is taught by Bhagavan)**. Then nobody remains to raise questions or formulate doubts or think thoughts, thus only the Self remains. Until the amount of *vairagya* needed to simply abandon the mind is gained, one must practise investigation along the lines of Who am I? *Athmavichara* is *sadhana*; complete surrender is the goal itself. Complete surrender is the immaculate state of pristine mental nudity.**

Complete surrender is merely another name for the Beingness of the Self; it automatically draws you into *Jnana* or Emancipation. There is no such affirmative act as 'surrendering' by means of which the Self may be Realised. To give up everything, including yourself foremost, is *Ananyasharanagati* [unconditional surrender]. Only one who has fully recognised *samsara* to be the horrific ocean of perdurable pain that it really is will be able to surrender the ego once and for all. Others carry on briskly with their usual nonsense, discussing, *'Now, I wonder which* sadhana *I shall pursue today...?'*

There is no such thing as 'surrendering' because surrender cannot be 'done'. Surrender is *Summayirutthal* [effortless consciousness]. The common man is so used to 'doing' that when asked to not do, he begins to ruminate, *'I wonder how I may do this thing called "non-doing"?'* Is it not absurd? Non-doing is just that, it is simply not doing; how can it be 'done'? Reality is not to be gained afresh.

If imagination is given up, Reality shines. It is you who are imagining your fictitious ignorance. Give up imagining and BE as you ARE. This is the way to Immortality from which there is no possibility of return. For one who has the burning, all-consuming *vairagya* to forthwith throw all his age-old mental baggage overboard, *sadhana* is a ridiculous proposition. Who is to do *sadhana*? However, partial surrender may be called *sadhana*; in due course, this would lead to complete surrender. *Vichara* and trying to surrender are not to be thought of as two different or mutually exclusive forms of *sadhana*, from which you may pick out either to follow. The one implies the other and the other the one. Do we not walk with two legs?

To Realise the import of self-investigation one must go on trying to completely surrender; to surrender completely one must relentlessly carry on with self-investigation. In either case what we are trying to do is to break the venomous, tenacious grip of the tyrannical ego in such a way that it is not able to rise again to arrogantly proclaim itself as 'I'. You may even pull out the roots of a poisonous plant and throw it away, but it might regenerate. The thing to do is to dig out the root, soak it in kerosene for some time, and then torch it. Then there can be no more nuisance. Soak the *ahamvritti* in the fuel of *vairagya* and torch it with the spark of the Guru's Compassionate Grace. Surrender will bring about peace only if it is completely unconditional: *'Anyatha sharanam nasti tvamaeva sharanam mama...'* [there is no other refuge, YOU alone are my refuge]. This is the way to the state of unceasing *mouna* or union with the Divine.

Observe Inwards

Q: Why is there no Order in this Ashram? If there were, I would have joined in it. Sri Ramakrishna, whom Sri Bhagavan seems to hold in lofty esteem, created an Order, and it is functioning till this day.
B: Realisation is a personal voyage into the Impersonal, J. Krishnamurti said, *'Truth is a pathless land.'*

Q: But unlike J. Krishnamurti, Bhagavan is not interested in touring around the world, giving speeches and lectures, and spreading his message. He keeps quiet. Why?
B: The message is the same: observe inwards. There it is delivered through the medium of the intellect. Here it is Heart-to-Heart. Whomever finds whichever compatible attends the respective presence.

Q: Is inner observation the same as Who am I?
B: Yes.

Q: How so?
B: The difference is in the nomenclature employed only. Continuously observing the mind, one finds there is no such thing, that no such thing could ever exist. The fruit of such observation is that the observer, the observed and the faculty of observation all collapse and disappear once and for all. Then only the Self, in all its pristine purity, is left as the residue. The mind is only a mistaken notion. If you look closely at it, it cannot remain. If you look at the snake in the twilight closely, it becomes obvious that there never was any snake. Then the question of killing the snake becomes an absurd redundancy.

Whether you call it *Vichara* or inner observation, the point is to give up or stop being aware of the not-Self. There is no need to cultivate awareness of the Self because that is an inevitable constant, a permanent 'given'. It is totally impossible to cultivate Self-awareness

because it is already here and now. If we stop paying attention to the not-Self, the Beingness of the Self alone remains. The approach therefore is one of elimination or negation. Total negation is the essence of the positive.

Q: So that is the meaning of Manasam tu kim marganae krite naiva manasam marga arjavat. *[When one enquires,* 'What is mind?'*, it is found that there is no such thing as the mind. This is the direct path.]*
B: Yes.

From Bhagavan's Upadesa Saram *verse 17. ED*

30th August 1936

The Grand Secret? LET GO

Q: Is Vichara *compatible with our day-to-day activities? Could I do it side-by-side with my domestic and official chores or is it to be done only at fixed hours during the day, when we have time to exclusively concentrate upon it?*
B: The former.

Q: Should then part of the mind be kept on the work? If attention is directed entirely towards the Vichara*, my work may suffer in quality and I may get into trouble at the office.*
B: Once the *Vichara* has taken firm hold of you, your mundane or temporal tasks will be executed by the Higher Power automatically, by using your body as a vehicle or tool. Everything is eventually taken out of your hands as you sink deeper and deeper into the delicious abyss of Self-awareness. It is like rowing downward along the current of a huge river whose course finally ends in a huge,

roaring waterfall. At one point of time, you observe the oars still clutched in your hands and start laughing at yourself, amusedly throwing them into the churning waters.

Those who desire to continue in *samsara* [cycle of birth and death] go on rowing in the opposite direction. Their fate is indeed miserable, but they will not listen to good advice. If you try to talk sense into them, they will become enraged and shout, *'What! Are you asking me to die, then?'* They keep on rowing ad infinitum, thinking themselves to be very cleverly escaping death, not knowing that the waterfall at the end is the gateway into Paradise, and all they have to do to get there is simply stop rowing and surrender to the current.

They are like the Greek king Sisyphus, who was forced to endlessly roll a massive boulder all the way up to the top of an enormous, steep hill, only to helplessly watch it roll back down just when the top was about to be reached, and then roll it up again and so on and so forth; he is supposed to be still there in the underworld, rolling and rolling with all the might of his arms, but to no fruitful end. Rowing in a direction opposite to the current is never going to get you anywhere, because all your labour is offset by the current, effortlessly. Wise *sadhakas* who have realised the true nature of *samsara*, on the other hand, know what to do – or rather what not to do.

The grand secret is, LET GO. Then you will be swept down automatically. Fear may sometimes force you to resume rowing, but eventually, you will see wisdom and throw away the oars. Then your boat will be wrecked by the rocks at the bottom of the waterfall. Further journeying, by now so wearisome, will have become impossible, and Paradise will be yours for all of Eternity. All you need to do, or rather non-do, is to LET GO. Yes, it really is as simple as that. *Summayirutthal* [effortless consciousness] is the secret whereby the Kingdom of Heaven may fall into your hands for perpetuity.

31st August 1936

All Vasanas to Be Completely Eradicated

Q: Can Jnana *once attained be subject to reversal? Is a fall-back into ignorance possible?*
B: Mind once destroyed can never return; but so far as your Realisation of the Real, or *vrittijnanam* [temporarily merged in the Absolute], is concerned, unless and until all the *vasanas* [habits of the mind] have been completely eradicated, you cannot remain steadily established in the *nivritti* state.

Q: How then to destroy the vasanas*?*
B: Surrender to the Guru and let his Grace do the work.

Q: Is it the vasanas *that ruin one's peace of mind?*
B: Yes. *Vasanas* channel the faculty of mental attention outwards, that is away from the source of thought. To merge into the source, it is necessary to harness the mind in such a way that it stands transformed altogether into the investigation or search for itself. As opposed to the mind flippantly flirting about with the question Who am I? on the level merely of the intellect, the aspirant who is burning with *Atmajignasa* [enquiry into the nature of the Self] allows the mind to be transformed into the investigation: Who am I? In the case of the latter variety of aspirants, his mind is not able to harbour any thoughts, being preoccupied solely and fervently with the search for itself. It is only then that the dormant power within asserts itself and bestows Grace upon him.

Q: Is not Atmajignasa *also a desire?*
B: It is that one thirst, the continuous attempt at satisfaction of which eventually bestows freedom from all thirst: *'...whosoever drinketh of the water that I shall give him shall never thirst, but the water that I shall give him shall be in him a well of water springing up into everlasting life.'*

The Guru's teaching that your actual nature is formless and timeless Reality, which, once it has entrenched itself firmly in your mind, will not let you escape. It pursues you all the way to the *Sahajastithi* [natural state], not resting and not permitting you to rest until the mind has been irrevocably extirpated.

Q: Is the intellect a help or hindrance for Vichara*?*
B: Initially, it is by using the faculty of intellect that the mind understands itself – including the world perceived by it – to be an unreal phantom. Once the intellect finally acquires the understanding that the only useful thing the mind can do is to not do anything at all, there is no further role for the intellect to play in bringing about Realisation. The intellect is the tool by which the mind is coaxed into getting convinced that it must disappear – or quietly subside into the Beingness of the Self – once and for all.

Intellect is not different from mind, intellect is only one of the possible forms that the mind can assume. Some of the other forms are memory, emotion, et cetera. So, while being helpful in the preliminary stage of *abhyasa* in facilitating one to distinguish between *Sat* [truth] and *asat* [untruth], the intellect also needs to eventually be forsaken, together with other mental modifications, before the *nivritti* state of mind can be regained.

Q: I am familiar with the Ajata Advaita *doctrine that is taught by Bhagavan, which says that creation is merely a mental phenomenon. But contemplating on this truth makes me feel uneasy rather than peaceful. Why?*
B: It is owing to the dense accumulation of *vasanas*.

Q: Although I am practising Vichara *every day, there is no improvement in me. My* vasanas*, if anything, are becoming even more vigorously assertive.*
B: You were told to go on pursuing *Vichara*, not to judge whether progress was being made.

Q: So, what Bhagavan is trying to tell me is that it is not of any great use trying to measure how much progress I have made. Is that right?

B: Not only is it impossible to measure how much spiritual progress you have made but also the attempt to carry out any such measurement is counter-productive since it causes detriment to what little introversion you might have managed to achieve up until now. By telling yourself that you want to measure progress, you are strengthening the 'I' that wants to measure its so-called spiritual prowess, the destruction of which 'I' happens to be the objective of your *sadhana*.

Q: It is said that without Guru's Grace, no matter how hard the jivatman *tries, Realisation will be unequivocally impossible. I pray for Sri Bhagavan's Grace to descend on me since I consider him my Guru.*
B: Grace is not denied to anybody. The present circumstance wherein you are yearning for Grace is a consequence of the fact that Grace has been working on you. The Guru is a delicious ocean of Grace without beginning or end that bestows everlasting life or Immortality, but only to those who dive in. Only if you lose yourself in the waters of Grace are you eligible for awakening into your actual nature of Immortality.

Q: Mere intellectual grasp of the teachings is useless; one must practise them assiduously and incessantly. Is that not what Bhagavan is trying to tell me?
B: Yes. What is the use of merely looking at the water?

Q: I want to plunge head-first into this ocean of Grace which Bhagavan tells me his devotees have access to. But although I am sitting at Bhagavan's feet, I am not able to find this ocean. Where is it?
B: Within you.

Q: Please tell me what I shall do to gain access to this ocean of bliss.
B: Don't do anything, simply surrender unconditionally.

Destiny Guides the World to Its Inevitable Future

Q: Shall I not try to effectuate Bhagavan's recommendation that I investigate along the lines of Who am I?

B: Certainly, practise the practice, but do not intellectualise the teaching. Remain entirely free from *vrittis*, be it belief, opinion, attitude, or anything else. If you make the teaching of *Ajata Advaita* fodder for the mind to think about or believe in, how can you meaningfully expect that very teaching to starve or bombard the mind out of its habit of functioning outwards?

Q: So, Who am I? should be investigated as a matter of course, and not with the idea that it is going to bestow Self-realisation or any other idea?

B: Exactly. Supposing you are unable to manage to undertake such motiveless investigation, go on investigating however you might be able to. Eventually, you will reach the stage wherein you are able to investigate without being encumbered by any motive.

Q: So, to tackle the obstacles to Vichara, *only further unflagging* Vichara *is the aid?*

B: That is correct.

Q: Should Vichara *be performed in Bhagavan's presence only? Suppose I do it at my home in Munich, or my vacation house in Tübingen, or anywhere else, will it be just as effective? Many Caucasians seem to have settled down here permanently, but I am unfortunately not in a position to do so.*

B: This or that place is there in your own imagination only. Places make no difference to *Vichara*. What is needed is *vairagya* [renunciation].

Q: What is vairagya?

B: Perfect *vairagya* is the *nivritti* [introverted] state of mind, where the mind has become altogether indistinguishable from simple, pure Subjective Consciousness; earnest and unremitting *Vichara* brings it about.

Q: Should I think of God whilst carrying out Vichara*? Shall I think of Bhagavan whilst practising it?*
B: No. All thoughts are to be avoided. There ought to be no possibility for thought.

Q: Bhagavan must be aware that the hometown of our winsome German people is now under the grip of a tyrannical Fascism. I am convinced the National Socialist ideology is exclusively destructive in character and ultimately lethally poisonous for our people, and, I think, not only morally. But what to do about it, I do not know. Any talk on these lines back at my place and I shall never be seen again – I am sure of it...
B: There is a destiny which guides the world to its inevitable future, be it good or bad. To the extent that we are ordained to have a hand in it, we shall find ourselves unavoidably taking part in it. Leave it there and do not fret unnecessarily and pointlessly about what you cannot help.

Q: Is there any efficacy in prayer? I am aware, of course, that Ajata Advaita *denies the existence of God.*
B: Surrendering yourself to what IS, is the loftiest prayer.

Vichara Cures Man's Biggest Ailment

Q: I have heard it spoken of that chronic illnesses become rectified by asking Who am I? in Bhagavan's presence. Can physical ailments be cured by means of practising Vichara*? Is it true?*
B: *Vichara* is the means to cure man's biggest ailment, that of physicality. Man imagines himself to be made out of gross flesh; whereas, in truth, he is pure Spirit only. If only you will open the eye of the mind to the real 'I', all is found to be well. It is the mind alone that is the cause of everything. Collapse the mind by allowing

it to become permanently submerged in its source, the Shining of the self-resplendent Heart, and only blissful Reality remains.

2nd September 1936

Vichara Will Obliterate the Ego

Q: So, annihilating the ahamvritti *leads to Self-realisation. But what is the bomb with which the* ahamvritti *can be killed? Is it* Vichara*?*
B: Yes.

Q: Some go on asking themselves Who am I? but see no result. Others put the question once and it suffices for them to Realise the Self. How to explain this?
B: *Vichara* is verily the *brahmashironamaka astra* [most destructive weapon in the *Mahabharata*] with which to obliterate the ego; as to this there can be no doubt whatsoever. The *astra*, being simply a mantra, was always the same. What was the potency of the person wielding it would be the question, for without considerable spiritual potency such mighty *astras* could not be wielded. Likewise, the question Who am I? is the same for all. What is the intensity of the particular individual's *vairagya* that drives deployment of the *astra* wielded by him known as *Vichara*? That is the question.

A dim-witted participant in a game of chess plods through the various ranks of the king's army before finally reaching the king and checkmating him. A warlord with no access to the weapons made available by recent developments in the applied physical sciences plods through the various battalions of the army of the country he wages war against, before finally forcing it to ask for

an armistice. Likewise, one practising the *Vichara* with a weak or insufficient quantum of *vairagya* may have to encounter and finish off one *vasana* after another before finally reaching the stronghold of the *ahamvritti*.

On the other hand, if your *vairagya* is remarkably great or immense, a single extraordinarily powerful instance of bombardment with the *astra* Who am I? will suffice to finish off the *ahamvritti* once and for all. The weapon is the same; how forcefully are you throwing it? The greater the velocity, the greater the impact. *Vichara* does not have any intended target, it is ideally deployed in the total absence of volition and also varies according to the initial momentum. If used with immense *vairagya, Vichara* lands upon the *ahamvritti* as a bomb. Else it lands upon some *vasana* as a few pieces of buckshot. It is left entirely to you how strenuously you throw.

Resign Yourself Completely to God's Will

Q: Is the Realisation of the Self difficult to achieve for those without a background of immense erudition in Vedantic *scholarship?*

B: No. What is all this talk about Realisation, as though it were something new? Is it not funny that people want to Realise the Self? Can the Self be reached with the mind or ego? Does the mind or ego possess any genuine existence? Is not the mind or ego merely a false phenomenon of reflection? If we would only keep the mind quiet or remain still, thus giving ourselves unreservedly up to the Self, Realisation is obtained then and there. But this we will not do. Instead, we want to Realise the Self. Can *sadhana*, which involves more doing and therefore more divergence away from the Self, discover the self-evident Self?

Q: Does not Bhagavan recommend the sadhana, *Who am I?*

B: It is the second-best approach, it is suggested because people

want a formula with which to Realise the Self. The direct and immediate way is only *summayirutthal.* Who am I? is not *sadhana* in any typical sense of the term. *Sadhana* presupposes the existence of the *sadhaka. Vichara* does not assume the existence of the *sadhaka* at all, but searches for him and finds him to be eternally incapable of existence. Then what remains is the bliss of the Self. Practising other *sadhanas* goes on reaffirming the false conviction in the mind that there is an 'I' which undertakes such practice.

In such cases, the question of 'I' always remains to be finally tackled in the end. In *Vichara* the 'I' is the only question and it is addressed right from the very beginning.

Q: Is everything pre-destined?
B: Yes, everything in the exterior world. Introversion of mind is the one and only thing not subject to pre-destination.

Q: I have committed an incalculable number of atrocious sins. I have sinned deliberately and repeatedly. What is the way out for me? Shall I confess to Bhagavan? Will that expunge or exonerate my sins? Please tell me what to do.
B: Surrender to God and He will take care of you. Surrender means unconditional surrender. Resign yourself completely to God's will.

Q: Bhagavan means that whatever happens in my life, I must accept the same as God's will?
B: Yes.

BE As You Are

Q: How shall I Realise the Self?
B: Why should you Realise anything? Why not BE or remain as you are?

Q: The truth is: I also want to become an omniscient Jnani *like Bhagavan.*

I am very eager to Realise the Self – as quickly as possible. Please encourage my ambition. Please tell me how I shall Realise the Self.
B: Only by BEing as you ARE.

Q: I don't understand.
B: Remain without thinking and without being overcome by drowsiness or lethargy.

Q: Impossible.
B: Practise *Vichara*.

Q: It seems difficult.
B: Remove the idea of difficulty and it becomes easy.

Q: Is it possible that having once attained Self-realisation, the same could be lost?
B: Yes. If one or more *vishaya vasanas* continue to remain latent in the mind, there can be no doubt that the Heart's Revelation stands unequivocally obstructed thereby, that is, on account of the mental contamination caused as a result of infestation by such *vishaya vasanas*. In the case of such a person, a fall from *manonivritti* [mind turned inwards] is altogether likely, but from *manonasam* [destruction of the mind] there can be no return to *samsara* possible. The mind of the Emancipated Soul is drowned and dissolved in the *Sahajastithi* of *Jnana*; he cannot be drawn back. It is like dissolving a salt doll in the ocean.

Q: Can such a person function normally in the world?
B: From his point of view there can be no world available to experience through sensory perception. Others may see him walking around, talking, et cetera; that is not his concern.

Q: Will the Vichara sadhana *[practice of enquiry] alone be adequate? I mean, by itself will the investigation Who am I? suffice to reach this* Sahajastithi*?*
B: Yes.

Q: Then is God's Grace also not needed?
B: Sincere and dedicated effort to introvert the mind will win Grace automatically. The deeper the introversion of mind accomplished, the more is the Grace won. There will arrive a point wherein Grace alone remains. That is to say the one who had been seeking it has vanished: this is referred to as *Jnana*.

Vichara Is a Watchman

Q: Is Who am I? also not sadhana? *After all, we must ask ourselves the question and asking involves doing something, the action of raising the question.*
B: Did I ask you to go on repeating Who am I? Who am I? Put the question when a thought emerges, not otherwise. Who am I? is meant to arrest further development of a thought process and return the mind's attention to its source, which is pure Subjective Consciousness. *Vichara* is a watchman for ensuring *summayirutthal.* Whenever rats try to carry away grain from your granary, chase them away. If no rats appear, well and good, let all the grain remain as it is. If and whenever it forms the subject matter of your observation that the mind, pursuing the form of thought, is deviating from its natural state of pure Subjective Consciousness sustained effortlessly and volitionlessly, put the question Who am I? to yourself and return the mind to such *nivritti* state; otherwise, let the mind remain in that state undisturbed.

Q: Is this nivritti *state of mind* Jnana?
B: No, but denuded mind *[nivrittiyanamanam]* is the only means to dead mind *[nashamagiyamanam]*.

The Self Is Really Always in Realisation

Q: Which is better – summayirutthal *or investigating Who am I?*
B: If and when thoughts arise, investigate to whom they have arisen. The investigation Who am I? is necessitated only to the extent that mental excursion takes place in opposition to the state of mind in which there is effortlessly and volitionlessly maintained, thought-free and languor-free Subjective Consciousness. In the absence of both thought and languor, the mind naturally remains in the state of *summayirutthal.* And that is the desired state.

Q: I have been carrying out the Vichara sadhana *for the past three years. I see no palpable improvement in myself. Can Bhagavan please tell me how close am I to Realising the Self?*
B: There is no such thing as being close to or far away from Realising the Self. Either you are emancipated or you are not.

Q: In what sense, then, does Bhagavan say, 'Liberation is in the here and now'?
B: In the sense that effort is made only to reach the effortless state. Effort is not made so that anything new may be obtained; effort is directed only at removing spurious modifications or accretions. That done, Reality is discovered to be as it always was. The Self is verily always in Realisation. It is we who have come away and therefore must now retrace our steps all the way back to our original Source. To the extent that thoughts arise, to that same extent make an effort to eradicate them then and there, and that is all the effort required on your part. The effortless and volitionless state of languor-free thoughtlessness is the objective of *Vichara.*

Q: I do not recollect ever having come away from any source.
B: Whatever is wont to rise or bubble up in contradistinction to reality must be cut down; only then will Reality be revealed. You say 'I'; that is the departure you make from the Self. It is not the Self that is saying 'I' because he does not possess the capacity to claim,

but something else. The Self, being Life Itself, is always silent. What is this something else? Find out.

Q: Is it the ahamvritti*?*
B: Yes.

Q: How to kill the ahamvritti*?*
B: Only by *Vichara*.

Q: Thoughts are like the waves of an ocean. They keep on coming. It is not really a pragmatic approach to ask 'To whom has this thought occurred?' *every time a thought presents itself. My mind is flooded with thousands of thoughts every hour of the day. What am I to do?*
B: Since you make the observation that in your case you find *Vichara* to be infeasible, I will give you another method. Keep watching the sense of 'I' keenly. Do not try to stop thoughts. Simply keep observing the *ahamvritti* or the thought 'I'. Instead of stopping thoughts, become aware of the thinker of the thought every time a thought occurs. Let your thoughts run riot, you remain with and eventually as the thinker. Do not feel any obligation to stop the flow of thought. Remain with 'I'.

Q: Will it do for Realisation?
B: Yes.

The Introverted Mind Invokes God's Grace

Q: What is the age limit for practising the Vichara sadhana?
B: There is none.

Q: I am an old man. I am 62 years old. I do not harbour any fixed notions about God's existence or otherwise, although mechanically I go to church on

Sundays. Is Self-realisation something quite beyond me, or is it something I can legitimately aspire to? Provided my efforts are not wanting in sincerity, can I also Realise the Self?
B: Yes.

Q: Will it succeed?
B: Provided God's Grace is obtained.

Q: Can I acquire God's Grace, although up until now I have never allocated much time for thought of God?
B: Yes!

Q: How?
B: Introversion of mind inevitably invokes God's Grace.

Q: How to achieve introversion of mind?
B: *Vichara* is the way.

Q: If what is destined to happen will happen, what is the use in making an effort to Realise the Self?
B: The completely introverted mind has transcended destiny.

Q: But to introvert my extroverted mind destiny must be favourable.
B: Yes.

Q: How to tell whether my destiny is conducive or non-conducive for introverting the mind and achieving Realisation of the Self?
B: While walking, do you doubt, '*Will the ground on which I propose to place my next step remain steady or will it suddenly waver owing to an earthquake or for some other reason? Without knowing the answer to this question, how can I continue to walk?*' Is it not absurd? Likewise, here. You incessantly pursue your *Vichara sadhana* and leave the rest up to Him.

Q: What I would like to know is whether my destiny in this lifetime is

conducive or non-conducive for introverting the mind and achieving Realisation of the Self. Please give me a direct answer.
B: It is not possible to carry out any such exercise of clairvoyance.

Q: So, I must throw away my life at God's feet like a wasted lover. If He accepts my love I am saved. Otherwise, I perish. He can do as He pleases. There is no possibility of appeal. This seems to be the line of opinion that Maharshi is taking.
B: Absolutely. But there is also the fact that for some persons, God is the only attainment considered worthy. I will marry him or die, says the fierce lover. I will try my best to get him to fall in love with me, but if I don't succeed, I can always marry somebody else, for I have charming looks and a nubile and voluptuous body, says the casual lover. God accepts the first kind of Love but unequivocally spurns the second. All this is applicable not exclusively to the path of *bhakti*. If you give your all to the quest for Realisation, without thinking a single thought about opportunity cost, you will succeed.

Otherwise, you may fall between two benches – spiritual attainment or worldly attainment – and become a failure altogether. Therefore, it is better that such half-baked persons not try to Realise the Self at all. Mr Patrick Henry said, *'Give me liberty, or give me death!'* That should be the attitude. If there is any option scrupulously arranged upon which to 'fall back' in case the quest turns out to be a failure, failure is made CERTAIN. Thereby, Realisation is rendered impossible. Such is God's design.

Q: It seems grossly unfair.
B: Are you and me to sit in judgement over Him?

Q: Are there really people who harbour such attitude of total maniacal vengeance to somehow attain God?
B: Yes, but not many. Their life has only one absolutely pertinacious, single-minded purpose: Self (or God).

Q: What happens when they fail? Do they commit suicide?
B: They never fail. It is the pusillanimous ones who fail.

Fall in Love with Arunachala

Q: But if investigating Who am I? will suffice to win Jnana, *where does the need for Arunachala come in?*
B: To succeed in the quest and sunder the knot of the Heart, Guru's Grace is a necessary condition.

Q: How to win such Grace?
B: Only by going on assiduously and incessantly with *Vichara*. However, in the case of a few rare individuals, a shortcut presents itself. If you happen to fall in Love with this magical Hill, no *sadhana* is necessary for you. Bear in mind that this Love must be not only unconditional, but also maniacal, and the potency or enormity of its intensity must be in perpetual climax. Such Love cannot be cultivated. Either it is there or it is not. If you fall under the spell of such fanatical Love, *Jnana* is automatic and inevitable in the incumbent lifetime. Love is verily God's most precious legacy unto man; it is Jacob's Ladder with which to unite into Him. Such Love is theoretically possible for all, just as theoretically all the buds of a tree may ripen into fruit. In actual practice, it requires an insanely firm, single-minded zeal and rank ferocity that the common man might find quite too impossibly sheer and stark to adopt in practice; that is why the gentler way of *Vichara* is recommended.

Love that is uncontaminated by volition invariably results in *Ananyasharanagati* [unconditional surrender], which is the same as *Jnana*. Love is the key to open the Gate of the Heart, to forever break the bonds of *karma*, and to escape once and for all from the fetid, obnoxious, horrifically excruciating putrid marsh known as *samsarasagaram* [ocean of *samsara*]. The mind must catch fire and burn away into nothingness before the Self can be revealed. If you are complacent about God, God will be complacent about you. People ask, *'Why am I not able to see God?'* What shall we say to them? *'You are sitting on top of Him, that is why. Clear off for good and He shall be Revealed.'*, is the fitting response, but

that may offend them, and so I keep quiet. Such all-consuming Love requires an object to long for.

God in His boundless mercy has given us Arunachala. One who, upon first sight, genuinely sees this Hill not as a mass of stone or collection of rocks, but as his Beloved Lord, will never again have to suffer the ignominy of being trapped within a woman's womb. *Jnana* does not come easily. It requires God to exert the entirety of His weight upon the strong knot of the Heart to sever it. There is also one more essential requisite for Emancipation: *Bhishma* (son of *King Shantanu*) could be killed only with the assistance of *Shikandin* (child of *King Drupada* – characters in the *Mahabharata*). It is not possible to conquer him in warfare.

Until the screen of *maya* [illusion] is lifted, there can be no Emancipation. *Maya* is simply the understanding that one is a transient subject spectating a permanent, objectively real entity known as the world. Equally harmful is the understanding that one is mere Subjective Consciousness or *Brahman*.

Any sort of conceptual framework should be avoided by one who wants to Realise the Absolute. The way to effect removal of this screen, being nothing other than a dense mass of arbitrary mental conceptualisations *[vrittis]*, is again only arduous, continuous, and unflagging practice of *Vichara*. However, for one who is burning in the fiery crucible of yearning Love for the Lord, the screen is removed in an instant.

Q: Love seems to be the quicker way, then.
B: Yes.

Q: But when asked which is the quickest and most effective way to Realise the Self, Bhagavan says Vichara.
B: *Parabhakti* [supreme devotion] does not come to all. *Vichara* can be practised by all. The prospect of practising *Vichara* attracts or captures the attention of anybody who has recognised *samsara* for what it is. *Parabhakti* cannot be forced, it must be present in seed-form amongst the *jiva's* latent tendencies. If it is not there,

we cannot do anything. *Vichara* gladly admits complete beginners also. It must be admitted that the *vasana* for *Parabhakti* [supreme devotion] is relatively rare.

Q: Can Parabhakti *be cultivated through* sadhana*?*
B: *Vichara* is quicker.

Q: Is God's Grace equally available to all?
B: Undoubtedly.

Q: Why do not all Realise, then?
B: God's Grace is like an ocean. How much you carry away depends entirely upon you. What is the size of the vessel you have brought? If you come with a cup you will get only a cupful. No purpose is served by accusing the ocean of parsimoniousness.

Q: I am unable to understand the analogy. What does the vessel in the allegory stand for?
B: The vessel is the mind. The bigger it is, the more introverted your mind is.

Q: So, the more introverted my mind, the more Grace I receive to Realise the Self?
B: Yes.

Q: But it is to introvert the mind that Grace is solicited.
B: Yes. It is like a boulder rolling down a mountain. The speed increases as more distance is covered. Take the first few steps in perfect sincerity. Thereafter you will find that a Higher Power is guiding you. Surrender to It unconditionally. All will be well. Everything will come aright in the end.

Vichara Should Be Practised Always

Q: Is setting time apart for Vichara *advisable, or shall I perform* Vichara *always? Can* Vichara *be practised whilst performing commonplace quotidian chores? There are tasks which necessarily involve a high degree of mental participation. Can* Vichara *be practised whilst performing these also?*
B: There is no point in setting time apart for *Vichara*, for it only makes the mind more ebullient at other times. Yes, *Vichara* should be practised always whether you are performing commonplace daily chores or tasks which according to you, necessarily involve a high degree of mental participation.

Q: The thoughtless state is the objective of Vichara*, it is said. How then can* Vichara *be practised at the same time as activities that require the expenditure of mental effort, such as thinking?*
B: This is not a matter that can be explained theoretically. Do it and see all this while you have been thinking that it is you who were doing the work. But now you will discover that the body goes on automatically with what needs to be done, whilst you, as the mind, remain blissfully quiescent in the Beingness of the Self.

Q: But how can that be?
B: Stop theorising. Do it and see. Then you will know.

4th September 1936

Mr Evans-Wentz

Among those who had turned up at the Ashram for a short stay, was an American author, Mr Evans-Wentz, whose books and translations of Tibetan manuscripts are well known. We had many enlightening talks and I was glad of his presence for another reason. Asking questions in the open Hall was rather an ordeal, but backed by him, I lost some of my shyness. We pooled our problems and came to the Maharshi with them, trivial or profound.

An interpreter was always on hand, for although the Maharshi understood English he was never willing to speak it. He knew immediately, however, whether the exact shade of meaning had been accurately translated, and if not, he persevered until one had understood him completely.

Mr Evans-Wentz, author of *The Tibetan Book of the Dead,* has written to the Ashram to convey his good wishes on the occasion of the anniversary observed here and the celebrations conducted for the purpose. Mr TKS handed over the letter to Bhagavan and was asked to read out the same since Bhagavan was presently busily engaged in feeding a squirrel with cashew nuts. (Reproduced from the best of my memory.)

> Dear Mr TKS,
> I am writing to the hermitage to express my warm compliments with regard to the celebrations planned for the 40th anniversary of Bhagavan's arrival at the Hill of the Holy Beacon; please convey the same to Bhagavan and the manager of the hermitage.
>
> It is my earnest desire and expectation that his fame should spread to every corner of the globe. Not that he would have any use for fame, indeed, most probably he would find it an annoying nuisance, but only so that as many people as possible stand to benefit from the existence

amongst us of this unique spiritual giant. Also, please tell the Master he always occupies the centre of my heart. Not that he would need to be told, but just so as for my satisfaction.

I will remain eternally grateful to you TKS for having explained Bhagavan's school of *Ajata Advaita* philosophy to me so admirably, my good friend. I find myself frequently poring over your translation of Bhagavan's *Forty Verses on Reality*. I have no doubt, sir, that they must be an excellent reproduction of the original *Sanskrit*, given the massive intellectual abilities I have been able to discern in you from our profuse discussions at the hermitage.

Many may be surprised to learn that apart from ensuring that the poor thronging the gates of the Ashram were not sent away with empty stomachs, the Master made it a priority to feed cows, monkeys, squirrels and other animals during his lifetime.

Whenever somebody brought fruit offerings, which in my observation even in those days was almost every day, a portion was not infrequently set apart for the monkeys by the Master himself. A portion would often be devoured by cow Lakshmi on her unfailing visit to the Hall twice a day and only the rest would go down human throats.

A small tin container filled with cashew nuts was kept in a shelf for the exclusive purpose of facilitation of the Master's feeding of the squirrels. Every morning and evening a few squirrels would punctually arrive to eat from the Master's own hand.

Mrs Piggot Comments about Bhagavan

During her visit, Mrs Piggot made some general comments about Bhagavan and his visitors. ED

Another problem discussed was that of the different kinds of yoga, and the comparative benefits offered by the various methods of spiritual discipline.

Bhagavan said that in the end there was only one approach to the goal and that was through the Realisation of the unreality of the thought 'I'. Why waste time on other roads which at best will only lead to the final path? Better be on that path itself all the time and waste no precious time on our sojourn on the earth. Meditate on the Beingness of the Self and on that alone. There is no other goal. Bhagavan's philosophy and teaching is the purest form of *Advaita*, known as *Ajata Advaita* [unborn non-duality; a particular philosophy of non-duality].

As the days passed, I saw more and more clearly that this was no theoretical philosophy. Bhagavan himself lived it continuously and joyously. He was one of the few I have met who were not only perpetually happy but also completely untroubled by the world. Not that the sorrows of the world left him untouched; on the contrary, he knew where they belonged and was not identified with them. To any sufferer his compassion was unlimited.

Every day, people with all sorts of worldly troubles came and sat in the Hall. The problems were sometimes narrated to him and he listened with a sympathetic ear. As far as solutions were concerned, mostly he asked people to walk around the Hill. Bhagavan never recommended *Vichara* when he saw that the *sadhaka* [spiritual practitioner] was pursuing a favourite method of practice that did not happen to be *Vichara*.

Other than the ones who wanted to get their doubts clarified by oral instruction, most people were quiet and taken up with their own thoughts. But sometimes there were Caucasians who were followers of *Swami Vivekananda's* or *Sri Aurobindo's* teachings, travelling monks, or Indian devotees who came for Bhagavan's blessing, and they would sing traditional songs and narrate stories from the *Puranas* [genre of ancient Indian literature] and *Itihasas* [the two great epics of ancient India – the *Ramayana* and the *Mahabharata*].

One day a man rushed in and flung himself face down before Bhagavan in a paroxysm of weeping. Great sobs tore his body. Bhagavan said nothing and no one else dared. I watched Bhagavan, His head was turned aside and he seemed indifferent. After some little time, the violence of the man's grief subsided and gradually he became quiet. Still, nobody spoke. Then at last, reverently, the man rose and made a deep salutation. Bhagavan turned his head and smiled upon him. I felt suddenly as if all the flowers of the world had poured their fragrance into our midst.

Another time a poor creature that had been bitten by a snake was brought in and laid before the Master. We all watched, fear gripping our hearts. Not so he, who sat looking into the far distance, while the victim writhed in pain. Fortitude and compassion were in that look and infinite peace. After what seemed like hours, the twitching ceased and the man appeared to be asleep. Then the one who had brought in the sufferer gently touched him. The man rose, prostrated himself before Bhagavan, and went out cured.

But this was an unusual occurrence. Bhagavan did not heal, at least not in the accepted sense of the word. Talking about it one day, I asked him if one could use spiritual power for healing. He remarked, **'Yes, if you think it worthwhile.'** However, he added that it required a great deal of spiritual force, which might be used more profitably in other directions.

6th September 1936

Investigation Is Only into the Not-Self

Q: Meditation on the Self is impossible because the Self is formless. If there is a form available in the Self, we can meditate on the same easily.

B: All forms are of the Self only. You can choose any form you like for your *abhyasa*. Meditation on forms or concrete objects is said to be *Dhyana*, whereas investigation into the not-Self is *Vichara* or

nirgunopasana **[meditation on the formless, attributeless Absolute Reality]. There can be no investigation into the Self. Investigation is only into the not-Self. Investigating into the not-Self, we find that it never existed at all. Then only the Self is left as the residue. This process is termed as *Jnana Vichara*. But there is nothing to be freshly got. Realisation only means the destruction of *purva samskaras* [old latent mind tendencies].**

8th September 1936

The Cosmos Is Mind Manufactured Fiction

Q: The answer to Who am I? is 'I am *Parabrahman* [supreme *Brahman*]'. *Is that correct?*

B: Is *Parabrahman* saying, *'I am* Parabrahman*'?*

Q: But I thought Parabrahman *is supposed to be the answer to the question.*

B: For those who are not driven by any impulse to venture into the practical (applied) dimension of *Ajata Advaita*, and who are contented, merely with an intellectual grasp thereof the answer being suggested by you will suffice. But in actual fact the thought '*I am* Parabrahman', has nothing to do with the *Sahajastithi* [natural state] of the *Jnani*. Thought is one thing and Realisation quite another.

Q: How shall I also reach this state? Is it only by interrogating myself Who am I? incessantly?

B: Yes. But do not do it because you want to obtain *Jnana*. Do it because you genuinely want to find out the answer to the question.

Theoretical or intellectual answers are mind manufactured fiction.

Find the Real answer. The Real answer cannot come from outside. It is within you. Concepts and words cannot bring about the discovery of the Self; only silence or stillness of mind can. Persistent practice is needed to attain that natural, primordial state of mind in which it has irrevocably been rendered indistinguishable from the Beingness of the Self. He alone who has been reduced into this state of mental nudity is pulled in and exterminated by the Beyond.

Q: Back where I am coming from, today's urbanised generation leads a fast-paced life where most people want instant gratification. This is why they resort to the usage of alcohol, morphine, cocaine et cetera. How shall we make such persons understand that the bliss of the Self yields greater happiness than experiences gained through employment of drugs?

B: It is not necessary to think of others when the question of who it is that perceives those others remains unanswered. The idea that the cosmos is mind-manufactured fiction disgusts a lot of people. It is not for them and they are not going to embrace it no matter how vociferously you endeavour to thrust it down their throats. Is it meaningful to expect all to be drawn towards *Ajata Advaita?* People usually want something they can 'do'. Some even come here and ask in English, *'How do I do* Vichara?' How shall we tell them that 'doing' is not the *lakshyam* [desired goal] of *Vichara?*

Q: Am I then to lead an idle and hedonistic life?

B: Keep the mind submerged in the Shining of the Heart and the body's activities will take care of themselves. If you are able to remain permanently submerged in the Shining of the Heart, you would never need to worry about anything. Freedom from thoughts, worries and anxieties comes naturally to one who has mastered the subtle art of self-abidance.

Q: So, attainment of Realisation is an art, not a science?

B: The tool, the method of *Vichara,* is scientific. But wielding it properly is an art.

Q: The expression 'Shining of the Heart', please explain what it means.
B: It refers to that perpetual state of mind in which there is effortlessly and volitionlessly maintained thought-free and languor-free Subjective Consciousness.

Q: How to be in that state without effort?
B: Go on practising with effort until remaining in that state has become effortless.

Practice Vichara and Surrender Together

Q: Desire for sensory experiences keeps cropping up in me. I am not able to concentrate my mind on Vichara. *Please tell me what to do.*
B: The idea 'I' or *ahamvritti* is only an arbitrary mental conceptualisation. Having no life of its own, it shines by the reflected light of the Self. You say 'I' am not able to concentrate. You were not asked to concentrate on anything. See if such a thing called 'I' exists. Scrutinise to see what it is. Try to examine it closely. By concentration we mean that the mind ought to pay close and unintermittent attention to an object of contemplation.

But in as much as *Vichara* is concerned, it is unnecessary and counterproductive that 'I' should concentrate on any object. *Vichara* does not involve concentration on any object, but rather the quest for the subject. Do not make 'I' concentrate on anything. Make the 'I' incessantly search for itself. Then it transpires that there never was anything called 'I'. That 'I' – which remains upon 'I' seeing that 'I' does not exist – is the Real 'I'; this alone is verily *Jnana*.

Q: In practice how is all this to be accomplished? Is it only by means of Vichara?
B: Yes.

Q: I have always imagined Vichara *to be meant for highly advanced ripe souls only. Will it not be too difficult for me to practise?*
B: The only difficulty is the idea of difficulty. Remain free of all ideas. Ideas choke the pure space of *Chidakasha* [pure consciousness] and convolute it into all sorts of bedazzling and befuddling imaginary shapes, names, and forms. Do not permit ideas to lead you. Remain with 'I am as I am'. Then ideas cannot cause any disturbance.

Q: If I should not think thoughts, how will day-to-day life go on?
B: Quite well, better than at present in fact. Try it and see that even in the absence of interference from thought, *prarabdha* automatically goes on placidly executing all its destined tasks for the body. We imagine we have free will, that is the reason for all our misery. People imagine free will to be freedom, but free will is really bondage. When the mind is dead, the myth of free will has faded away and only the bondage of automatic acceptance remains; this is veritably the bliss of freedom beyond imagination.

Q: Am I right in my understanding that thought-free, pure Subjective Consciousness is the Self, provided the absence of thought is volitionless and effortless?
B: No. It is only *chidhabhasa*, a reflected ray from the Self.

Q: Then what about the actual Self?
B: It cannot be comprehended by the mind.

Q: How do I reach it then?
B: There is no reaching It. Surrender yourself to It and be absorbed by and dissolved in It. Like a salt doll in the ocean.

Q: Can we practise Vichara *and* sharanagati *[surrender] at the same time?*
B: Yes, it is the best approach.

Vichara Prepares for Unconditional Surrender

Q: Yogis are said to divest themselves of body consciousness and remain in the absence thereof for decades together.

B: Yogis try to eliminate body consciousness by practising *kevala kumbhaka* [advanced breath retention] for abnormally large spans of time. But the trouble with adopting such an approach is that the volition or intent to remain bereft of body consciousness remains still to be tackled. For this reason, it is better to not try to forcibly eradicate body consciousness, which after all is only a harmless *upadhi* [limitation]. Once you have given up the notorious delusory habit of false identification of the Self with the not-Self, all possibility of volition and effort must be destroyed before *Jnana* can dawn.

As per the body's *prarabdha*, let the *upadhi* of body consciousness drop off automatically. We need not bother about it, not regard it as any hindrance to be resolved or tackled. You need not try to destroy the body or somehow subsume it into nothingness, simply cease to identify or associate with it in any manner. That will do. Trying to get rid of the body implies paying further attention to it. Instead channel attention away from the body and into the Self, that is the thing to be done.

As for the supreme spiritual state which you asked about, it is the *Sahajastithi* of the *Jnani*. It cannot be attained by *sadhana*. No effort can reach it. Surrender yourself to it unconditionally and you will be absorbed into it. *Vichara* is only to prepare the mind for unconditional surrender. If you can surrender absolutely, where is the need for *Vichara* and where is the possibility someone would then be left to investigate?

Q: Is the Self located on the right-hand side of the chest?

B: Only up until it is necessary for you to admit that you have a body. Do you?

Q: Yes. How can I deny it? Does not Bhagavan see this body talking to him?

B: The body does not say, *'I am you'*. You say that you are it. When you have weaned yourself away from this erroneous attitude that you are somehow linked with the body, then you will know where the Self is. The Self is not anywhere, it IS.

Perfect Vairagya Realises the Self

Q: Is it my own vasanas *which create this world I see about me?*
B: Yes.

Q: Including the other people I see in the world?
B: Yes.

Q: For Vichara marga, *is* diksha *[spiritual initiation] necessary?*
B: Longing or craving to escape from *samsara* is the one and only *diksha* required in relation to this path.

Q: How to cultivate such craving?
B: No separate efforts are necessary for it; steadfast and relentless practice of *Vichara* will take care of the requirement automatically.

Q: My Guru is the Shankaracharya of Sringeri (head of a monastic centre established by Adi Shankara). Must I renounce him and accept Bhagavan as my Guru if I want my practice of Vichara *to culminate in success?*
B: No such thing is necessary. If unequivocal *vairagya* is there, *Vichara* cannot fail to result in success. Perfect *vairagya* is the sole essential thing needed to Realise the Self.

Q: What exactly is meant by vairagya*? How to measure the same?*
B: *Vairagya* means the absence of inclination to part or slip away from the Beingness of the Self. The intensity of one's desperation to escape from *samsara* is a sound indicator of how earnest one's *vairagya* is.

Q: What is samsara*?*
B: One's mundane, apparent bodily existence.

Q: Thoughts pertaining to the body's mortality are plaguing my mind. What is the remedy?
B: Find out their origin and stay there, never to return thence.

Q: What are the qualifications needed to successfully practice Vichara*?*
B: Perfect *vairagya*, which is the same as perfect introversion of mind, is necessary and sufficient.

Q: How to cultivate such vairagya *or mental introversion?*
B: Only by continuous practice of *Vichara*.

Q: It sounds cyclical.
B: Stop theorising and start practising.

Q: But how to know whether I shall succeed on the quest or not?
B: No guarantees for success can be given.

Q: Then where is the incentive to try?
B: If the desperation I mentioned is there, the option to not try is sealed off. Then you will automatically succeed.

Q: But to cultivate such desperation we must start the practice.
B: True. Start.

Q: But this state is said to be exceedingly hard to attain, so the odds stacked against me are high. It is improbable that a weakling such as me should succeed.
B: That is your opinion. But even so, what is the harm in trying? What are you going to lose?

Q: What is the auspicious hour to start the practice?
B: Here and now.

The Cosmos Is a Dream

Q: Even after one or more persons die the world continues. If it were all only a dream, the death of one or more dreamers should in some way affect its continuity.

B: When it is said that the cosmos is a dream, it means that it is your dream. It is not correct to think of the world as being a collective dream. The other people you see in your dream are also your own mental creations. 'You' as you incumbently imagine yourself to be are unreal. What you actually ARE is Real, because Reality is your Self.

Q: The difficulty lies in reaching the Self.

B: There is no possibility of reaching the Self. Are there two selves according to you so that with the one we can reach the other or with the other the one? The only thing to do is to merge the mind in the Shining of the Heart. So that the screen of *avidyamaya* obscuring the Self is set aside. Then the Self alone is found to remain without a second.

Q: What is this screen?

B: The *ahamvritti*.

Q: If I get rid of this ahamvritti, *would I too become a* Jnani?

B: 'I' cannot get rid of 'I'. All 'I' can do is to surrender itself so that the Self stands revealed. Steadfast and incessant *Vichara* culminates in absolute surrender, which is the same as *Jnana* or Emancipation.

Vichara Is Easy

Kunju Swami: How is it that without a mind Bhagavan is able to conduct rational conversations with us and engage in many other tasks and functions besides?

B: Causality is unknown to the *Jnani*. The Emancipated Soul's actions therefore are always bereft of motive, purpose or volition. Bhagavan does not act at all. Action is alien to the Self. He is Life Itself but yet absolutely motionless. He is simply AWARE. Other than the fullness of Being – consciousness which he abides as – he does not know anything. The body may act in the world or remain idle. He cannot know. The faculties of sensory perception may remain inactive or function so as to take cognisance of objects in the world. He cannot know. Being the Self, the *Jnani* is totally ignorant of anything and everything but the Self.

He is referred to as the witness consciousness transcending space, time and causality, but that is exclusively from the point of view of objects with name, form and shape that take their origin in Him, subsist in Him and dissolve back into Him – Being merely appearances in Him of Him, and by reason of Him. He Himself has nothing to witness or see.

The body might be working day and night like a steam engine, but no *karma* can touch Him. His sensory organs might be caressingly assailed by the greatest of pleasures, but He enjoys nothing. His body might be racked with debilitating pain, but He does not make the foolish mistake of coming under the influence of the notion that the one undergoing an experience of pain is He. No matter what manner of work the body might be engaged in doing, He never does anything.

K: Maharshi, please clarify this one thing for me: are you or are you not now talking to us?

B: No. 'I' am not talking to you.

K: (reflectively) That's right. Maharshi is not doing any talking, He simply IS.
Chadwick: I am sometimes given to wondering how a Jnani's *awareness of the Self could formerly have been obscured or obstructed by prior ignorance. Was there ever ignorance for a* Jnani?
B: No.

C: Are Jnanis [*Self-realised sage*] *born* Jnanis *then?*
B: One's idea that one took birth is merely mental information. When the mind is annihilated, there is nothing to falsely inform the *Jnani* that he was born. Therefore, the Emancipated Soul abides in perpetuity as the Unborn, to which time, space and any other firmament of transformation or possibility of measurement are wholly alien.

We point to the body of the Emancipated Soul and give it the name *'Jnani'*, thinking that such a person must have awareness of the Self. But what is the fact? Is there anybody who can both stand apart from the Self and yet know the Self? The only way to know the Self is to BE It. So, the *Jnani* is verily *Jnana* [spiritual knowledge] and nothing but *Jnana*. There are no *Jnanis*. *Jnana* IS. *Jnana* alone IS, and *Jnana* alone could ever BE.

K: (in an over-awed cadence of voice) Maharshi, you inspire me. I also want to become great like you, I want to attain your same greatness, I want to become as great as you. I consider it my life's mission to emulate you. You are my idol, my superhero. Please tell me what I should do to attain the same greatness that you have attained; you the incomparably great Bhagavan Ramana.
Chadwick: Impossible and inconceivable. How could anybody become our Bhagavan? He is God Absolute.
B: (smiling) **What is there in it? Only remain still *[summayiru]*.**

K: Maharshi, I would like to know how I shall get rid of all my sins.
B: Original sin and original ignorance are all one and the same thing. To get rid of the one is to get rid of the other and the other the one. One certain repercussion of pursuing the investigation Who am I? all the way to its successful culmination in Realisation is the total effacement of all your sin.

K: Is the investigation Who am I? easy or difficult?
B: It is the easiest thing there can be. If attending to other things is readily possible for you, imagine how much more easy should be attending to yourself and attending to yourself exclusively!

K: Some say that it is exceedingly difficult.
B: Pay no attention to their words. Do you trust Bhagavan or not?

K: Implicitly and absolutely.
B: Then never mind what others are saying. Regard only what is said here. Bhagavan (tapping right cheek with palm multiple times rapidly and then pointing to own face) **says *Vichara* is easy. Will you practise it or not?**

K: (eyes swimming in barely suppressed tears voice choked, and face convulsed with emotion) Yes, Bhagavan.
B: (smiling) **Good.**

This text was also published in Aham Sphurana. *ED*

Mental Activity Cannot Take You Beyond Mind

Q: Despite engaging in the practice of Vichara *for a prolonged span of time, I see no improvement.*
Q2: (another questioner sharing the same sentiment) *I have been investigating Who am I? for several years. I see no result. What is the reason? Where am I going wrong? What am I doing wrong? Please help me.*
B: What is meant by *Vichara*? Is it to intellectually analyse oneself along the lines of the question, Who am I?

Q: Isn't that it?
B: No. *Vichara* means the effort to trace thought back to its source.

The culmination of this effort is the discovery of such source being the Shining of the self-resplendent Heart, the Beingness of the Self. The penultimate triumph in *Vichara* has come about when effort is needed in order to leave the Shining of the Heart rather than in order to plunge and merge into It.

If you incessantly hold on to the source of thought, there will come a time when emergence from such source becomes altogether impossible. Realisation of this state is what *Vichara sadhana* seeks to achieve. *Vichara* means hunting for the source of thought so that we might abide exclusively and permanently there practising *Vichara.* Simply seek whence within yourself it is that thought arises, having found such source, stay there once and for all.

Q: Since the ego is said to emerge from the right-hand side of the chest, can we say that this is the source of thought? Shall I therefore concentrate on the right-hand side of the chest?
B: Trace back thought subjectively, not conceptually. Do you need a mirror to enable you to ascertain that you exist?

Q: I don't understand.
B: Any sort of concentration of mind, be it upon the right-hand side of the chest or otherwise, is a mental activity which cannot take you beyond mind. There is only one way to get rid of the mind, that is, to transcend or bypass it. If you catch hold of the 'I'-'I' consciousness that manifests itself when the mind remains submerged in its source and holds on to the same indefinitely, the mind will fade away of its own accord. This alone is the way to earn the undying state of *Sahajastithi* from which there is no return possible. No amount of concentration of mind or other mental activity can result in Revelation of the Self.

Q: How shall I search for the origin of the ego? Please explain to me in such way that I shall be able to understand.
B: Whenever you find the mind wandering, pull it back by asking yourself Who am I? and fix it in pure Subjective Consciousness. Who am I? is like a mongoose patiently but vigilantly waiting outside the

termite mound, so that when the snake should emerge, the animal can spring upon it, break its neck and eat it. If the mongoose is resolutely determined to feast upon the snake, can anybody save the snake from certain annihilation? If it remains inside fearing for its life, it eventually dies out of starvation. If it emerges from the termite mound to look for prey, it itself becomes prey and dies.

This analogy becomes splendidly appropriate when the mongoose happens to be an aged creature. He would not have the stamina to kill a living snake. So, whenever the snake's head pops up, he hisses ferociously and the terrified snake beats a hasty retreat back inside. Eventually, the snake, living in perpetual terror of being devoured gives up the attempt to go outside and perishes inside the termite mound out of starvation. Then the mongoose, sensing that the snake has given up its life, breaks open the mound and gleefully consumes his dead prey.

Likewise, the mongoose, known as Who am I?, cannot by itself kill the snake, known as *ahamvritti*. *Vichara* is a watchman. When the troublemaker shows itself, he drives him back inside, so that he eventually perishes on account of lack of food to feed on, thoughts to think about or concepts to ruminate upon.

Immediately a thought presents itself, arrest its further progress by means of asking yourself, *'To whom has this thought presented itself?'*, and then and there return your attention to being aware of the one who is having the thought, that is, to pure Subjective Consciousness, sustained effortlessly and volitionlessly. This is how *Vichara abhyasa* should be deployed (smiling)**. Is it clear now?**

Q: Yes. But without thinking thoughts is it possible to run the household or attend to office duties? Our day-to-day activities require usage of the mind.
B: Do not speak from theoretical presumption. Try it and see. Do you know what your observation will be? In the absence of thought, work is found to go on even more efficaciously and efficiently than before.

Q: They say a Guru is needed to Realise the Self. There is no order of monks in this Ashram. Where shall I go?

B: Where is the need to go anywhere? BE as you ARE.

Q: Without Guru's Grace there cannot be success on the quest.
B: True. But such Grace is automatically vouchsafed unto him and him alone, who sincerely goes on with his *abhyasa*. There is no need to separately look out for a Guru. Go on practising and the Guru will come to you. His form and shape would depend upon your mental predilections and predispositions. He may or may not be in the human form. It is unnecessary to fret over not being able to find a Guru. You go on with your practice steadfastly and incessantly. See if one day the Guru comes in search of you or not.

This text was also published in Aham Sphurana. *ED*

Priority

Q: Some practise Vichara *for a short while and succeed in Realising. Others try for decades; their efforts are rewarded only with failure. What is the explanation?*
B: What matters is the extent of intensity of introversion of mind. There must be desperation to Realise the Self. The thirst to discover Reality, the yearning, the longing must burn brightly in the mind, burn with enough force to reduce the mind into ashes. Half-baked and half-hearted efforts are not going to get you anywhere.

Once you know that all this is fiction, can you remain content until and unless Reality is gained? The more actually unacceptable the mundane existence is – as opposed to the mere intellectual understanding or conceptual notion that existence in the form of the body is undesirable to you – the greater your chances are of Realising the Absolute Existence. Perfection in *vairagyam* [renunciation] automatically brings about *Jnana* in its wake.

9th September 1936

Bhakti Alternates with Vichara

Q: Continuous Vichara *makes the mind fatigued. What must be done to overcome this problem?*
B: Plunge yourself in the heavenly ocean of *bhakti*.

Q: And when that becomes tedious?
B: Get back to *Vichara*.

To Know Self Is To BE Self

Q: Would it be correct to say that Vichara *and concentration on the right-hand side of the chest are one and the same practice?*
B: This is like the long-standing belief that the goose barnacle gives birth to the barnacle goose.

Q: So, such a view is totally absurd?
B: Yes.

Q: What is the relationship subsisting between Jnana Vichara *and the Heart, which latter forms the subject-matter that constitutes the object of the former's effort?*
B: On the seabed of the oceans surrounding the Indian subcontinent, there lives a peculiar, colourful animal known in English as the 'peacock mantis shrimp'. This creature is related neither to the peacock, nor to the mantis, and nor to the shrimp, yet it has been given such name because it resembles each of these three inasmuch as certain specific characteristics are respectively concerned. Likewise, the Heart has nothing to do with our efforts to discover the same

and Shines all by Itself in perfect isolation. Yet we use terms such as 'Heart-centre', *'Jnana Vichara'*, and so on, in order to facilitate our supposed understanding. But any understanding we think we possess related to Realisation is unequivocally ridiculous nonsense.

Self cannot be understood or apprehended by what is not-Self, for not-Self does not exist at all. On the other hand, to know Self is to BE Self and therefore, Self does not even know Himself. He simply IS. So, in this sense, we can say that knowledge of Self is impossible. He cannot be reached at all. All that is possible to do is to surrender unto Him and keep quiet. *'Fear ye not, stand still, and see the Salvation of the Lord, which he will shew to you today...'*

The moment the mind has relapsed into total silence or stillness from which no return is possible, Salvation or Realisation has become a certainty. The mind presently sees itself as a physical body with an intellectual personality, the combination of which is understood to be one's 'person', which one then feels the need to deploy so as to facilitate one's functioning in the 'world'. If this wrong superstructure of ideas collapses and perishes, pure Subjective Consciousness is the remainder.

10th September 1936

Complete Obliteration of Vasanas Is Necessary

Q: But is not Who am I? explicitly mentioned?

B: *Vichara* does not mean repeating like a well-trained parrot, Who am I? Who am I? Mind seeking its own source incessantly is *Vichara*. The question Who am I? is only the linguistic component of the actual investigation. As you progress more and more in introverting the mind, the need to ask yourself the question repeatedly becomes less.

The moment it directs itself inward, the mind finds itself spontaneously dissolved in the Heart – for the time being, at least. However, if the process of extirpation of the *vasanas* is yet to attain completion, the mind resurfaces.

Q: When the mind temporarily plunges into and remains withdrawn within the Heart, does the sadhaka *then temporarily experience the state of the* Jnani?

B: No. Any experience that precedes the comprehensive annihilation of the *vasanas* cannot be the *Sahajastithi* of the *Jnani*. There is no such thing as a 'temporary experience of the *Sahajastithi*'. The *Sahajastithi* is not merely an elongated version of the state in which the mind remains one and identical with effortlessly and volitionlessly maintained, thought-free and languor-free Subjective Consciousness. Nor is it an elongated version of the *Spandabhraja Samadhi* state, nor yet is it an elongated or upgraded version of any other state. The *Sahajastithi* of the *Jnani* is in a class all by itself. It simply cannot be conceived by the mind, whether an active mind or a denuded one.

Q: There is a popular notion prevailing that Sri Bhagavan is of the opinion that there is a class of vasanas *known as* bhoga vasanas *[attachments towards worldly pleasures], and that these can remain latent in the* Jnani *even after his mind has been destroyed.*

B: No, it is not so. Complete obliteration of *vasanas* is necessary before the mind can be destroyed.

Q: From what Bhagavan has been telling me, I am able to infer that the question Who am I? is actually unnecessary after a certain stage of spiritual maturity has been reached, although the investigation itself must never be abandoned till the Self stands Realised. Is that right?

B: That is correct.

Depend on Grace from Moment to Moment

Q: Can one lead a life that is totally dependent upon Grace from moment to moment?
B: Why not?

Q: But practically speaking, is it really possible? Will God take care of all my requirements if I give up my individuality?
B: Provided one has surrendered without reserve unto the Higher Power.

Q: How to achieve such surrender?
B: Cease to imagine yourself as being the ego and remain as you really ARE.

Q: So, the ego is in fact simply an imaginary entity?
B: Yes.

Q: Why then does it appear so real?
B: Because of the long-established habit of cherishing one's individuality.

Q: How to break this habit?
B: Steady introversion of mind is required; the same is possible only with continuous *abhyasa*.

Q: Which is the most efficacious abhyasa *that can be followed?*
B: *Vichara*.

Jnana Is Nothing but Love

Q: Is the loss of body consciousness a necessary pre-cursor to experience that which Bhagavan refers to as 'Aham Sphurana'*?*

B: No. People long for an experience of absence of body consciousness without understanding the simple fact that what is not permanent is not worth striving for. Even if you were to happen to remain plunged in *Nirvikalpa Samadhi* for a thousand years, thereafter, you would still have to return to experience the *jagrat-swapna-sushupti* triad [three states of consciousness: waking state, dreaming and deep sleep] as usual if the *vasanas* have not been destroyed. Desiring for *Nirvikalpa Samadhi* is simply yet another *vasana* and yet another distraction or diversion from the straight path of *Vichara* that is characterised by the fact of its leading directly towards Realisation.

Why do you hanker after *Nirvikalpa Samadhi?* Because within your mind you regard it as the highest spiritual experience possible whilst still retaining the ego. While as a matter of principle we can say that such a view is not incorrect, why do you wish to retain the ego? The ego is a mischievous thief. He is ruining your natural state of incessant happiness. Rather than wanting to taste what it would be like to be divested of one's mind for a brief span of time, or rather than permitting the ego to encourage itself, so to speak, to taste what its own absence for a while would be like, rid yourself of the ego once and for all; then you will be at peace forever.

It is not *Nirvikalpa Samadhi* that is the goal, but the destruction of *vasanas*. If all *vasanas* are destroyed, only *Samadhi* remains. Any *Samadhi* that is experienced whilst one's *vasanas* are still alive could only ever be a transient, ephemeral experience. Do not aspire for that which comes and goes. Rather set your sights on That which never moves. *Jnana* should be our aim – and be satisfied with nothing less than That.

Q: What is the meaning of the expression, 'Prema purna thaya jnanam' *[the wisdom arising from complete love]?*

B: It means that *Jnana* is nothing but Love.

Q: Love of what?
B: *Jnana* is simply Love; It is not love of or love for anything.

Integrating Vichara into Worldly Life

Q: Why do some persons fail so lamentably despite making earnest efforts to Realise the Self?
B: One must hold fast to the mental pursuit Who am I? to the exclusion of every other mental activity, only then is success rendered possible and not otherwise.

Q: If I go on asking myself Who am I? all day to the exclusion of every other activity, who will take care of my family, and how shall I earn a living so as to be able to financially support myself and my family members?
B: Worldly activity and *Vichara* should go on side by side.

Q: Impossible. Vichara *aims at eliminating thoughts whereas thinking thoughts is essential if worldly activity is to go on.*
B: After some practice, you will discover that the mind effortlessly abides in the blissful beatitude of the Self whilst the body automatically carries on with its allotted activities according to its *prarabdha*.

Q: It is hard to understand how this could be possible.
B: That is because you are under the mistaken impression that it is the mind which is responsible for governing, controlling, administering, and executing the activities of the body. In other words, you still believe in free will. Free will is a myth. There is no such thing called free will. The mind spuriously pretends that it is in charge of the body's actions, which are in fact always going on of their own accord. By taking on such false or fictitious sense of responsibility, the mind tricks itself into believing that it is real and that it exists.

Do not make the mistake of taking the mind's presumptions and presuppositions seriously or for granted. Examine them ruthlessly and watch with detached satisfaction as they disintegrate.

Mind is only a wrong notion or assumption. If examined or scrutinised closely, it fails or breaks down or fades away. Constant enquiry into the question of what the mind is leads to its disappearance. Who asked you to take the mind's existence for granted? See if it exists. In the irrevocable discovery that it does not, you will lose yourself once and for all. This self-destruction is known as *Jnana.* Remain fixed in the Beingness of the Self and worldly actions will go on of their own accord.

Q: How will they go on unless I perform them?
B: You remain as you are and let the body go on with its destined duties.

Q: This may be possible for the Jnani*, others need their minds to tell their bodies what to do.*
B: Just now you were told not to take the mind's existence for granted.

Q: If there is no mind, then all are verily Jnanis.
B: *Ajnanis* are simply potential *Jnanis.*

Q: In practice we do not find it possible for actions to go on in the absence of the mind that supplies the body with instructions.
B: Steady practice of mental introversion will make you change your opinion and see things differently. Only those who think they have a mind are afflicted with the disease known as mind, the mind is an imaginary disease.

Q: How to remain free from such imagination?
B: Why are you asking for a formula for it? There is no formula. Remain as That which IS. What could be more simple? Yet for those who are not able to understand this, we have to say that *Vichara* is the principle means to Realise the Self.

Q: So, in actuality, the simplest way is to really…?

B: Remain as you primevally are. Do not try to reach the thought-free state with the thinking mind, it is impossible. Rather, give up the thinking mind. That is the thought-free state needed.

13th September 1936

Gajapathi, Muruganar, Knowles and Chadwick Sharing a Joke with Bhagavan

Q: If everything is an illusion, is God at least Real?
B: Are you aware of God in your deep sleep?

Q: No.
B: What is the inevitable inference?

Q: So, God also is just a myth, as is the case with the world, is that right?
B: God is real only if and until mind or ego remains.

Q: What about the Impersonal Absolute, which Bhagavan says is my actual Self? How can it be ascertained definitively that even this is not unreal?
B: In His case who do you think is available to raise this or any other question?

Q: What about the not-Self?
B: What is meant by 'not-Self'?

Q: That which is not the Self.
B: Impossible. There cannot be anything apart from the Self.

Q: What about the ego?
B: Whose ego?

Q: So really the ego does not exist at all?
B: That is correct. Mind or ego is fictitious fiction. The moment 'I' tries earnestly to know itself, it finds itself to be the Self. But this cannot happen whilst any *purvasamskara*, or other *chittavritti* lies latent in the mind. That is why the practice of *Vichara,* which steadily destroys all *chittavrittis* [fluctuations of the mind] is advocated. *Vichara* succeeds only if it is deployed continuously and incessantly.

Q: How then is worldly work to be carried on?
B: Both *Vichara* and worldly work can be carried on side by side, concurrently.

Q: Vichara *aims at a state of mind wherein there is no movement of thought waves.*
B: Correct.

Q: On the other hand, worldly work requires me to think thoughts.
B: Not correct.

Q: I am an architectural engineer. While drawing up plans, do I think 'Who am I?' *or do I think* 'What measure of length shall this facade extend up to?'
B: That is the mistake.

Q: Swami, piteously dim-witted mortal creature that I am, I am not able to identify my mistake. Please be so gracious as to point it out to me.
B: You seem to be under the impression that practising *Vichara* merely involves asking yourself Who am I? But that is just the first step. As you yourself said, *Vichara* aims at a state of mind wherein there is no movement of thought waves. This cannot be brought about just by asking yourself Who am I? and thereafter permitting the mind to meander about as it pleases. The question Who am I? is only meant to arrest further progress of the thought that you incumbently happen to be thinking.

After the present thought has been curtailed, take the mind back to its source, which is the primordial state of pure Subjective

Consciousness, sustained effortlessly and volitionlessly. When you are in this state, neither the thought Who am I? nor any other thought should disturb you. If it does, ask yourself Who am I? and come back immediately to such a state of mental stillness. Who am I? is an axe with which to chop down thoughts, at once, as and when they occur. After the current thought has been struck down, the mind must retreat into its natural state. The question itself is only a tool to help you move from the realm of thought to the realm of effortless and volitionless stillness of mind. It is vital that the mind recognise the error of its extroverted ways and make a determined effort to not stray away from its source.

A still mind is a mind that is exclusively subjectively conscious, when – by means of and as a result of having extensively practised in this manner – you are able to remain effortlessly and volitionlessly still. All the work that it is the body's *prarabdha* to carry out will go on of its own accord like clockwork. You will then be surprised at the efficaciousness and efficiency achieved by you, although you never in fact did anything! So, whilst drawing up plans for constructing buildings, think neither Who am I? nor think any other thought, but keep your mind still, merged in its source. Then the work will go on of its own accord. If your practice has been sufficiently intense, at one stage thereof you will discover the intuition has taken over the intellect. When you realise the fact, make no attempt to logically judge the decisions taken by the intuition or to scrutinise them in the light of reason.

The more you surrender, the more your worldly actions would be guided by intuition. The movements of the surrendered mind are not its own.

Q: Is the natural thought-free state of mind mentioned by Bhagavan the same as the Parabrahman *mentioned in the* Upanishads *[sacred scriptures in Hinduism]?*

B: No. He is the Beyond.

Q: How then shall I know Parabrahman, *which is the final goal of human birth according to the* sastras *[spiritual scriptures]?*

B: The primeval thought-free state of mind to which thought, desire, aspiration, volition, or effort are altogether alien, will of its own accord take and plunge you There. But you cannot have It overnight. Sustained practice is necessary to uproot all your ancient *vasanas* and other *chittavrittis.*

Q: If the mind must be destroyed before there can be the possibility of Realisation, the question arises, how did the mind arise, and why?
B: There is already no mind. Searching for the mind, we arrive at the Self. Mind can never be found. How to find something that is not there at all? What never could be, never was. What cannot be is not. What IS, is only That alone which IS, and That is the Self. Speaking from the point of view of mind, it certainly will not be possible for you to deny the existence of mind. The only way to genuinely discover the mind's non-existence is to Realise the Self and vice versa.

Q: Bhagavan's words make a powerful impact on me. But will I remember them?
B: There is no need to force yourself to remember anything. The words of sages are not meant to be verbatim memorised. Practice *Vichara* when you remember Swami but don't try to 'do' anything else with whatever you have listened to here. Let the words sink deep within your mind. When the time comes, they will do their work.

Birds drop their seed containing excreta on all sorts of terrain. In some terrain the sprouting is immediate. In others it takes time because favourable conditions have to arrive before germination can take place. There will come a time when you cannot rest content until you have Realised the Self. The longing to wake up or discover Reality grows slowly in the mind of the beginner. In due course of time, it kills all other thoughts and emerges as the one sole thought or concern supremely dominating or exclusively occupying the mind.

That is the stage when the aspirant is ready to plunge the mind in the Heart so that it stands annihilated there once and for

all. The thirst for *Jnana* must be permitted to wax undisturbed in the mind. It is like the pernicious water hyacinth weed irrevocably choking the entire ecological system of a water body to death. The weed drifts in upon the pond as a tiny seed. In due course, it multiplies itself rapidly and shuts off access to sunlight to the other living organisms inhabiting the pond. How? It covers the entire surface of the pond. Nothing in the pond can survive.

Likewise, if Guru's Grace is available, the seed of *Jnana* planted by the Sage multiplies into the great destroyer *[mahaviksheenaka]* of illusion which chokes the mind to death. How? It covers the entire surface of the mind with the blazing fire of *vairagya*, revulsion towards *samsara*.

Q: So, until then I just have to wait?
B: No, go on with your effort in investigating Who am I? But only when the present, mundane bodily existence has become completely, intolerably unacceptable will the effort bear fruit.

Q: I hope I am not a barren wasteland. I hope Bhagavan's seed in me will sprout into Jnana. *Will it? Or am I a desert in which nothing will grow?*
B: Do you think that Swami explains this matter to all and sundry who come here?

Whilst the delighted gentleman was exiting the Hall, he came across the entering Mr Knowles with whom he was evidently acquainted and told him, *'Do you know? Bhagavan has planted his seed in me!'* and went hurriedly on his way. The comical expression of mortified horror that appeared on the face of Mr Knowles as he walked into the Hall made me regret for the first time in my life until now that I was not the owner of a camera!

He slowly and cautiously turned his head towards the Sofa, as if expecting to find some loathsome scene, penned by the quill of Aristides of Miletus (ancient Greek writer), being enacted there. He seemed extremely relieved to notice Bhagavan serenely reclining on his sofa as usual, but with a wide smile, a steadily widening smile, sitting on his lips. Just then I burst into an unpardonable peal of loud laughter. To my surprise, everyone in the Hall who understood what was going on joined too. Bhagavan particularly; he was racked with coughs as he was laughing, and resultantly the Sofa started quivering!

Mr Knowles now looked, or perhaps tried to look – in which case he was not meeting with much success – apologetic and shame-faced. He came and sat down. The attendant looked puzzled. Once the laughter had died down somewhat, Mr Knowles addressed Chadwick.

K: I say, Major, what the deuce is going on here? What on earth did that idiot mean when he said that to me? I mean, imagine Maharshi, the nonsense. Of course, I wouldn't presume anything to the contrary to what that bugbear must have been thinking to say such a thing I can't quite begin to...

Amidst convulsive spurts of snortful, chucklesome giggling, Chadwick told him all about Bhagavan's message to the other gentleman. I was trying to wipe the smile off my lips, fearing Bhagavan should take offence. But the Master seemed to be taking it all jovially, in fact to all outward appearances, he seemed to be enjoying himself!

K: Oh! So that's the matter, eh?! Of course, that's what I thought it would be too...

The Master glanced at him and smiled blithesomely. Presently, surprising everybody, Sri Muruganar spoke seriously; he sounded quite emotional:

The Sage implanting the Seed of Jnana *into the mind of a deserving aspirant is, without doubt, akin to a heroic man impregnating a loving, fertile girl's womb. There is nothing improper about the comparison. It is quite altogether fitting. But why is everybody posturing in this pretentiously moralising fashion all of a sudden?*

The Hall was dumbstruck. Bhagavan smiled quietly.

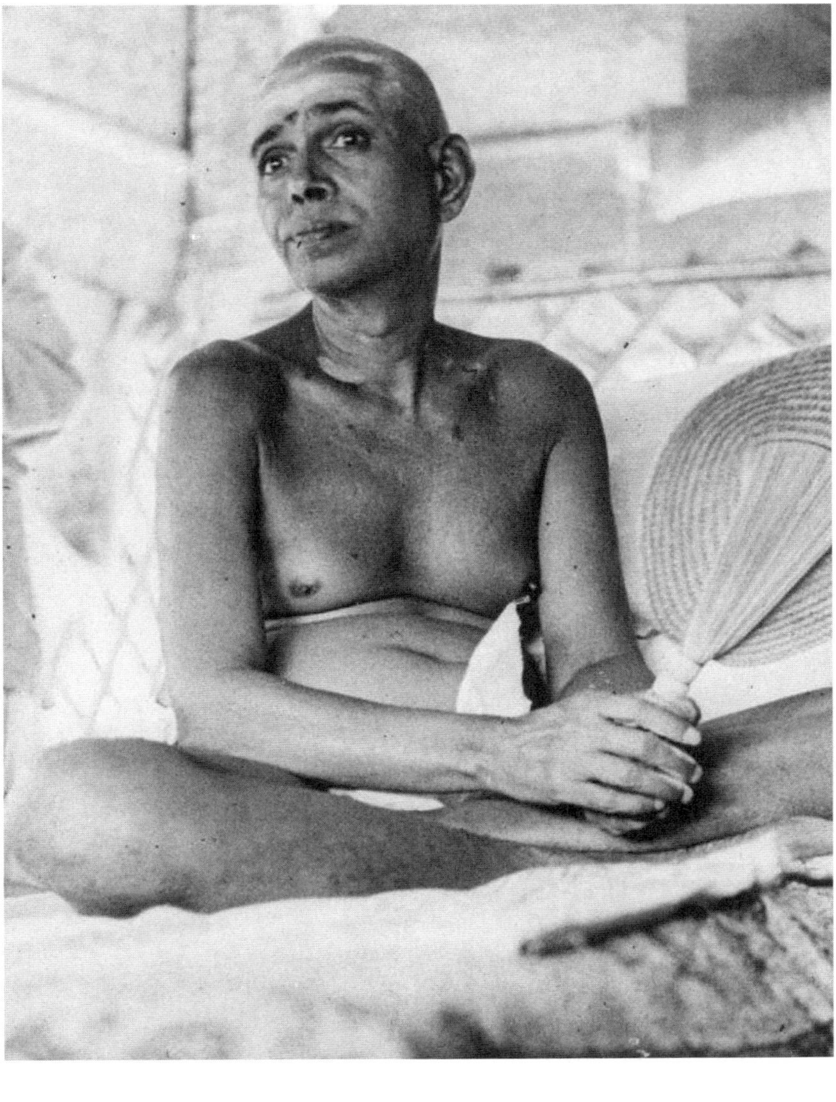

Paul Brunton – sitting in suit – who wrote *A Search in Secret India* which brought many Western devotees to Ramana Ashram

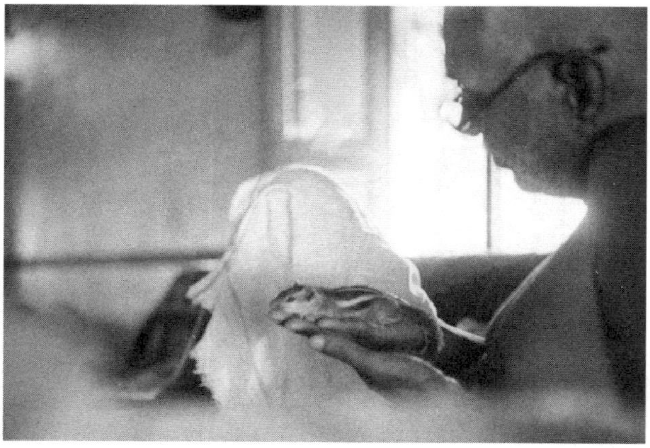

(below) **Chinnaswami** (brother) with Bhagavan on Arunachala

(bottom left) **Guy Hague** with Bhagavan

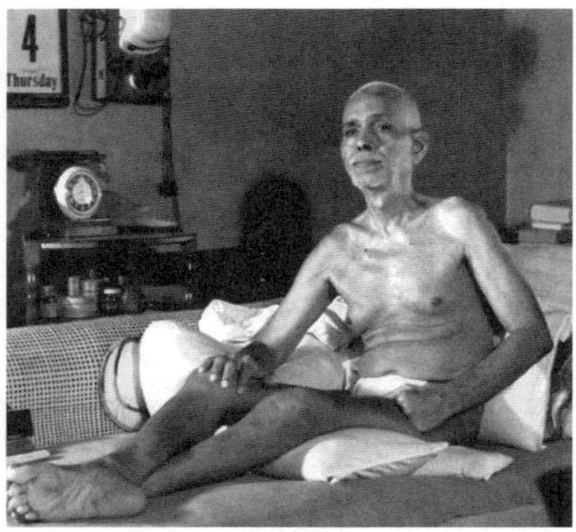
4
Thursday

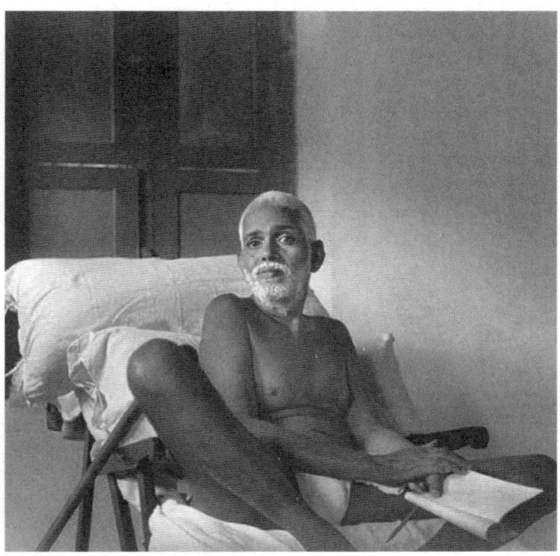

Bhagavan's Original Drawing of Arunachala, as on the Book Cover

At Ramana Ashram in 1934, Chinnaswami (1); next to Bhagavan, Dr W.Y. Evans-Wentz (2) (compiler of the *Tibetan Book of the Dead*); Grant Duff (3); Munagala Venkataramiah (4) (compiler of *Talks*); T.K. Sundaresa Iyer (5); Annamalai Swami (6)

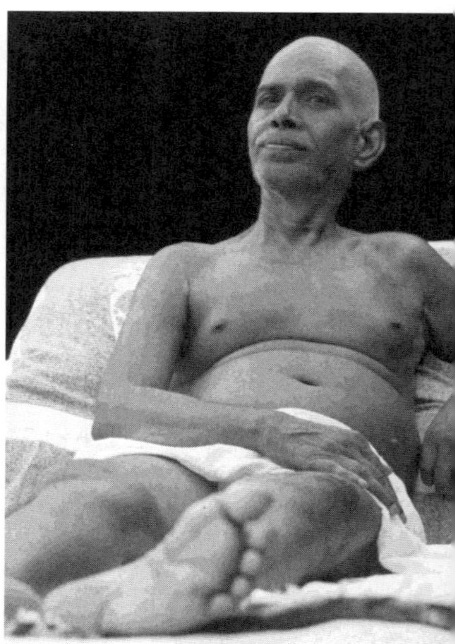

Sacrifice the Ego and Be at Peace

Q: He alone Realises the Atman *who is chosen by the* Atman. *Is that right?*
B: Yes.

Q: Please tell me if I am chosen or not. If I am not chosen, what is the point of making an effort? Please tell me whether it will be productive for me to try to Realise or not. You are known as the Sarvagnar *[one who knows everything]. You should be able to read the letters on my brow. If I am not destined to Realise, let me not waste my effort, time, and energy on a pointless wild-goose chase. What is it going to be? Please tell me...*
B: Do you think those who Realise were given certificates saying, *'I, God Almighty, hereby guarantee that this person is destined to Realise Me, so he may occupy himself busily with* sadhana?' If such a proclamation is made to a man's knowledge, will he thereafter ever make any effort to Realise?

Q: I feel God is a sadist. Why play games with people? There should be a way to find out whether a given somebody is destined to Realise or not.
B: We want to do business with God. That is the problem. *'It is easier for a camel to go through the eye of a needle, than for a rich man to enter into the kingdom of God.'* The poverty required is intellectual poverty. The shrewd, calculating mind, which wants to 'strike a deal' with God, has no place in His Kingdom. Whereas the innocent, guileless simpleton with the mind of a toddler is ushered inwards with profuse fondness. Know this, nobody deserves to gain His state, *Jnana* can NEVER be earned. It is exclusively His compassion or mercy that sunders the knot of the Heart and brings about Emancipation.

Q: I thought Vichara *was a scientific method whereby which one could attain* Jnana. *Now I find that some nonsensical sentimental garbage is thrown in my face.*
B: The doorway leading into *Jnana* is exceedingly low. If you want to get inside, the only way so to do is to CRAWL.

Q: I am reminded of Colonel Dyer's notorious 'crawling order' in the Punjab. Sir, what about my self-respect?
B: There is no harm in losing it for God.

Q: But the Upanishads *declare that I am myself – that my Self is God.*
B: The Self is not the ego's property. The ego is an appearance in, and of, the Self.

Q: Will God or the Self accept my efforts to Realise Him or not?
B: He might or He might not.

Q: So, it is a gamble...
B: Yes.

Q: I have understood Maharshi's doctrine of Ananya Sharanagati *[unconditional surrender] to be as follows: I am expected to throw away myself and everything I have, yet there is always the heftiest of chances that I may not gain Realisation at all. That is what you are trying to say. Is that right?*
B: Yes.

Q: Which madman would be willing to do such a thing?
B: One who has recognised rightly that he has nothing left to lose here. To bring about this understanding in a man, Grace is needed. Why? Because he who has something to lose or forgo in the world will never be able to bring himself to that state of uncompromised surrender in which he gives himself up once and for all, so that God may shine forth from his Heart as the blazing sun of his Self.

Q: So then, the sort of sacrifice required to obtain Realisation seems to me to be totally absolute.
B: Yes.

Q: The Lord has said, 'And he that taketh not his cross, and followeth after me, is not worthy of me.'

B: Yes. The cross stands for sacrifice. Sacrifice the ego on the altar of *Jnana Vichara* and be at peace.

17th September 1936

Vichara Is Without Doubt the Best Means

Q: Should I attempt to endow myself with a more advanced spiritual condition prior to taking up Vichara*?*

B: Those who find that *Vichara* attracts them need not endeavour to endow themselves with any qualifications by using other methods. *Vichara* is the best preparation for *Vichara*. It is only for those who seem to think that *Vichara* is too abstract for them that we may suggest other methods as preliminary, preparatory exercises. For those who are desirous of obtaining Realisation, *Vichara* is without doubt the best means.

For those who do not find *Vichara* attractive, they are asked to travel by the path of their choice until the time arrives when their mind has become ripe enough to feel tempted to explore the question, Who am I? of its own accord. The mind must feel the fascination or allurement to probe into the 'I', that is essential. Can *Vichara* done as a *sadhana*, with the ulterior objective of achieving something called Realisation remaining established as a mental concept, be successful?

This chapter was also published in Aham Sphurana. *ED*

Annamalai Swami's Story

Annamalai Swami was clearly a close devotee. He started as an assistant to care for Bhagavan. Later he was the organiser for constructing the ashram. Major Chadwick, who shared a cottage with Annamalai Swami, was surprised to discover that he came from a village and had no formal education. In later years he created a small ashram neighbouring Ramana Ashram and had his own devotees. ED

For the most part of today, I was unable to go to the Ashram. Since Sri Cycle-Pillai seemed to be indisposed for the time being with one of his occasional abdominal ailments and was thus not in a position to do his usual chores for the Ashram, the *sarvadhikari* has asked me to fetch by way of purchase, roots of the *shathavari* [asparagus] plant from a herbs dealer who put up his wares in different parts of the town on different days. The *sarvadhikari* gave me three annas. This meant I was to purchase three annas worth of roots and take them back to the Ashram as soon as possible.

I was not inordinately delighted with the chore but still agreed to do it because I knew who it was for. I had been given the task because the herbs dealer sometimes spread out his wares at the beginning of the street where I was incumbently put up. But today he was missing there. Every day he went and squatted at a different place, spreading out his condiments before him on a piece of khaki-coloured canvas. He himself would not sit on the canvas, I know not why, he would unwind the ragged towel around his head, spread it on the floor and seat himself on it. At the end of the day, the towel would be back on the head and he would gather up his inexpensive wares in a little brown bundle and carry it away in the crook of his arm. Fondly hugging it to himself as if the thing was his newborn baby. He would invariably leave when the sun's light began to fade, perhaps he could not afford a kerosene lamp.

After making inquiries, I finally found him today near the *Ammani Ammal gopuram* (gateway tower of the Arunachaleswarar Temple), bought the necessary item and made haste to return to the

Ashram. The sun was not merciful, but the fact notwithstanding I walked to the Ashram because I did not like to haggle with the town's rude horse-drawn carriage drivers. All along the way, my thoughts were with poor Major Chadwick, for whose sake this purchase had been made. He had been suffering for the past few days from an acute and relentless attack of dysentery, forcing him to keep away from the Hall and stay amidst vegetation on the nethermost slopes of the Hill. Bhagavan noticed his unusual absence from the Hall and sent for him. Feeling sorry for his plight, a gentleman known as Lakshmanan, a Congress worker from Pondicherry and a devotee of the Master, has volunteered to take care of him. The gentleman is apparently an ace at practising Ayurvedic remedies. He told the Master that he had the other ingredients but needed just one more, *shathavari* [asparagus] roots.

The task was assigned to me. Evidently, since I am neither eating nor sleeping at the Ashram, the *sarvadhikari* did not relish giving me work, but consequent to the fact that I sincerely felt sorry for Chadwick, I agreed to help him by fetching the roots. As I walked towards the Ashram my thoughts were with Chadwick. He was a war veteran from the Great War. He could lead a comfortable life in England. Yet he had opted to mortify himself in this manner, all for his Love of the Master. I wondered if I had been born as a Caucasian and were to be in the retired Major's position, I would still be interested in Bhagavan. Probably not, I thought to myself, for I must be honest in my self-appraisal. I would read books by and about him, certainly. But personally, come and stay here and get attacked by dysentery? No. The Major, did he feel bored here? It was a question that sometimes popped into my head whilst I set eyes upon his towering frame. He did not have many friends here, five at present, at most. Bhagavan, Cohen, Annamalai (Bhagavan's rudraksha-adorned attendant), Mr T.K. Sundaresa Iyer (see photo page 200), and myself.

Was it proper to include the Master in this list, since his state was transcendental and thus did not permit him to see anybody as an 'other'? I do not know, but certainly, the Master was more than a friend to Chadwick. One did not leave England and come to some corner of an unknown land in order so as to be in the vicinity of a mere 'friend'. How much joy did Bhagavan's presence fill him with? Evidently exceedingly a great deal, because he had never turned back and left. The surprising thing was that even before he had met Bhagavan, he had decided that he would stay with him till the end. In other words, at the time of leaving England, he had been determined to leave Her for good! And what about his other friends? The rudraksha-adorned attendant, he told me, was an extraordinary fellow. Although his actual name was something else, the Master called him Annamalai the moment he set his eyes on him, and so this was his name at the Ashram.

Since he is executing more than one construction project here, I assumed he was a professional engineer who had come to serve Bhagavan. Chadwick astonished me by saying that he had never been to school. Chadwick informed me about many other fascinating details related to this man's life, which he knew owing to the fact that they were staunch friends. He had come to the Ashram a decade back and had been assigned to work as Bhagavan's attendant. In a week or so, he had grown tired of his role and had left, but poverty had forced him to return. He came back to the Ashram and clasped hold of the Master's feet in a gesture of solicitation of pardon, since he had discourteously left without telling anybody. The moment he made contact with Bhagavan's flesh, he heard the sound of a bell ringing followed by the Master's voice reciting the *shloka* [verse]: *'Indeed, this one (the Self), having experienced in the dream state, having wandered and seen both virtue* [punya] *and wrongdoing* [papam], *returns again, in accordance with the natural law, to the waking state, just as it transitions to the state of deep sleep.'* Both the sound of the bell and the sound of this *shloka* being chanted in the Master's voice were, peculiarly enough, heard by him inside his body and the same were not heard by anybody else among those who were at the time present in the Hall. At that very moment, owing no doubt to Bhagavan's Grace, memories of his previous lives returned to him.

In his previous life, he had been Mr William Talman, the great English architect who had single-handedly rebuilt much of that country after it stood thoroughly mangled by the great fire that totally conflagrated it during the 17th century. Yet while he remembered all his previous architectural knowledge, he could not recall how to speak the

English tongue. The Master smiled at him and told him that henceforth, he should take care of all the building works at the Ashram. Mr Talman, that is to say, Annamalai Swami, agreed eagerly. Although de facto on that day he had ceased to serve as the Master's attendant, he did not relinquish the post altogether. He helped the Master by rubbing oil all over his body whenever the latter needed to take anointment with an oil bath. Mr Talman being a fellow Englishman and fellow devotee of the Maharshi, I thought, it was natural that immense affinity should develop between the soldier and the architect every day. They even shared the same room at night.

It had happened that when Chadwick had moved into the Ashram, the *sarvadhikari* had asked Annamalai Swami to vacate his room so that the towering Caucasian should exclusively be able to stay inside it. Although the architect attendant immediately endeavoured to comply, the kind-hearted Major did not wish to see another inconvenienced for the sake of fortification of his own comfort. To the surprise of one and all, he summarily announced that he would have no objections to sharing the room with Annamalai Swami. For some reason, Chadwick said, Bhagavan had never permitted this architect attendant to spend any time in the Hall, even before the massive construction projects incumbently going on in the Ashram had begun. This has been my observation also. As soon as he entered, he would be sent out on a fresh building assignment or to the care of some structure that stood out as being in need of repairs. My own surmise is that his desire during his lifetime as the original Mr Talman to construct buildings for God Himself is being played out in this life.

Bhagavan wants his desires to fulfil themselves fully so that there can be no more births for him, thus he keeps him busily engaged in construction work all the time so that this desire can be exhausted sooner and he can attain *Moksha* expeditedly. Chadwick has remarked to me more than once, *'I wonder whether Annamalai Swami regrets the fact that he is unable to spend as much time in the Hall with the Master as a regular attendant would be able to.'* This remark on the Major's part betrays how deeply sensitive his nature is, though he seems casual and unconcerned on the outside. He puts himself in the shoes of another and then wonders about that person's problems from his perspective! The Major had once rescued Annamalai Swami from a grave crisis that had gathered itself together so as to be able to pounce upon him.

More than a year back, a group of devotees constituting the Ashram's managing committees had decided that Annamalai Swami was to be regarded as being a villain because he was wasting the funds of the Ashram by unnecessarily constructing grandiose buildings that in their opinion the Ashram would never feel need for. They asked him to stop all his construction work and surrender his responsibilities to them. Henceforth, they said, he would have to be content with being the Master's attendant. Annamalai Swami firmly refused. The upset group asked him on whose authority he was putting up buildings left, right, and centre inside the Ashram premises. Annamalai Swami replied that he was acting on his own authority. The gentlemen constituting the group secretly conferred amongst themselves and decided that the police must be called in the middle of the night to have Annamalai Swami ejected from the Ashram. The actual fact was that Annamalai Swami was putting up the many buildings he was constructing here only because Bhagavan had privately asked him to do so. The Master had told him that he must never disclose the fact that he was acting under his orders, but must always pretend that he was acting of his own independent volition.

Annamalai Swami told nobody, but Chadwick had guessed that he would not be engaging himself so strenuously were not the Master's orders behind it all. He asked Annamalai Swami if that were not so. On being confronted with the question from his dear friend, Annamalai Swami laughingly admitted that the Major's surmise had been correct. Now, the group discreetly contacted Chadwick and told him not to be surprised if a policeman knocked on the door of his cottage in the middle of the following night. Chadwick asked for the reason and was horrified when informed of it. He told the group that the entire idea of putting up so many elaborate buildings one after the other on the Ashram premises was Bhagavan's. The gentlemen were initially sceptical but later, in a dilemma as to whether to believe the earnest-sounding Major or not, asked Annamalai Swami if it were not so.

Annamalai Swami, not one to break a promise of confidentiality he had made to the Master, stubbornly maintained that he was doing everything solely of his own accord. The group then went to the Maharshi himself, in order to get matters clarified. But Bhagavan would not even look in their direction. Chadwick arrived in the Hall at that moment and said to the Master agitatedly, *'They are planning to forcibly evict Annamalai Swami from the Ashram.'* That very moment the Maharshi thundered in an uncharacteristically powerful voice, ***'The moment Annamalai Swami is forced to leave the Ashram, I will also go away.'*** The group, upon hearing these words, went away quietly and never made any further attempt to disturb the construction work going on in the Ashram. Realising that it was indeed the Master who must have issued orders for all these works to be carried out. Soon after it had become common knowledge in the Ashram that Annamalai Swami was merely carrying out Bhagavan's orders in executing all his elaborate building projects. Thereafter, nobody dared to comment on how resources were being wasted on putting up huge buildings when smaller ones would suffice. Chadwick had told me of all these little interesting incidents, and more, whilst I sometimes visited him during the late evenings in his little cottage, which he happily shared with Annamalai Swami during the night. Some of his other anecdotal rambles I recollect were:

(a) When the Major had first arrived in the Ashram, he had prostrated in front of Annamalai Swami, imagining that the latter was Sri Maharshi!

(b) Soon after Chadwick moved into the Ashram, a letter addressed to the Master arrived from one Arunachala Mudaliar living in town. It carried the baseless complaint that Chadwick was regularly and clandestinely purchasing beef from a vendor in Matthalakkaran Street, secretly roasting or barbecuing the same on a fire he lit every Sunday near Palakothtu and every day consuming it inside the Ashram precincts, silently sitting next to Bhagavan's mother's *Samadhi* [tomb of an enlightened being] whilst so doing. The letter was also signed by one Gopal Rao, a former manager of the Ashram!

(c) Bhagavan once told the story of how in the early days of the Ashram there was a big fight between one Dandapani Swami, a former manager of the Ashram, and the *sarvadhikari*. Dandapani Swami became excessively enraged and tried to push the *sarvadhikari* into the Agatthiyar Tirtham (holy water tank). The *sarvadhikari* would have drowned if the Master had not scooped up from the ground some cow turd and flung the same squarely at Dandapani Swami's face. The humiliated Dandapani Swami stopped fighting at once. Bhagavan had then explained to one and all present there, that his intention was not to insult Dandapani Swami, but only to ensure that *sannyasis,* in general, did not acquire a disreputable or reprehensible name (for causing to drown those of their kind). With these and other thoughts roaming around the inside of my head, I entered the Hall and prostrated to the Master as usual. Then I told him that I had procured the required roots. The Master acknowledged the fact with a smile and stretched out his hand for the condiment.

He held it close to his face, smelled it carefully from various angles, remarked, ***'It is of marvellous quality, thoroughly dried, with no fungus infestation; good...'***, and handed it over to me so that I could give it to the *sarvadhikari*, which I then did. *'It is precisely for three annas – is that not so?'*, he said, good-humouredly, *'Good fellow! See how much he has given for three annas'.* I was then asked to hand over the same to Mr Lakshmanan. I went to the cow shed, where I was told he could be found. He was tending to a sick cow, administering unto the uncertain, reluctant animal a frothing and foaming herbal decoction. The cow was attempting to withdraw its head away from the bucket into which the man was pushing it, coaxing it to drink what I guessed would be some not-delicious substance of his own contrivance and manufacture. I was asked to hold the unfortunate animal's snout, which I did. Mr Lakshmanan fastened a rope around the cow's head and her mouth was now confined to the bucket. *'This is what we must do with the rebellious mind'*, he remarked to me grimly as I handed over the roots to him.

But the moment he finished saying it, the cow violently tilted her head and most of the mixture splashed out of the bucket. We heard a familiar laugh and it was Bhagavan! He caressed the cow gently and she relaxed her mouth into the bucket. He waited for a minute. Then he took the rope off, but the cow made no attempt to extract her mouth from the bucket. ***'No, this is what we must do with the mind,'*** he said, and Mr Lakshmanan smiled feebly. I laughed. Then we went back to the Hall. As we approached, my ears pricked up, for somebody was saying the Führer's name. Mr Knowles was reading out from some magazine he was clutching in his hands: *'...judge that the sufferings imposed on Jews are unjustified. Thus, reserving to himself and Hitler, as Germans, the right to judge themselves.'* Presently the Master entered and all rose, although he motioned everybody to remain seated as he was walking in. It was then given unto Mr Knowles to understand that the Maharshi had no objection to the man continuing to read out whatever it was that he had been reciting at the time of the Master's temporary absence from the Hall.

B: (laughs) **Yes! He has got the idea that he is also a *Jnani*, but that nobody is respecting him or worshipping him. So, he is coming and sitting here so that his ego may feel appeased. What can we do? Can we say it is wrong? In the absence of the distractive, sleep-inducing, and concealing phenomenon known as mind, all are verily *Jnanis*.**

19th September 1936

Absolute Surrender Crushes the Ego

Q: If summayirutthal *is the way to Realisation of God, why does Bhagavan ask people to carry out the investigation Who am I?*

B: To Realise the Self simply be still *[Summayiru]*, that is to say, remain without emerging from that state in which the mind is perfectly indistinguishable from the Beingness of the Self. That is all

that is necessary. But inasmuch as there is deviation or derailment from this natural or pristine state, get back to it by means of investigating Who am I? *Vichara* is a tool with which to get back to *summayirutthal* when and whenever there is fall from there. To the extent there is distraction from self-attention, exclusively and precisely to that same extent *Vichara* stands having become necessitated.

Q: Is surrender the same as bhakti*? Then dualistic practices of worship such as chanting God's name are worthless?*
B: Did I say so? Such practices prepare the mind for introversion. Thus, they have their use.

Q: Is Ananya Sharanagati *[unconditional surrender] a loftier practice in comparison with* Vichara*?*
B: Yes. Absolute surrender is to crush the ego in a single stroke. But for those who find this impossible, the suggestion might be made unto them to practise unrelenting, intermittent attempts at partial surrender. In due course of time that will lead to complete surrender.

Absolute surrender is another name for Realisation, whereas partial surrender or surrender as *abhyasa* means making attempt to surrender. Except in the case of *paripakvis* [a fully ripe person]**, repeated attempts to surrender are generally necessary before the ego can be finally toppled off completely and before complete surrender can be achieved.**

Q: Will Vichara *be effective even if performed away from Bhagavan's physical presence, say in Europe?*
B: (smiling) **There is no such thing as physicality and it is impossible to be away from Bhagavan's presence.**

The questioner's face lit up with joy.

Concepts Are Obstacles to Vichara's Success

Q: Why is it that certain persons find practising Vichara *to be an easy task? whereas others find it exceptionally hard?*

B: Among those who pursue the investigation Who am I? there are those who do it because they are under the impression that by performing the practice they are going to obtain a state they refer to as 'Enlightenment'. This is *Vichara* that is motivated by conceptual understanding as the underlying foundation. And then there are those who do it because they feel burning curiosity about 'I' and its origin. This is *Vichara* that is motivated by *Atmajignasa* [enquiry into the Nature of the Self] as the underlying foundation.

Q: Which category of aspirants is more likely to obtain success?

B: The former category of aspirants cannot succeed unless and until they have undergone conversion so as to fall into the latter category. Why? When a person wants Enlightenment and with that aim undertakes the practice of *Vichara*, the conceptual fabrications which function as the supportive bulwark or foundation for this effort are numerous. There is the 'I' that wants *Jnana*, there is the arbitrary, mental conceptualisation of there being something called *'Jnana'*. And there is the idea *'I am going to metamorphose into the state of* Jnana *by supportively performing this* sadhana.' All these subtle intellectual formulations are obstacles and they prevent the *Vichara* from resulting in any genuine progress. The *sadhaka's* mind may manufacture spurious, seemingly lofty, counterfeit spiritual experiences to convince him that he is making sound progress.

On the other hand, consider the one with a burning curiosity to probe the 'I'. There are no conceptual formulations in his case, there is something called 'I' arising from within him and he wishes to scrutinise it closely, that is all. It is like a tiny splinter of wood that gets stuck in the gums in some remote corner of your mouth that you are unable to pinpoint with your finger with any precision. The tongue engages in an aggressive war to dislodge it, without any

conscious motive or volition on your side. Who am I? does not mean wondering who I might be. It means being fascinated and enthralled by this entity 'I' and resultantly holding on to and watching it all the time. When 'I' pays attention to anything other than itself it is not *Vichara.* 'I' incessantly attending to 'I' is *Vichara.*

Q: Bhagavan has frightened me by saying that the mind may play tricks on me by deluding me into thinking that I am making spiritual progress. Please tell me how I can ascertain for myself whether I am making progress or not.
B: Inasmuch as the mind stays in the natural state without feeling the need, urge or inclination to deviate therefrom you are on the right track.

Q: Please tell me what this natural state is. Bhagavan must know how much progress I have made. Please tell me how long I have yet to journey in order so as to Realise Jnana.
B: This desire to measure progress is at this very moment preventing you from abiding in the natural state. Such desire is also an obstacle. Remain free from this obstacle also. You can give up the idea that it is you who is responsible for your Emancipation.

Q: If I am not responsible for my own Salvation, then who is? Is it the Higher Power whose responsibility it is to ferry me safely across the foul, treacherous waters of samsara, *so that I may one day land on the cherished shores of* Jnana*?*
B: Yes.

Vasanas Create Our World

Q: Does submergence of mind in the source of thought prevent reincarnation at the time of death?
B: Provided the *vasanas* have been stripped away. The important thing is to get rid of all of one's pre-existing, outdated tendencies and predispositions *[samskaras and vasanas]*. In deep sleep and

comatose states, there is no awareness of the external world but neither is there conscious awareness of the Self. The reflected light of the Self falls on one's *vasanas* and produces the phenomenon of reflection we call 'mind'. Each person finds himself in a different world depending upon his *vasanas*. It is exclusively the individual's *vasanas* which produce in front of or before him the world he imagines himself to be living in. Apart from one's *vasanas* there is no such thing as 'world'.

Even before one lights fireworks, the various colours it will explode in whilst rocketing up into the sky are already pre-determined in the form of the chemical combinations packed inside. Likewise, the world experienced by one in one's life is already printed like exposed film deep within the mind. This is why free will is regarded as being mythical by the wise. The *Jnana sadhaka* crushes his *vasanas* by refusing to pay them any attention. His *lakshyam* [aim] is on pure Subjective Consciousness exclusively, his mind is restrained from attending to anything else. What is the result? The individual's *vasanas* get destroyed and so the reflection cannot possibly continue. The light of the Self does not fall on anything. It is unable to find anything to fall upon or strike.

So, the Self remains without reflection. This is Emancipation. Reincarnation is made possible only when consciousness still has contents. If the contents are fully expunged or wiped off, rebirth is rendered impossible. This is the way to *Mukti*. Wipe the slate of your mind clean, make it a tabula rasa (clean slate). A slate with the words 'tabula rasa' written upon it is not a genuine tabula rasa. So, instead of thinking about how to Realise the Self, simply remain as the Beingness of the Self.

Q: I feel peace in Bhagavan's presence. How to get the same peace in Vellore?
B: Bhagavan is within. Can there be any Bhagavan outside you?

Q: May I repeat my question?
B: There is nothing. BE.

An Immense Revulsion to Samsara

Q: How can someone judge for himself if he has the necessary competency to take up Vichara marga *[path of Self-enquiry]?*

B: There must either be intense longing or thirst to awaken to one's true Self or immense revulsion or abhorrence towards *samsara*. These are two sides of the same coin. But of its own accord continuous practice of *Vichara* itself brings about these necessary qualities in an earnest aspirant. So, there is no need to bother with the question, anybody can endeavour to practise *Vichara*.

The Other Side of Beauty Is Pain

Q: They say that the path of Vichara *involves enormous mental agony because of the need to relinquish all of one's* vishaya vasanas *and* purva samskaras.

B: Pain involved in eliminating *vasanas* cannot be avoided. How is a pearl formed? Something enters past its clamshell and somehow pierces the soft flesh of the oyster, and, unable to bear the pain of it, the animal secretes layer after layer of nacre (substance forming the inner layer of clamshells) over the intruder. What is pain to the animal, humans relish it as a priceless item of decoration. If the animal could choose to live with the pain of something constantly irritating the underside of its belly, we would not know that there ever could be such a thing known as 'pearl' and Bhagavan would not be saying these words to you now.

What is the moral of the story? The other side of beauty is pain. *Jnana* is the supreme beauty among beauties, for there is none to rival Her. To reach *Jnana* any amount of pain is worthwhile. So, don't harbour or give scope for the feeling that pain is something to be shirked. Be convinced of this firmly in your heart. Even if the way to Realisation were to be paved with pain and pain only, your need

is to unhesitatingly traverse the path because the pain is imaginary but *Jnana* or Reality is Real.

What is expended is fictitious but what is earned is Real. Therefore, there is no harm in experiencing pain in order to Realise the Self. You are not asked to wantonly mortify yourself. But whether pleasure comes or pain, accept it without question. Don't feel mental perturbation or exultation. If you are able to inhere in the Beingness of the Self as a matter of course, events taking place or circumstances prevailing in the external world will never affect you.

Do Senses Cease to Function with Vichara?

Q: Will eyesight and hearing, as well as the other senses, gradually cease to function as one makes progress along the Vichara marga*?*

B: The normal biological functions of the body do not become dilapidated on account of the mind being turned inward. *Chittam* [conscious awareness] intrinsically remains as It IS. It is we who channel it towards the direction of thought and suffer unnecessarily. Once extroversion ceases altogether, the *prana* [life force] in the body keeps the senses functioning for as long as that body's *prarabdha* demands. The presence of *prana* in the body does not unequivocally imply or indicate presence of any mind underlying that *prana*. The light of *chittam* is directed away from the intellect, which is the fraudulent entity responsible for attributing spuriously authorship for sensory perception to a fictitious entity called 'I', and driven back into its source, the Heart.

This is the point of *abhyasa*. The guideline to direct mental attention away from tendency for sensory perception does not mean that you should close your eyes, cover your ears, et cetera. It is the mind that counts, go straight to the source of the mischief and tackle it there. 'I' is the reason for all your misery. Find out what is 'I' and all your problems are solved. You can prevent the outer senses

from functioning using pieces of cloth and cotton to cover the eyes and ears, but will that solve your problem? No, the one enemy is the mind, and it must be made to submit to the Higher Power one way or the other so that its apparent separate existence is put to an end. Gradually shift attention away from perceived to perceiver, this is what is meant by destruction of tendency of directing *chittam* towards satisfying proclivity for sensory perception. Not tearing out one's eyeballs or gouging out one's ear drums.

A Remote Place

Q: Would I get more benefit by going to a remote place to do my practice?

B: Always the same question: *'If I isolate or seclude myself from humanity and go away to some remote location and so place myself in solitude, will I not stand a better chance at Realising the Self? Is that not what you did?'* What can we say to this? Is it the Self which discerns the difference? This Ashram is a place where humans are going and coming, yet, on the other hand, it is a deserted place. Is He not always quiet even if a war is raging on in the empirical world? Is it not the mind that invents otherness? In Truth are there any others to be aware of? How then could they become a nuisance to you? If you find anybody to be a nuisance it means you have become a veritable nuisance unto yourself. So, investigate Who am I? and get rid of yourself so that the nuisance stands eradicated. What else can we say?

Q: But during meditation, a silent atmosphere is conducive and preferable. It is observed by us to be so. We feel we make more progress if the room is silent whilst one is meditating.

B: These mind-manufactured notions of progress are totally false. In fact, such notions constitute the triumphal war cry of the ego. The ego is a cunning demon who wants to be in total control of the situation all the time. When his desires are fulfilled, he ever so

slightly steps aside and permits more light to flow from the Self. This is received by you as 'I' experiencing happiness and this is what you mistakenly refer to as progress. Do you see now how you are being deluded? Everybody deserves to experience, in its entirety, the boundaryless tranquil ocean of Self.

You are the sole rightful inheritor of this blissful Kingdom of Heaven known as *Parabrahman*. But have you successfully realised this invaluably precious legacy? No. What is happening? A scandalous fraud is taking place. Namely, the non-dual experience of Absolute Awareness is smothered and thereby rendered unaffordable by the ego. *'Fear not, little flock, for it is your Father's good pleasure to give you the kingdom.'* God does not mind sharing with us his state of *Sahajajnana*. But something seems to stand in the way of one's Immortal Hereditament being obtained by one in its unlimited entirety. Somebody called 'I' is giving you a few drops from the delightful ocean of *Atman* now and then and you feel grateful to him for such a considerate act on his part.

What is the truth? Is this 'I' your friend? He is keeping back your priceless Eternal Treasure from you and giving you titbits every now and then to keep you satisfied and complacent. Is it not an outrage? Slay this unholy foe known as 'I' here and now! Arise and take your Kingdom back. Realise the deathless Self! Can you afford to permit the ego to say, *'This place is comfortable for meditation, that one is far too distracting'*? Remain as That which IS, no matter what the place, situation or circumstance might happen to be. Never let the ego take control. Whenever one thing seems attractive and another repulsive, know that it is the handiwork of the ego.

Q: Bhagavan exhorts everybody to ask Who am I? Who is he?

B: I am You. Before going to sleep from within the previous dream, you left a watchman behind to wake you up if you happened to go on dreaming for far too long. Ramana Maharshi is that watchman. He now enters your dream and says loudly. *'Wake up!'*

Will you not pay attention?

Q: (emotionally) Yes.

How to Control the Mind

Q: How to control the mind?
B: Realise the Self and see for yourself whether there is any mind remaining to be controlled.

Q: Whilst practising Vichara, *I am carried away by various obstacles and impediments which keep distracting me. Apart from trouble caused on account of thought, there are also external disturbances, such as noises that perturb me. Somebody talks or someone arrives to greet me, or some other interference presents itself, just whilst I happen to be carrying on meditation. I feel frustrated and irritated. What am I to do?*
B: Those obstacles are part of this mind-generated delusion known as 'world'. They cannot be avoided because they are not in our control. The only thing we can possibly bring under our control is the mind. The events of one's outer life are determined by *prarabdha* [inevitable karmic consequences] which is absolutely unchangeable.

There is no use in stubbornly endeavouring to change what cannot be changed in the slightest. Why try to irrigate a desert? Instead, try to work in a field wherein there is available fertility. *Prarabdha* is totally unyielding. The only thing you can do is to sink the mind in its source so that *prarabdha* no longer has any power to affect you, so that *prarabdha* has no influence over you anymore.

Q: But prarabdha's *sway over the body is inalienable.*
B: Be it so. You don't identify yourself with the body or its sufferings. What then can *prarabdha* do to you? *Prarabdha* is helpless to taint the totally introverted mind.

The Buddha's Last Words

Q: It is said that the Buddha's last words were as follows: 'Therefore be ye a lamp unto yourself, be a refuge to yourself. Look not for a refuge in anybody besides yourself. Those who shall be a lamp unto themselves shall betake themselves to no external refuge. But holding fast to Truth as their lamp and holding fast to Truth as their refuge, they shall reach the topmost height.' *Can I, without needing to depend upon outside help, Realise the Self by virtue of my own efforts?*
B: Grace is needed. Grace comes from within not from without. There is no such thing as without. Everything is within the Self only.

Q: How to acquire Grace?
B: By means of introverting the mind and keeping the same perennially merged in its source. Practically, *Vichara* is the way.

The Stages in Practice of Vichara

Q: What are the stages in the practice of Vichara*?*
B: Find the source of thought. Having found the same, stay there once and for all. This is all that needs to be done.

Q: How does one remain merged in pure Subjective Consciousness or the state of choiceless awareness which, according to J. Krishnamurti, is the natural state, while simultaneously dealing with illusion in the life of the world?
B: By giving up the wrong idea that you are the doer of actions performed by the body. Ask yourself, *'Who works?'* Remain as That which IS. Then the work will not bind you, it will go on

automatically. It is like an actor on a stage. He plays the role given to him exceedingly well. But he is not deluded, he knows that in real life he is not that person whose appearance he has taken on for the purpose of entertaining the show's audience, but somebody else.

Likewise, remain as pure Subjective Consciousness to which volition and effort are wholly alien. Let the events of the outer world pass you by without affecting you. Take part in them – without imagining yourself to be the doer or confounding yourself to be the author of the deeds the body carries out – to the extent necessary, but do not fall prey to the delusion of thinking that it is real.

Q: Is the world only a drama then? Are we all merely actors fulfilling an immutable script that somebody has written for us in advance?
B: Quite so.

Give up Thought Once and For All

Q: How shall I become a devotee of Sri Bhagavan?
B: By remaining permanently submerged in the Shining of the Heart.

Q: How to dive into the Heart?
B: By giving up thought once and for all.

Vichara Is the Best Preparation for Vichara

Q: Is Vichara *a practice specifically intended for use by the ripest and most advanced among* sadhakas *only, or is it meaningful for the common man also to take it up?*
B: Anybody might pursue it.

Q: Prior to commencing Vichara, *is it a good idea to better qualify oneself by preliminarily undertaking preparatory practices such as* murti dhyana *[meditation on a form of God],* pranayama *[breath control],* mantra japa *[repetition of mantra], et cetera? Or can the common man start with* Vichara *straightaway?*
B: It is not for us to suggest what *sadhana* an individual ought to opt for. The form of *sadhana* chosen depends on the latent mental proclivities of the individual. Each one chooses that path which, based on his *samskaras*, appears to him to be the most attractive.

As for preparing for *Vichara,* there is no need to seek out any other separate practice that is to be used as preparation for *Vichara*. *Vichara* is the best preparation for *Vichara*. There is no need to interminably ponder over the question. *'Am I mature enough to undertake the quest of* Vichara *or not?'* If it attracts you, plunge.

Vichara Is Itself the Guru

Q: Does Vichara *need to be learnt from a Guru? Or can I try it on my own?*
B: *Vichara* is itself the Guru.

22nd September 1936

How Did the Ego Arise

Q: How did the ego arise?

B: It is unnecessary and counter-productive to make such futile enquiries which are based on the intellect. Your enquiry must be of such a nature that it uproots the mind and not of such a nature that it fattens the mind. When the one who is asking how the ego has arisen is that very same ego, what meaningful answer can be arrived at? It is like running after your own shadow when the sun is directly behind you or like searching all over the earth for your own eyes. The intellect only paves the way for more intellectualism.

Abandon the quest for objective knowledge and instead seek the subject. What is this 'I'? Some persons invent or manufacture some mental concept to which they bestow the name 'I' and go on looking at it. This is not *Vichara*. One component of the mind paying attention to another can never be *Vichara*. Mind unceasingly seeking itself alone is *Vichara*.

All People Cannot Do the Same Sadhana

Q: Why does Bhagavan not ask all those who come here to practise Vichara*?*

B: All people cannot be expected to do the same kind of *sadhana*. Each one acts according to his *purva samskaras* [past impressions] and *vishaya vasanas* [worldly tendencies]. *Jnana, bhakti, karma,* these are all intertwined. *Sagunopasana* [worship of a deity] may be more suitable for the common man. It is aimed at ridding oneself of other forms and confining oneself mentally to one form exclusively. Carried on with steadily and unremittingly, it leads eventually to

nirgunopasana **[formless worship], which is the same as *Vichara.***

For most, it is impossible to straightaway drown the mind in the Heart. So to begin with, other aids such as *pranayama, mantra, japa,* et cetera, might be necessary. But in due course, everyone must come to *Vichara.*

Vichara **is the ultimate route. Each individual conceives of God according to his own degree of spiritual advancement. There is nothing wrong with it. You say that you are the body in a wakeful state, but there is no body to be found in deep sleep. The presence of the body is contingent upon the incumbent mental state at the level of an individual. Why should there not be infinite possibilities for God? Whichever method one wants to follow, according to his *purva samskaras* and *vishaya vasanas,* that method is encouraged by the Guru. When the time is ripe, the Guru converts him over to the path of *Vichara sadhana.***

The Unknowable Cannot Be Known

Q: Jnana *means Realisation.* Jnana marga *is also the name for the method of* Vichara *leading up to Realisation. Why so?*
B: Because it is only by the Grace of the Unknowable that the Unknowable is to be known.

Q: How can it ever become possible to know something that is already correctly recognised as being unknowable?
B: The Unknowable cannot be known by you as the mind. If the mind shatters, only the Heart is left. Then the individual is said to have knowledge of *Parabrahman.* However, this is only a linguistic convenience. Actually, there is no such thing as knowing Him. It is like the funny allegorical fable of the salt doll that wanted to measure the depth of the ocean. Of course, it never succeeded; but in making the attempt it got merged into the ocean.

Likewise, nobody actually succeeds in obtaining *Jnana* and nobody can because He is the Beyond. What happens is that in making incessant and wholehearted efforts to scrutinise itself, the mind gets killed. That is the goal of our efforts. There is an ancient Egyptian symbol of a snake devouring its own tail. That is an approximate pictorial representation of *Vichara*. Instead of using the mind to concentrate on objects, use it to concentrate on itself.

Q: Shall I then devote all my energies concentrating on the thought 'I'?
B: No, that is not what was meant. When asked to seek the 'I', why do you invent something called 'I' and then try to pay attention to it? You are so used to employing the mind to work with concepts that when asked to remain without conceptualising you are unable to do so. *Vichara* does not involve the need to concentrate on anything. Concentration means focused or pinpoint extroversion, whereas *Vichara* means unequivocal introversion.

Q: I am unable to understand what I should do.
B: There is no need to do anything. BE, that is all there is to it. When there is a departure from the state of mere Beingness, return there as soon as you have discovered that the mind has wandered away. Then, there is the question of tackling the subtle 'I' that is aware that it is spectating Beingness. On paying close attention to it, it starts to sink within the Heart.

With prolonged practice, the mind learns to remain permanently submerged in the Heart. Once the mind has lost all volition to leave the Heart and is no longer conscious of there being any world available for itself to live in apart from the Heart, it is automatically destroyed by the Heart. This is how the dawn of *Jnana* is made possible.

Q: What is the first step in this process?
B: The first step is to turn the mind away from the juvenile pleasures of worldly life and expose it unintermittingly to the Beingness of the Self. The more you practise introversion of mind, the greater your

***vairagya* becomes conjointly. The greater your *vairagya*, the easier your practice will become.**

Q: How many years will it take me to get Jnana*?*

B: Allowing the mind to assume control over or be in charge of your *sadhana* is a capital mistake. The mind will never consent to its own destruction. It might go to the trouble of creating sophisticated mental experiences for you so as to delude you into believing that you are in the state of destroyed mind. But never will it allow itself to be led into the gallows of the Heart unless and until it has conclusively seen the futility of its own phantasmal existence. It is not so easy to break the tyrannical grip of the ego. Unless the Higher Power shows you mercy by revealing to you your own utter helplessness – that is to say, your ineptitude – you will never surrender. So, do not let the mind plan your Realisation for you. Leave everything to the Higher Power and persistently go on with your *sadhana*.

Q: But will it not be encouraging to know how much progress I am making?

B: No, it will be discouraging. (The visitor seemed too shocked to say anything. Smilingly, Bhagavan continued.) **There is no need to occupy ourselves with thoughts of any kind, including thoughts concerning the question of when *Jnana* is finally going to arrive. You need not and cannot take responsibility for your Emancipation. Leave it to the Higher Power to do as He pleases with you, but never slacken your grip over the quest for the mind.**

Q: Bhagavan must have meant to say, 'The quest for the Self'.

B: Bhagavan says exactly what he means to say.

Q: Is not the Self the goal of our sadhana*?*

B: No, the presence of a goal implies the existence of the one that happens to harbour such goal. If you take your existence for granted while pursuing the quest, how can you make any progress in relation to it – since the objective of the quest is to prove your non-existence? So, there is no goal. Investigate Who am I? just for the investigation.

The spiritual quest is not a quest for the Self. He is the Beyond, and there is no contacting or reaching Him. Your quest is for yourself. *'What is this thing which I keep referring to as my 'I'?'* This is the quest. *'What is the Self? What is* Parabrahman?' This is a noble way to waste your energy, time and effort. See 'I' with 'I', this is *Vichara.* One component of the mind studying another cannot be *Vichara.* Mind incessantly seeking itself is *Vichara.*

Q: I wish for Bhagavan's Grace to descend on me in order that I might succeed in the quest.
B: You have it already.

The visitor's face beamed with profuse joy.

Life Is a Mere Game

Q: Is life a mere game?
B: Yes. Till you win the effortlessly and volitionlessly thought-free and free-from-drowsiness state of mind, you play again and again the game of *Vichara.*

Q: Achieving Realisation of the Absolute Self constitutes victory in the game of life. Am I correct?
B: Yes, to awaken into Realisation is to conclusively win at losing everything.

Hatha Yoga

Q: Is hatha yoga *necessary?*

B: Not for all, but only for those who are altogether incapable of otherwise stilling the mind. The question of whether *hatha yoga* is needed rests upon individual temperament. *Vichara* is the best weapon for killing the ego. Yogis reach *Nirvikalpa Samadhi* by practising *kevala kumbhaka*, which suppresses the *prana*. But the best way is to trace out the source of the mind or *buddhi* [the subtle intellect] and remain merged in that source permanently.

What is yoga? It is said that yoga refers to the merging of the *jivatman* into the *Paramatman*, but this explanation gives rise to the question of how they got separated from each other to begin with. *Yoga marga* [path of yoga] and *jnana marga* [path of knowledge] both have as their *lakshyam* [aim] the retrogression of the mind into its primeval condition of pure Subjective Consciousness sustained volitionlessly and effortlessly. To this end, yoga tries to use *prana,* which is a gross manifestation of the *jivatman's bimbithachittam* [reflective consciousness], whereas the *Vichara sadhana* directly uses the *bimbithachittam* itself.

The highest yogic state is not different from the actual Realisation that the *jivatman* never existed. It is not the same as intellectual understanding of any concept explaining the non-existence of the *jivatman*. In such Realisation, duality is wholly wiped out and thus the Self does not lend itself to be experienced by anything. Such a state of non-duality is verily the goal of yoga.

Q: Hatha yoga *is said to cure the diseases of the body.*

B: The body consciousness itself is the biggest disease.

Q: Is there any individuality for the Jnani *after Realisation?*

B: No.

Q: I am trying Bhagavan's Vichara *method. But it is not working.*
B: The entire mind must be harnessed and channelled into its source. Applying part of the mind's faculties of concentration will not do.

Q: What is the difference between neti-neti *[neither this nor that] and* Vichara*? Is the former of any use?*
B: The latter includes the former automatically. *Neti-neti* stops at the level of the intellect. If you will Realise the Self, then your task is to find the source of the *ahamvritti* – to see whence it springs. For Realisation, you must reach the source of 'I' without fail. Then, the false 'I' will disappear. The disappearance of the false 'I' automatically results in Revelation of the Real 'I'. The quest needs *vairagya*, otherwise, your half-hearted attempts could only ever result exclusively in futility.

Q: How to cultivate vairagya*?*
B: Again, *Vichara* is the way.

Q: How long does it take to annihilate the ego using the weapon of Vichara*?*
B: Why are you asking this question? No matter how long it takes – do it.

Pain

Q: Sometimes while investigating Who am I? I feel pain in these regions. (touches himself successively at the regions corresponding to the cranial-bregma and the abdominal-fundus)
B: You are telling me. When I was in Madurai I also felt these same pains, but I did not tell anybody. I would be lying down with my head tightly clutched in hands and my aththai (aunt) would ask what the matter was. But from me, no reply would be forthcoming. So she

would rub my forehead vigorously with wintergreen oil of her own accord. There was no relief. The pains subsided only after I came here.

Q: I cannot follow the remedy of renunciation. I have dependent family members at home for whom my earning is the sole source of sustenance.
B: Ask yourself *'Who feels this pain?'* Shift your attention away from the pain to the one who becomes aware of the pain. Then the pain will fly away.

No Need to Fight

Q: The famous Chinese military leader Sun Tzu is reputed to have said, 'The supreme art of war lies in subduing the enemy without having to resort to fighting.' *Likewise, Maharshi's* Vichara *seems to kill the mind or the ego without having to fight him.*
B: How to kill something that is not there at all? How to kill a snake that one sees in a rope? Likewise, here. If the mind exists it can be killed. See if it exists.

Q: I think thoughts; therefore, I infer that I have a mind.
B: Turn your mind completely back on itself and see if it remains. See mind with mind. Then you will know that there is no such thing by name as 'mind'. The Mind is useful for seeing objects and worlds. But when the mind is kept persistently and incessantly turned inward to look at itself only the Self remains.

Q: What is the cause for arising of maya *[illusion]?*
B: Who is complaining that *maya* has arisen? Is it the Self that so complains or is it *maya* that so complains? The one who complains of being affected by *maya* is himself the one and only *maya* and there is no other *maya*.

Who Am I? Is not an Intellectual Exploration

Q: Is 'I' a myth?
B: Yes.

Q: Then who am I?
B: (smiling) **Find out.**

Q: But really, what is the answer to the question?
B: The answer cannot be discovered by the intellect. The *Jnana Vichara* Who am I? is not an intellectual exploration. The purpose of the practice is to sink the mind in the Heart and prevent it from straying outwards. Destruction of both thought and the faculty of thought manufacture is the goal of investigating Who am I? – not searching for the answer with the aid of the intellect. Incessant submergence of mind in the Shining of the Heart alone genuinely leads to Emancipation.

The Buddhists Deny Reincarnation

Q: It is said that the Buddhists deny the individual soul. But on the other hand, Hindus believe in a reincarnating ego. Which of these two conflicting views is correct? Is the individual soul a continuous entity which reincarnates again and again or is it a mere agglomeration of purva samskaras *or* vishaya vasanas*?*
B: The latter. The actual Self is the only continuous entity. It remains eternally unaffected by the activities of its egos. The reincarnating ego belongs to the illusory dimension or plane of thought; it is transcended by means of Realisation of the Real Self. The Buddhists deny reincarnation because of their belief in the non-Reality of anything but the Self.

The states of *jagrat* and *swapna* are neither of total darkness as in sleep, nor of total light, as in *Samadhi*. They arise on account of the fact that we mix up *chit* [consciousness] and *jada* [insentient, inert matter]. *Chit* refers to one's own Beingness, whereas *jada* includes sensory perceptions and the apparently objectively real and permanent cosmos which they seem to reveal. If you go on investigating the true nature of *chit*, *jada* disappears completely and only infinite *chit* remains. What is known as *Vichara* is nothing but an investigation into the *chit* aspect of the ego. One's interest in one's interminable streams of thought has to dry up before *Vichara* can result in needed mental introversion.

What Is Vichara?

Q: Can you please explain in detail what Vichara *is and why it is necessary?*
B: The mind presently sees itself diversified as the cosmos. If it remains in its own essence, namely pure Subjective Consciousness maintained effortlessly and volitionlessly, such diversity can then be understood to be merely an appearance. Our real nature is formless consciousness to which limitation is alien. Yet we mistake ourselves to be this body, which was born one day and will certainly perish one day, which is insentient and lifeless like a log of wood, and which cannot say 'I' or anything else.

It is thought which creates the body and the cosmos perceived by it. It is thought that prompts us to presume ourselves to be this inert body made of flesh and blood, whereas our true nature is unqualified bliss. We undergo all sorts of miseries because of the fact that our mind keeps extroverting itself in the form of thought. If the habit of thinking is given up and the mind is made to effortlessly and volitionlessly remain as pure Subjective Consciousness on a

permanent basis, the mind returns to its source, which is the Self and is dissolved there like a salt doll in the ocean. This dissolution is the goal of all our spiritual practice and Hindus refer to it by the name *Mukti* [Liberation]. The effort to transform the thinking mind into a simple expanse of pure Subjective Consciousness, which is its primal nature, may be accomplished in many ways. The safest and easiest way is that of *Vichara,* or the investigation Who am I?

Q: There is a feeling among followers of Bhagavan that constantly watching the thought 'I' will lead to the same results as Vichara. *Please comment.*
B: No. Watching the 'I' thought is only a preliminary level practice meant for neophytes who are new to the path of *Vichara.* It cannot serve as a substitute for *Vichara.* Once he intuitively feels that sufficient maturity has been gained by means of constantly watching the 'I' thought, the aspirant should switch over to *Vichara.*

Q: Does Vichara *involve concentrating on the heart centre on the right-hand side of the chest?*
B: No. The practice of concentrating on the heart centre on the right-hand side of the chest has its own benefits such as the increase in mental ability to concentrate, focus, et cetera; but the same has nothing to do with *Vichara.* Furthermore, the same is not a fit practice to lead to Realisation of the Self.

Q: Can I, while remaining in the life of the world, practise Vichara*?*
B: Why not?

Q: Our day-to-day life requires us to think thoughts and take decisions. But as far as your method is concerned, the goal is to remain without thinking thoughts, to remain as pure Subjective Consciousness. Is that correct? How can day-to-day life go on in the state of absence of a thinking mind which takes decisions and solves problems?
B: When one has mastered the art of simply BEing, all his worldly concerns are automatically taken care of by some Higher Power, which works through his body in some mysterious way – using it

as an instrument in its hands – and gets the job done. It might be hard to understand how this could be possible. By long-established habit, we are used to considering ourselves to be the doer of all actions performed by the body. But the body is merely a tool in the hands of the Higher Power, which alone, in truth, does everything.

The gargoyle figures at the base of the sculpted towers forming part of the Annamalaiyar Temple (main *Shiva* Temple in Tiruvannamalai) appear to be carrying the weight of the entire structure on their shoulders. They have been sculpted in such a way that the looks on their faces indicate that they are under great strain on account of bearing so much weight. But the whole idea is a creative sham because the sculpted figures are part of the tower and the entire weight of the tower, including such figures' own weight, is borne by the earth and the earth only.

Likewise, here the actions destined to be carried out by the body in the present lifetime will be executed whether you wish it or not. The body has a pre-written script according to which its actions proceed automatically. If you associate or identify yourself with the body, misery is bound to result. So, remain as you blissfully ARE. Let the body work or be idle as destined, pay no attention to the matter.

Q: But without my participation, how can my day-to-day routine go on?
B: Once we cease to believe, pretend, or behave as though it is ourselves who direct and control the body's actions – which are in fact only according to the body's pre-written script – exclusively the Higher Power takes complete charge over the body's functions and directs it to act accordingly. In fact, all along this is what was happening, but we unwisely believed otherwise!

Q: Should an individual who wants to practise Vichara *retire into solitude?*
B: Mental solitude or absence of thoughts is necessary.

Q: Is it not necessary to avoid fellow human company and physically and mentally isolate oneself?
B: Solitude depends upon your mind only. One man might be in the

thick of the world and maintain serenity of mind; he may be said to be in solitude. Another may be camping in a remote forest all hours of the day, but his mind may be running riot. Can we say that he is in solitude? So, solitude does not lie in physical surroundings; rather, the same is a function of the mind.

Moreover, where you stay depends upon the body's destiny. It is not up to you to decide. But your mind is always at your disposal. Keep it in perfect solitude, wholly free from thought and from lethargy. Work performed with any sort of attachment is a shackle. But work carried out in absence of attachment does not affect the doer; even while working he remains at peace and in solitude.

Q: Will aspiring for occult powers distract one from the quest for Realisation?
B: Certainly. With limited powers man is unhappy. With extended powers, his misery will increase exponentially.

Q: It is said that without a living human Guru, Realisation of the Self is not possible. What is your opinion on the matter?
B: Guru is certainly necessary for Realisation. But there is no mandate that he ought to necessarily be in human form. As in the case of *Dattatreya* [Avatar considered to be *Brahma*, *Vishnu* and *Shiva* combined], even inanimate objects may be Gurus.

Q: But for the vast majority of people it needs a living human Guru to show the way. Am I correct?
B: Yes.

Q: Is diksha *or initiation required for the path of* Vichara*?*
B: Commencement of *Vichara* is itself the necessary initiation into *Vichara*.

Q: It is said that in the absence of the descent of Guru's Grace, Realisation is impossible.
B: Grace is earned by means of introverting the mind. The further or deeper the introversion of the mind, the more is the Grace earned.

Enlightenment Takes Only a Moment

Q: Some say that Enlightenment takes only a moment.
B: To remove darkness from a cave that has remained in the dark for thousands of years, it is enough to roll away the boulders at the entrance and let the sunlight come in. The sunlight which has gained admission into the cave's interior takes only a moment to illumine the entire space of darkness inside the cave. But to roll away the boulders at the entrance needs centuries of toil.

Q: If it takes lifetimes to Realise the Self, I have a feeling I don't even want to try. It seems to be too hard.
B: What purpose is served in feeling discouraged? It might be true that it takes many lifetimes but how do you know what the ordinal position of this birth is? You might perhaps even be in your last lifetime. So go on making effort: *Vichara.* And please do not bear any resentment towards those who try to make you believe that Liberation consists exclusively in getting rid of the thought that you are not liberated. Everything has a purpose in God's creation. Let these people do as they please. After all, does it not serve the purpose of some comic relief?! (laughter in the Hall)

Q: Who am I? needs effort. But effort is said to be an obstacle to Realisation.
B: All effort is made only so that we can remain without any effort.

Q: Please explain further.
B: The effortless and volitionless state of thoughtlessness is the goal. Until it is attained, effort is necessary. Effort is made only to get rid of predispositions. Effort is only to get rid of the not-Self, not to Realise the Self. The Self is already Realised. Yet true freedom is not already there for the taking. It can be Realised only after all latencies have been burnt into annihilation in the fire of *Jnana.*

Q: Can Surrender *and* Vichara *be all practised together?*

B: Certainly. Complete surrender is another name for *Jnana* or Liberation. There is also partial surrender, or attempt made to completely surrender. This is surrender in the sense of *abhyasa* or spiritual practice, about which you are evidently asking. Whatever path you might be following, loss of interest in not-Self is essential. The seeker must learn to distinguish between sentience and insentience.

Q: All living things are said to be sentient.
B: Yes. But look at it from your point of view. As far as you are concerned, your own feeling of being in existence is the only thing that is sentient. Everything else is just sensory perception supported by intellectual activity. Suppose you are seeing, shall we say, Ramana Maharshi. Ramana Maharshi is now sitting on this Sofa and delivering a lecture on what is sentient and what is insentient and how to tell the difference. Is that so?

Q: Yes.
B: No. It appears so to your eyes and ears. That is all. There cannot be anything 'out there'; there is no 'out there'. What is seen is only that image that is cognised and nothing more, and so on for other sensory perceptions. On the other hand, your own Beingness is self-evident or *pratyaksha* [an immediate experience] to you. The aim of *Vichara* is to cleanse this beingness that lies underneath the effervescent mind as its quiescent substratum of the faculty of thought manufacture.

If, to begin with, you find *Vichara* too hard, hold on to the feeling of being subjectively conscious to the exclusion of everything else and this by itself will take you to the degree of spiritual maturity needed for commencing *Vichara*. Pure Subjective Consciousness alone is *Sat*. Everything else is *asat* or *jadam* [insentient]. Subjective self-consciousness is not to be confused with the thought of one being self-conscious. Self-consciousness has nothing to do with thought. It is unrelated to the intellect and unrelated to anything. Pure Subjective Consciousness shines as the self-luminousness of the Heart in spontaneous fashion. Realise it by BEing it.

Q: What are vishaya *[sense objects],* vasanas *and* purva samskaras?
B: They are latent predispositions. Thought in seed form. They cause thoughts to arise again and again.

Q: How shall we put an end to their existence?
B: By the investigation Who am I? That is the safest and surest way. *Vichara* becomes easier and easier as you go on practising the same.

Q: Cannot Sri Bhagavan help me to Realise? I am after all a weak creature.
B: The Guru is only an aid. Your constant effort is a necessity. Divine Grace is also a sine qua non but the same is vouchsafed only to him who is a true *sadhaka,* who has striven hard and ceaselessly on the path towards Emancipation. To even think about Liberation means that God's Grace has been operative in you.

Q: Are even good thoughts inconsistent with Realisation?
B: Yes. Thoughts are one thing and Realisation quite another.

Q: Some people have visions of God. Is it in their own imagination only?
B: Even this conversation you now think you are having is within your own imagination only.

Q: Even in Vichara *there is perception of an 'I' which wants to engage itself in the practice of* Vichara.
B: *Vichara* does not take the existence of 'I' for granted. You are not told: *'This thing known as 'I' exists. Discover it.'* Many misunderstand *Vichara* thinking that they are being asked to discover the non-dual Self. What is the purpose underlying the investigation of oneself? Who am I? is not to discover the not-Self. There is no second self with which one may affect the discovery of the first. The purpose of investigating Who am I? is to scrutinise this thing called 'I', whatever it might be, and whether it might exist or not. Go about practising *Vichara* without assuming that something called 'I' exists.

Q: What is the consequence of such scrutiny? Is 'I' found or not?

B: Intellectual answers are not of any use. Find out for yourself; that is the only way.

Q: I shall do so. But I would like to hear the answer from Sri Bhagavan's mouth.

B: Searching for 'I', 'I' is never found. The searcher himself vanishes and 'I'-'I' manifests itself spontaneously. But this is an experience, and you must yourself undergo the same to find out what it is. Intellectual explanations are of no use.

Q: What is this 'I'-'I'? Is it the same as Jnana?

B: No. 'I'-'I' is the stage before the *Sahajastithi* of the *Jnani.* It is known as *Aham Sphurana.* When the *Sphurana* becomes continuous, unstoppable and spontaneous, and when it has solidified itself, so to speak, into a permanent phenomenon, it leads to the *Sahajastithi* [the state of the *Jnani]*. In Vedantic parlance *Aham Sphurana* is known as *vrittijnanam.* It may otherwise be known as cosmic consciousness.

It is called 'cosmic' because the mind in that state is in a generic form. It is not held captive by the primordial mental modification 'I' for the duration of the experience. If the destruction of *purva samskaras* [latent predispositions] is incomplete, the *ahamvritti* reasserts itself afterwards and the usual flow of thoughts resumes itself as usual. The *Sphurana,* when held onto continuously, weakens the *ahamvritti,* which alone is the cause of the *hridayagranthi* [energetic knot between the sentient and the insentient] and bestows *Mukti* [freedom from embodiment and future births].

Q: How to hold on to the Sphurana *continuously?*

B: The effort, will, or volition to do it is itself an obstacle to the shining of the *Sphurana.* If you remain as you ARE, the *Sphurana* shines forth of its own accord.

Q: Has Bhagavan said that the experience of the Sphurana *is accompanied by a prickly sensation on the right-hand side of the chest?*

B: Leave alone the physical sensation; it might be brought about by the *Sphurana* but it is profitless to think that merely having experienced the sensation means that you have accomplished something. The important thing is to always remain in a state of effortless and volitionless thoughtlessness. The subtle 'I' which witnesses the fact of the mind remaining in this state must also vanish. Only then is Realisation made possible.

Q: All this sounds highly difficult. I am only a mere layman. What can I do?
B: Go on with *Vichara*. Perseverance is the secret of success. Mind control is not your birthright. The few who succeed owe their success to perseverance and perseverance alone. Go on being maniacally persistent in continuing with your *Vichara*; one day you will see the Light.

The Happiness of the Self

Q: While practising Vichara *there is often felt an urge to give up everything and retire to some remote forest uninhabited by mankind.*
B: Within a few days of having gone to such forest, you will again feel like moving somewhere else. The mind, in order to divert our attention away from the one and only actual issue at hand, namely itself, comes up with such tricks to delude us. Pay no attention to the mind but only continue to seek and abide at its source, namely the Shining of the Heart.

Q: What is the difference between the happiness obtained on Realising the Self and that obtained by means of enjoying objects of sensory enjoyment?
B: The happiness of the Self is of the nature of *shanti* or Abiding Peace. Sensory enjoyments are of the nature of fleeting pleasures. However, it may be borne in mind that any kind of happiness is

made possible only on account of the Self. When the mind imagines itself to be enjoying objects of sensory perception, what it is really doing is temporarily submerging itself in the Shining of the Heart, although unconsciously, the resultant happiness – we presume in our unwisdom – comes from the object that we are interacting with. But what is the truth? Such happiness also comes from the Self only. If you dive consciously into the Shining of the Heart, the same is known as *abhyasa* or spiritual practice.

Q: In the introductory paragraph accompanying the essay Who am I? why does Bhagavan write, 'Everybody loves himself most of all.' *Does this statement actually hold good in all cases? For instance, I love my son more than my own life.*

B: Everything is dear to us only because of the Self. The paragraph in question itself indicates that happiness is the reason why the feeling of Love is possible, and the explanation as to how any happiness derives its origin from the Self only has been given to you. You say that your son is exceedingly dear to you. Examine your own statement closely. You love your son. He is dear to you in so far as it is true that he is your son. How is this affection made possible? Because of the idea that this other human being is your child who has been crafted out of your flesh and blood.

The central idea supporting this feeling is 'my son', the idea of this other person being related to YOU. When you say 'my' an 'I' is implied. Without 'I' there cannot be 'my'. What is this 'I'? 'I' is the faculty of intellect which takes yourself to be this body and the other body as being your son's. The faculty of intellect derives its origin from the mind and the mind is in essence a reflected ray of light emanating from the Self. So, we see that when the mind loves something, what it loves is not anything apart from itself. Whether I love myself, my son, anybody or anything else, it is only myself that I love. The other things emanate only from this primordial 'I' which is the origin of all I perceive. You love your son more than you love yourself, you say.

Suppose a man's infant son goes missing. The man and his child coincidentally cross each other after several decades and do

not recognise the relationship that exists between them. The two men become good friends but remain without the slightest inkling that they are father and son. Suddenly the son dies. When the news reaches the father, he feels sad for a few days because he thinks he has lost his good friend. If he had known it was his son, his grief would be vastly greater. What does this show? Our responses to the world and its events are conditioned by how we perceive them. The boy is the same boy whether he is friend, foe, or son. But we react differently based on how we look at the other person.

There is a similar story in Sri Vidyaranya's *Panchadasi* (renowned fourth-century Sanskrit philosophical text on *Advaita Vedanta*). Two young men from a village went on a pilgrimage to Uttarkashi. One of them died there. But the other, having picked up some occupation, decided to return to his village only after some time. Meanwhile, he came across a wandering pilgrim and sent word through him to his village about himself and his dead friend. The pilgrim conveyed the news and in doing so inadvertently interchanged the names of the living and the dead man. The result was that the dead man's people were rejoicing that he was doing well and the living man's people were in grief that he was dead.

You love not that other human being; you love your son. He is dear to you exclusively and only because he is your son. 'My' is in turn based on 'I'. 'I' is based on the Self. So, everything dear to you is so because of the Self only. No matter what it is that you love, you love yourself only. The *Jnani* alone knows the meaning of unselfish love.

Q: So, I am really formless consciousness?

B: You are not being asked to believe intellectually that you are consciousness. Instead of mentally believing that you are consciousness, BE consciousness, which you ARE. Be as you are, that is all. The practice of *Vichara abhyasa* is not for any fresh gain. It is only to get rid of predispositions and latent tendencies which obstruct one from remaining or abiding as pure Subjective Consciousness, which one already is.

Q: If I am already at the goal, where is the need for practice?
B: Since you are of the nature of consciousness, you ought to be content to remain simply as consciousness. But does it happen so? No. There is a constant stream of thoughts which passes over and obstructs one from remaining as what one really is: pure, volitionless, motiveless Being. It is at getting rid of thought that our practice is directed.

No efforts need be made for cultivating awareness of the Self because it is already there and is forever shining as 'I'-'I' in the Heart. All our effort is made only to eliminate the not-Self, in other words, thought and the faculty of thought manufacture. Freedom from thought is bliss, it is your real nature. It is the contrariwise tendencies which must be eradicated.

Reality Is Simply the Loss of the Ego

Q: Why should I agree that Vichara *alone is the direct means to Enlightenment?*
B: All other methods are exercised only by means of retaining the ego. In these other paths many doubts might arise along the way and the eternal question Who am I? remains to be tackled – finally. On the other hand, as far as this direct method is concerned, the final question is the only one and the same is raised from the very beginning. Reality is simply the loss of the ego.

Transcend the false idea of the ego's apparent existence by means of continuously and incessantly pursuing the search for its identity. This search is the same as the investigation Who am I? Since the ego is no entity at all, it will result in incessant and intense practice of *Vichara*. Automatically ego vanishes and Reality is Revealed of and by Itself. The quest Who am I? is the axe with which to strike down the ego.

Q: I feel dejected and despondent because I am not able to Realise the Self. Please show me your Grace and thereby help me.

B: Instead of falling prey to the web of thought-stuff spewed out by the mind and in consequence roaming around without peace, trace the mind to its source and remain there once and for all.

Q: What is the mind's source? Is it pure Subjective Consciousness?
B: When you hold on to pure Subjective Consciousness by means of making an effort to do so, it cannot be said then that you have successfully traced the mind back to its source. The mind's source is pure Subjective Consciousness in which there is not the slightest trace of thought, volition, effort, individuality or personality. Pure Subjective Consciousness is always here and now and it is unrelated to anything. It is self-luminous and it is always spontaneously self-evident. No effort or volition is needed to inhere in and as it, because you verily are it. If our experience is otherwise, it means that our mind is clouded with latencies and predispositions, these must be eliminated if Reality is to be regained. For this, Who am I? is the means.

Q: Will it be enough to raise the question once?
B: Wield the weapon of *Vichara* whenever you find that the mind has strayed away from its source. As and when you find that the mind has forsaken its natural place in the Shining of the Heart drag it back gently by means of deploying Who am I?

Q: Is it possible that knowledge gained by means of direct experience could be lost at a later point in time?
B: Experience gained without rooting out all of one's *vasanas* cannot remain steady. Efforts must be made to destroy all *vasanas*. Even if a single *vasana* is left in the mind, permanent Realisation *[Sahajajnana]* is an impossibility and rebirth into ignorance is inevitable. Realisation can remain unshaken only after all *vasanas* stand extirpated.

Q: How shall the grip of the ego be loosened?
B: By refraining from adding new *vasanas* to it.

23rd September 1936

The Self Can Never Be Understood by the Mind

Q: Is it true that the experience of the Jnani's Sahajastithi *cannot be comprehended by the mind?*
B: Yes. The Self can never be apprehended by the mind: It is the Beyond. *'Eye hath not seen, nor ear heard, neither have entered into the heart of man, the things which God hath prepared for them that love Him.'* Here we may take the word 'heart' as connoting 'mind'.

Q: I have been practising Vichara *for the past few months. It is my experience that after tracing thought to its source, I find that a certain nothingness remains. Shall I ask,* 'Who becomes aware of this nothingness?' *Or is experience of this nothingness the intended fruit of the investigation, Who am I?*
B: No. Ask yourself who experiences what you refer to as 'nothingness'. The sought-after consequence or result of *Vichara* is that pure Subjective Consciousness sustained effortlessly and volitionlessly spontaneously manifests itself. This awareness is not divisible into subject (experiencer), object (experience) and process (act of experiencing) by means of which the former becomes aware of the latter. This awareness is not itself the Self but is only the means for Realising the Self. Remaining without moving away from this awareness leads to the Realisation of the Self.

You mention that nothingness is experienced by you, that means that you are there to experience it, never mind nothingness or somethingness or anythingness. Focus on that 'you', merge into it and become one with it; this is the way. The phrase *'holding on to subjective awareness'* should not be misinterpreted to give scope for the perverse understanding that there is anything apart from such awareness when one is so holding on. There is a limit to which language can be used to explain such a simple matter. You may understand 'holding on' to be connoting 'remaining as'.

24th September 1936

Who Is Eligible to Practise Vichara?

Q: For taking up and practising Vichara, *who is fit and who is unfit and who is eligible and who is ineligible?*
B: There are no restrictions, anybody may. However, one's chance of succeeding may be unlikely to be adequate unless there is any one or both of the following present in the aspirant. (a) An all-consuming desire for Emancipation. (b) An all-consuming *vairagya* or aversion towards *samsara*. It may be noted that these feelings must themselves disappear before Realisation can be achieved. Determination to get Emancipated must be so strong that it allows no scope for any other thought to arise in the mind. Ultimately, this one thought also disappears, and the Self reveals itself.

Q: How is one to cultivate the desire to obtain Emancipation?
B: Your question sounds strange. A man is standing in the middle of a desert. On all directions around him, he is able to see only miles and miles of sand stretching away before him. He is exceedingly thirsty and it is a few days since his lips have touched water. He suddenly chances to meet a fellow traveller. Instead of asking for water, imagine this is what he is saying: *'Brother, how can I or how am I to cultivate the desire to drink water?'* What would you make of such a man?

Q: I would instantly surmise that he suffers from serious mental illness.
B: Exactly.

Q: The desert stands for samsara *and water for* Vichara. *Thirst is* vairagya. *Is that right?*
B: Yes. That is it.

Q: Some fools do not even realise that they are wandering about parched, hot, and thirsty in a desert; they go on wandering. What shall we do to help these poor, lost souls?

B: First, you exit the desert, and then let us think of others. One blind man cannot lead another.

Q: Some find samsara *acceptable and tolerable; they even enjoy roaming around in this desert.*
B: They are merely on the outskirts, where they can find plenty of shrubbery and large oases. Eventually, they will wander deeper and deeper. It is then that the value of this teaching will really become readily apparent. When you are having a pleasant dream and at that time somebody tells you how to wake up you feel like throttling him to death out of annoyance, but when you are undergoing a horrible nightmare and at that time somebody tells you how to wake up, you feel like falling at his feet and worshipping him as a saviour.

Q: So, going through a terrible life is really good?
B: Yes, you will feel, *'Enough of this nonsense, let me wake up once and for all and be done with it.'*

Q: But mere determination to Realise is said to be insufficient. God's Grace must be obtained, is that not so?
B: Take one step towards Him. He will take ten steps towards you. But the first step must be from your side. To begin with, the ball is always in your side of the court.

Q: I have no faith in existence of God or any Higher Power. My outlook is not sceptical, but rather rational in character. Can I also practise Vichara*? I am burning with curiosity to know who I really am. Is there any use in me practising* Vichara *or are only theists meant to take it up?*
B: Certainly, you may. (smiling) **In fact, you will find it easier than many others sitting in this place.**

Who am I? Is the Direct Method

Q: Sri Bhagavan says that Who am I? is the direct method to Realise. This being the case, why is chanting of the Vedas *[The oldest and most important scriptures in Hinduism], worship of Bhagavan's mother's sarcophagus, et cetera, going on in this Ashram? Where is the need for all these ritualistic practices if* Vichara *is sufficient?*
B: Not all minds relish taking up *Vichara* to begin with. Over a period of time these other practices make the mind relatively calm. Thereafter, it might come to relish practising *Vichara*.

Q: Vichara *is used to kill the mind. How then could the mind ever relish practising* Vichara*?*
B: All minds, whether they are aware of the fact or not and whether they are prepared to accept the fact or not, long for peace and happiness. The practice of *Vichara*, which plunges the mind into the contentless silence of boundaryless self-absorption, will be accepted by the mind as being relishable only after it has once had a taste of what it is to be like when 'I' is submerged in the Shining of the Heart.

Q: How do we get this first taste of or first glimpse into the peace of the Self?
B: Constantly practising *Vichara* is the means.

Q: We seem to be moving around in circles.
B: Our problem is that we always crave conceptualisation and intellectualisation of everything we come across. *Vichara* cannot be tackled that way. Start the practice, stick with it constantly, and the rest will follow.

Q: How can I gain steadiness in practice?
B: Only by means of more practice.

Q: Which is the most potent mantra*? Is it the* Gayatri Mantra *[prayer directed towards the Supreme Consciousness]?*
B: The most potent *mantra* is the silence of the Self. This *mantra* is always automatically going on in us. Only we interrupt it with other *mantras*.

Q: It is said that the purpose of all efforts is to give up all efforts. What does it mean?
B: Does remaining without thinking involve effort in your case?

Q: Yes.
B: Then make effort to remain without thinking until you are able to remain effortlessly without thinking. This cannot be accomplished overnight. It requires patience and perseverance.

27th September 1936

Bhagavan's Enemies in Tiruvannamalai

Learnt firsthand today that Bhagavan has many enemies in Tiruvannamalai. The Master's complaisant and docile nature would upon juxtaposition make the most bashful amongst lambs seem unduly pugnacious. To think that there are people in the world who would bear in their hearts anything but limitless Love befuddles me. To have to accommodate myself to the fact that of all places here in Tiruvannamalai there are people who loathe and malign him, breaks my heart into smithereens.

During the wee hours of the morning today, I was as usual proceeding to the Ashram. When I was passing near the Pai Gopuram, a gang of roguish *sadhus* descended on me. They were about two dozen in number; they started by talking politely to me but went on to abuse and slander Bhagavan in the vilest language imaginable. The apparent leader of the band was an elderly ochre-robed personage with matted beard and bald head; countless garlands of *rudraksha* beads bounced off his chest as he walked.

Ostensibly, he looked highly respectable. He started by saying: *'Considering you as my own younger brother, I am now going to tell you something. I watch you going to that man Ramana every day; seeing it I feel enormous pity for you because you have unwittingly placed yourself in profound danger. Many young men like yourself have been trapped by that devil and have gone completely astray. Please listen to me whilst I divulge to you a few truths about Ramana.'*

During the interaction, the leader and his group spoke critically of Bhagavan, expressing baseless accusations attempting to sow doubt in my mind. I tried to maintain my composure and play along, sensing it was better to avoid confrontation.

Now we were walking near Agni Tirtham; at that precise moment I spotted walking on the opposite side of the road a familiar face – it was Yogi Ramaiah! I called out *'Ramaiahgaru...!'* repeatedly to him in a screeching, beseeching voice and he came rushing to this bandit-like group. I immediately jumped to his side and firmly clasped hold of his comforting hand. The irate gang-leader glared at me like he would like to decapitate me. As soon as we reached the Ashram, I tried to make my way to Bhagavan as usual.

My head was swimming with questions. The yogi, the *sarvadhikari* who had heard about the incident, some others and myself all marched into the Hall. One look at our faces and Bhagavan asked smilingly, ***'Ennayittru?' (What happened?)***

The *sarvadhikari* lamented: *'Last week he has intimidated Raja besides snatching away from him all the Ashram's mail that day; now it is Gajapathi – the offences of these villains seem to go on never-endingly.'* Even as his ears were processing their exasperated complaints Bhagavan quietly held out his hand in my direction. I instinctively reached out to him and only then noticed the small book handed over to me by the dastardly ex-attendant still clutched in my hand.

I tried to seize my hand back, because I was sure that the material constituting the book would contain nothing good, and I did not want Bhagavan to undergo what I felt would be a disgrace in perusing it. It was too late; the depraved volume was in the Master's deft hands already.

The *sarvadhikari* began a fresh tirade against the enemies who were raining down incessant troubles upon the Ashram.
B: (placidly) **Why do you begrudge them their little joys? They are doing their job properly, likewise let us do ours.**

With that he gave the *sarvadhikari* to understand that the matter stood dismissed. The latter reluctantly trudged out of the Hall after prostrating in front of the Sofa. Now the Master patiently perused the villain's book; after sôme time he laid it aside, laughing, saying:
B: Why is he complaining that if he had more money, he would have printed a bigger book with more content? If he had come here, we could have gladly given him all the money he needed! Possibly he thinks I am angry with him, poor fellow.

TKS: (sadly) It is Perumal again, is that not so?
B: Yes, yes...

TKS: Bhagavan is not allowing the Ashram to prosecute him, we ought to file a suit alleging criminal defamation. Justice is on our side. Why should we not approach the court? If we leave him like this, there will be no end to his atrocities.
B: Why is everybody perturbed? He is only doing good. You may take it that I have myself authorised him to write and publish these things. I have permitted him long ago. Let more such books be published. Let many others bring out such works. If on account of

such publications, no one comes to me, I shall consider it a great favour shown to me. In fact, books containing scandals sell better than others. It is really an excellent, novel method to make money. I wish everybody in the Ashram would start bringing out such books about me. (laughs)

After some time, Bhagavan addressed me thus of his own accord:
B: Why are you so dispirited?

G: Why does the omnipotent Bhagavan allow such negativistic occurrences to take place?

The Master did not make a response but gazed at me steadily, and eyes streaming with uncontrollable tears, I repeated word-for-word everything. I could not help it. The Master listened with a steadily, widening smile. At the end, he said: **'They have spoken and you have listened; it is finished. Why do you go on dwelling upon the matter?'**

G: Their harsh words have left a strong impression in my mind; how am I to erase it?
B: This is where people go wrong. Listen to the following story:

> ***Once upon a time, two disciples of a Guru were travelling together. At one point in their journey, they came to a huge river that was flowing with a terrifically strong current. As the disciples readied themselves to cross the river, they beheld a young and beautiful woman also attempting to cross it. The woman pleadingly asked if they could help her cross the river.***
>
> ***The disciples were confused as to what to do because they had taken both these vows under the instructions of their Master: to help all living beings out of distress and also to never touch the flesh of a woman. Suddenly the older disciple tore off a part of his dhoti and made a hammock out of the torn piece. He asked***

> ***the woman to get into the hammock and deposited her gently and safely on the opposite bank of the river. He lifted her not bodily but by means only of holding on to the cloth of the hammock he had fashioned for the purpose.***
>
> ***Then the two disciples continued on their trip. The younger disciple was burning with resentment. He felt that the older disciple had violated a direct commandment of their Guru. In helping the woman, he felt that the other disciple had obeyed the letter of their Guru's covenant but not the spirit.***
>
> ***For some time, he kept quiet, but after many hours had passed in silence, the poor man could contain himself no longer. He burst out, addressing the older disciple,*** **'Brother, what a foul deed hath thou committed in carrying that woman across the river!'** ***The elder disciple replied with a smile,*** **'Brother, a long while ago I did set her down upon a bank of the river but why are you still carrying her?'**

TKS: What is the moral of the story?

B: Do what is right at a given moment and leave it behind. Anything which carries you away from the present is harmful divergence. Live in the present. In the HERE and NOW.

TKS: Bhagavan does not prevent ill occurrences from happening. Are we then to give ourselves to understand that everything happens for the greater good?

B: You may do so. But try to abide in that state wherein worldly appearances have no power to perturb your inner tranquillity.

G: This former attendant of Bhagavan's, Perumal, seems to have become a complete enemy of the Ashram and Bhagavan. If, at least in cases related to such depraved persons, Bhagavan will slightly deviate from his routine policy of not showing any display of siddhis *[spiritual powers], such persons will come to cultivate fear of Bhagavan. Thereafter they will not do any*

mischief. If I have said something wrong, I crave Bhagavan's pardon.
TKS: I also agree with this.
B: (smiling) ***Summayirutthal* [natural being] is the greatest *siddhi* [spiritual power]. One who has mastered this *siddhi* need not know any other.**

TKS: But believing Perumal's rumours people may stop coming to our Ashram.
B: Exactly. Let us finance the poor chap; if we do not come to his aid, who will? If you meet him, ask him to come here if he has run out of money for printing additional copies of the book.

One feels sorry to see such a thin book. Already many splendid ideas for the next edition he has communicated to Gajapathi here. I also have many good ideas, let us also invite suggestions from everybody in the Ashram. In the second edition, a lot more scandals can be added.

TKS looked horrified by the joke.

G: I never saw the Perumal character again, nor the band of rowdies he came with that day. Sometime after the above incident took place, a formal summons arrived at the Ashram from the District Munsiff's Court of Tiruvannamalai, summoning none other than Bhagavan himself to Court!

By virtue of his contacts with Caucasians in eminent official positions in what was then His Majesty's Government, it was Mr Nambiar, I think, who managed to obtain exemption for Bhagavan from appearance in Court – subject to the condition that the Maharshi agreed to be examined at the Ashram premises.

I am stating all this here to highlight one thing only. Even after all this, the Master's attitude towards Perumal remained stoically empathetic. I heard he even solicitously arranged for the villain to be provided with medicines at a time when he himself was critically ill during the months of adverse health that led to his death. *'Father, forgive them, for they know not what they do.'*

Transcend the Mind and Find it Non-Existent

Q: I carry out Vichara *in the following manner. That is to say, I investigate thus: Consciousness does not by itself think any thoughts, yet thoughts are made up of consciousness in fact. Again, thoughts must have their common origin in a thinker. This thinker cannot be consciousness itself. Yet he manufactures thoughts all the time. Where does he come from? Who is he? Why does he come up with thoughts? It all seems to be most puzzling. Is that right?*

B: This is not *Vichara* in the sense that is useful towards the purpose of Realising the Self. The thief cannot apprehend the thief. You can never find or catch hold of mind with mind. It is like a dog chasing its own tail, or like a man chasing his own shadow. Transcend the mind and find it non-existent. But how to do this? It cannot be done by doing at all. No mental activity can ever discover the Self. 'Be still.' This is the direct technique for Realising the Self. Who am I? is for those who are, for some reason or another, unable to keep themselves mentally still.

Q: It is said that owing to vasanas *we are unable to keep the mind still.*
B: Quite so.

Q: How to eradicate these vasanas?
B: By eradicating that one called 'I' who possesses them.

Q: Now we are back at square one.
B: Commence the practice, get on with it and thenceforward do not worry about anything. You need not see all the way to the goal and mark out your route before commencing the journey. Take the first step and then the next one and so on and so forth, until one day you find that you have arrived. Realisation cannot be intellectually planned. There is no need for any plan. Planning is just another excuse to deliberately procrastinate the journey. Have you not heard the lines: *'Lead, kindly light, amidst the encircling gloom, lead Thou*

***me on! The night is dark, and I am far from home, lead Thou me on! Keep Thou my feet. I do not ask to see the distant scene; one step is enough for me.'* So, start NOW.**

Vichara Is Wholly a Risk-Free Practice

Q: Will engaging in spiritual practice impair my ability to function normally in the world?
B: *Vichara* carries no such risk.

Q: Can I engage myself in Vichara *and attend to office duties at the same time? Is it possible? Is it feasible? Is it advisable?*
B: Yes.

Q: Will not Vichara *make the mind go into a blank and make worldly activity impossible?*
B: No.

Q: But suppose I do it incorrectly or improperly. Then my mind might go into a blank and make my normal functioning in the world impossible. Is that right? I am terrified of becoming like a statue. I have a family to support.
B: *Vichara* does not carry any such risks. It is wholly a risk-free practice.

29th September 1936

The Self Alone Is Permanent and Real

Q: Can I engage in Vichara, *even whilst remaining in the entrapment of* samsara*?*

B: Yes, but who told you that you are now trapped in *samsara*? Why should you think, *'I am trapped in* samsara*'* and so on? The fact is, there is neither bondage nor liberation. One simply remains as one really IS.

Q: Is not the householder's life a hindrance? Do not all the sacred books advocate leaving one's house and moving into a forest? For Realisation, should not one's life in the world be given up completely? Is not sannyasa *[renunciation of worldly life] necessary for Realisation?*

B: *Samsara* and *sannyasa* are only in your own mind. You talk of life in the world, but what world? Is there a world apart from one's mind? The world does not speak out saying *'I am the world.'* For if it did, it would always be there even when you are in the *sushupti* [deep sleep] state. But in deep sleep is there any world? No. Since it is not in sleep it is impermanent. Being impermanent it has no possible capacity for *svagruni* [self-luminosity]. Having no capacity to shine by its own light it is easily subdued by the Self.

The Self alone is permanent and real. You talk of *sannyasa*. What is the true import of *sannyasa*? It is to remain without identifying yourself with this or that. It is by grasping and feeding upon forms that the ego fattens itself. If the ego is interminably starved of opportunity for identifying itself with thoughts and objects, it begins to fade away. On eradication of ignorance, not-Self, which is already non-existent, is found by itself not to exist and never returns after making such discovery. This is known as *Jnana*. Real renunciation does not involve leaving the house and moving into a jungle or desert. It simply means giving up not-Self. If not-Self is abandoned, the Self stands revealed.

Q: Why then did you leave your house in your youth?
B: My *prarabdha* lies this way, yours that way.

Q: Shall I not also leave my house?
B: If that had been your *prarabdha*, the question would not have arisen.

Q: Then it seems I am fated to remain in the world and engage in spiritual practice. That being so, can I Realise the Self in this lifetime?
B: Yes. You are always the Self only you are yet to relinquish the realm of thought that veils the Self. With sincere, continuous and persistent practice of *Vichara*, thought is snuffed out and the Self is revealed. Earnest efforts never fail. Success is bound to result.

Q: Yes. I shall try to practise Vichara. *But I beg Bhagavan to bless me with his Grace so that I can Realise the Self in this lifetime.*
B: (smiled but offered no reply)

30th September 1936

The Power of Intense Practice

Q: But sleep and waking are two different states having different characteristics.
B: How does the fact affect you? The Self is the same all through.

Q: The mind is not steady in meditation.
B: Whenever it wanders, turn it inward again and again.

Q: When mental perturbation overpowers me, Vichara *becomes impossible.*
B: It is because the mind is too weak to turn inward. Make it strong.

Q: By what means?
B: It depends according to the maturity of the aspirant. Those who are fit for it can take up *Vichara* directly. Others have to go through *pranayama, murtidhyana*, et cetera. The point is to gain introversion of mind.

Q: What is the result of all this abhyasa*?*
B: Misery is removed; our aim is removal of misery. You do not acquire happiness. Your very nature is happiness. Bliss is not newly earned. All that is done is removal of unhappiness. These methods do it.

Q: Association with a Jnani *may strengthen the mind. But there must also be practice.*
B: Yes. Practice is definitely necessary. Practice means removal of predispositions. Practice is not for any fresh gain; it is to kill one's predispositions.

Q: What is the ideal practice that ripens the mind and makes it ready for experiencing Realisation?
B: *Vichara*.

Q: Will practising Vichara *give me the power to Realise* Parabrahman*?*
B: Practice is in itself power. If one's thoughts are reduced to a single thought, the mind is said to have grown strong. When the effortless thought-free state gained as a result of unremitting practice has become unshakable, you abide in your natural state.

Q: What is the aim to be kept in view whilst practising Vichara*? Practice requires an aim.*
B: We are ourselves our exclusive aim. What other aim can there be? All other aims are for those who are incapable of *Atmalakshya*

[having the Self as the aim]. Other practices lead you ultimately only to *Vichara.* Mental introversion is the fruit of all kinds of practice. One may get it quickly, another after a long time. Everything depends on the intensity of the practice.

Q: Peace is extolled more than anything else. How shall we gain the same?
B: Peace is your very nature. Forgetfulness never overtakes the Self. You have confounded yourself with that which is non-Self and therefore you speak of paucity of peace, forgetfulness of the Self. Oblivion will never rear up its head if this confusion is not put an end to.

Q: How is that done?
B: *Vichara* is the way. Introversion of mind means cessation of mental activities. Forgetfulness can never overtake the Self. There is nothing for the Self to either forget or remember. There is not more than one Self, and such multiple selves might take it in turns to remember and forget each other. Practice is only meant to remove one's *vishaya vasanas* and *purva samskaras.*

Q: But samskaras *and* vasanas *are infinite and eternal, they come from beginningless time.*
B: This thought in itself is merely a *samskara.* Give up such notorious ideas and be at peace. Peace is ever-present *[Nityapratyaksha].* But you hold it down. Rise over it as the ego and thus disturb it. Thereafter you say, *'I want Peace.'*

Q: Will mental stillness be gradually obtained?
B: Yes. Gradually, step by step, one should withdraw the mind, holding it steady with the intellect controlled by determination. Fixing the mind upon the Self *[Atman]*, one should think of nothing else.

One Day You Will Reach the Summit

Q: Which is genuine Vichara *– asking myself Who am I? every time a thought arises or keenly investigating the problem of who I am?*
B: The latter. If you want to get rid of a poisonous tree, do you lop off its leaves one by one? What is the use of such an approach? In the time it takes for you to cut down one leaf, leaves multitudinous in number and multifarious in variety would have sprouted forth from the vicious tree. Instead, attack the poisonous root of illusion, namely the *ahamvritti*, straightaway!

Q: But I have heard it spoken of amongst Bhagavan's devotees that Vichara, *according to Bhagavan, can be compared to an aged mongoose waiting for a snake to come out of a discarded anthill that the latter happens to be using as its place of residence.*
B: Yes. The sword can be used for slicing as well as for stabbing. In the preliminary phase of *sadhana,* when thoughts rush out furiously one after the other, *Vichara* is used as a tool to go on returning the mind to its native state of thought-free pure Subjective Consciousness. It is always to be practised as and when it is discovered that the mind has strayed away from this natural state.

However, there is also the subsequent stage, where thoughts have largely subsided. Now, the investigation Who am I? is used to seek the mind with mind. Use the mind to scrutinise closely what 'I' is. Rather than creating something called 'I' and then looking at it so as for fulfilling the instruction to closely scrutinise 'I', seek 'I', whatever it might be and whether it might exist or not, without harbouring notions as to its existence or non-existence.

Q: I am trying to follow Bhagavan's instructions. But my vasanas *prove to be an obstacle. What can I do?*
B: Never mind obstacles. Keep on going. Do not sit down or pause to moan or complain, but keep on going. The only important thing is to keep on going. If you try to take stock of progress yet to be

made, you will feel alarmed and then further progress would have become impossible. So, never stop, but go on escalating. One day you will reach the summit, or rather, realise that you never left it. Until then, climb relentlessly and incessantly. Do not bother about obstacles, progress, and the like. Simply and only, go on scaling.

Doubt the Doubter

Q: In his Meditations on First Philosophy, *Descartes opines that if only he could find some reason to doubt each one of his present opinions in his quest to seek sturdier foundations for knowledge, such quest would surely succeed. Rather than doubt each one of his opinions individually, he reasons subsequently that he might cast them all into doubt if he can doubt the foundations and basic principles on which all of his opinions are founded. Is Bhagavan's* Vichara *method analogous or comparable to this sort of radical self-doubting?*

B: Yes, doubt the doubter. Doubts may be many and never-ending. Doubter is only one. Solving the doubt concerning the doubter's apparent existence, all doubt is put to an end, once and for all. King Janaka said, *'At last I have discovered the thief who has been ruining me all along. Now I shall execute him summarily.'* So, once you come to know that the *ahamvritti* is the cause of all your misery, what are you waiting for? Finish off the thief and rest in peace forever more.

Q: How to get rid of vasanas *which are preventing me from Realising the Self?*

B: Ignore the mind and its contents, including *vasanas, samskaras,* et cetera. If the mind is rebellious let it be. You pay it no attention but rather repose blissfully in the stillness of pure Subjective Consciousness. When you pay attention, the mind obtains more fuel. If you ignore the mind, it will die away of its own accord.

Only by means of keeping it in perpetual inactivity can the mind be killed. This game is to be won only by means of perpetual non-participation.

The Real God Lies Behind the Mind

Q: It is said that Shiva *in the form of a yogi is sitting somewhere on the Arunachala Hill. Where can we find him on the mountain? Is the saying true or just a myth to fool the credulous? Will having* darshan *[auspicious sight of a deity or saint] of this yogi make me Realise the Self at once?*
B: Seeing God is not Realisation. Visions of God *[Ishwara]* are on the mental plane. The Real God lies behind the mind. Investigating Who am I? is the one infallible means to find Him in His true, eternal abode, the Heart.

Q: Is the ahamvritti *itself just a* vasana*?*
B: Yes, it is the primordial or principal *vasana* without which no other *vasana* could exist. All *vrittis* are strung upon only this one single parent *vritti*. If the *ahamvritti* is snuffed out, other *vrittis* are automatically rendered impotent and powerless. Destruction of the *ahamvritti* is known as *manonasam* or *Jnana*.

Q: Should all other vasanas *be destroyed before we can proceed to annihilate the* ahamvritti *– or can a* sadhaka *tackle the* ahamvritti *straightaway?*
B: It depends upon the *vairagya* of the aspirant. To ruin the *ahamvritti* all at once requires *vairagya* as boundless as the sky.

Q: How may we cultivate such vairagya*?*
B: *Vichara* is the way. Constant *Vichara* steadily introverts the mind and gradually, gently turns it self-wards, eventually plunging and submerging it completely into the Heart. When *purnapakkuvam*

[state of total maturity] has dawned, then the mind, being altogether denuded of *vrittis,* is destroyed by the Heart. This is the only genuine Emancipation. Introversion *[antarmukabhavam]* means inherence of the mind in its entirety in the lustre of pure Subjective Consciousness emanating from the Self. *Vairagya* means persistently shunning the not-Self. Thus, can there be any difference between introversion and *vairagya*?

Q: How shall I obtain the Grace to Realise the Self?
B: By introverting the mind through *Vichara.*

Q: It is to introvert the mind that Grace is solicited.
B: Yes, it is cyclical: through *Vichara,* Grace is earned. It is Grace that makes *Vichara* possible. It is like dislodging a large boulder situated at the summit of a huge mountain. Initially, great effort is needed. Thereafter you can sit back and enjoy the ride. Start with the practice. The rest is automatic, and it is only a matter of time before the mind is dissolved in the Heart. Once a certain critical level of introversion is reached, the mind can no longer stay away from the Heart.

Normally the mind is like a piece of rock in space orbiting around the sun. To break the centripetal force propelling the object on its circular orbit, application of immense energy or effort is required. But once the body has started to accelerate towards the sun, the sun's gravity will take care of the rest of the work and no other effort would be needed.

Q: The body may also break its orbit by falling away from the sun and becoming lost in the dark, fathomless depths of empty space.
B: The danger you mention is very real for those on the *raja yoga marga* [path of meditation and self-discipline], because some people imagine the mindless state of *shunyam* [emptiness] to be *Jnana* and will not listen to sense when told otherwise. That is why for the *raja yoga marga* a genuinely Realised Guru in human form is a sine qua non (necessity). Otherwise, the aspirant will in all likelihood unknowingly mistake the *shunyastithi* [state of emptiness] to be *Jnana* and rest in it, eventually becoming hopelessly lost.

***Vichara* poses no such danger. The orbit-breaking force exerted by this *sadhana* is always applied in such an inclination as to precisely drive the mind solely towards and into the blissful Heart. For *Vichara* the Heart Himself lovingly assumes the role of Guru and if the aspirant is sufficiently mature, no other Guru is necessary.**

Q: How shall I tell whether I am in the shunyastithi *or in* antarmukabhavam *[inward-facing consciousness]?*
B: The former is a variant of sleep. The current of awareness is either dim or, in severe cases of affliction, not there. In *antarmukabhavam* the mind is fully alert, aware, or conscious, but not extraneously active, not effervescent in relation to any craving to satisfy proclivities for sensory perceptivities and intellectual exploits. It is an unfortunate fact that many quack practitioners or teachers of meditation tutor *shunyastithi* and purposely delude their pupils into believing that it is *Jnana*.

***Shunyastithi* is deadly spiritual poison. It drives one away from the Heart, and thereafter the lost ground has to be recovered all the way – by means of doubling back – if *Jnana* is to be reached. That is why meditation is not encouraged here, but only *Vichara*.**

Q: So, this kind of malapropos meditation, far from helping me to Realise the Self, is actually harmful.
B: Undoubtedly.

Q: Will Bhagavan agree with me that Meher Baba (an Indian spiritual Master) is actually teaching only this shunyastithi*? I hear that many people, particularly Caucasians, are falling prey to all his devilish tricks.*
B: (no response)

Q: What shall we say to those piteous deceived persons who are falling prey to such harmful teachings of charlatans?
B: (no response)

G: *We can ask them to come to Bhagavan!*

What Fault Am I Committing?

Q: All my efforts to sink the mind in the Heart have proved to be in futility. What fault am I committing?

B: If the desire to sink the mind in the Heart is still present, how can it be said that you are completely free of desires, which is the essential condition for effortless submergence of the mind in the Heart? The mind cannot sink into the Heart as a consequence of the fact that you desire it to do so. If all contents of or knots *[vrittis]* in the mind stand destroyed, what remains is merely pure Subjective Consciousness – to which formulation or sustenance of thought is wholly alien. Such pure Subjective Consciousness cannot remain apart from its source for long; soon it sinks into the Heart and is dissolved there once and for all like a salt doll in the ocean. This is how Emancipation naturally takes place. One cannot succeed in forcing the mind to sink into the Heart; apart from other considerations, which might turn out to prove a hindrance to such submergence, the effort will itself obstruct you from so doing.

You are asking this question because you are applying everyday logic in trying to tackle the Self. In worldly life, when you want to attain something, you make effort to get it. So here, in relation to the question of Realisation also you are trying to do the same thing. But can it work? To realise the Self, the effortless and desireless state must first be gained. For this, the mind must be made steadily inward-pointed and free from distraction or restlessness. It must develop perfect introversion *[antarmukabhavam];* for this, incessant and continuous practise of *Vichara* is necessary.

Trying to use force to lead the mind into the Heart will not work. The mind must sink into the Heart extemporaneously and effortlessly owing to the absence of distraction, *chittavrittis.* We see therefore that whilst distractions still remain latent in the mind, Realisation is altogether impossible. The mind's distractions have been accumulated over a long period of time; they will not go all of a sudden. To root them out, steadfastness and *Vichara* is necessary.

Q: Should Vichara *be taken up even whilst the mind is at peace?*
B: Yes. It should be practised until the mind stands destroyed. Even when at peace or whilst in a mood of happiness, the mind must not be permitted to rest. Happiness or peace is also just another mental mode. The happiness you mention is the happiness of *manolayam* [a state where mind structures are temporarily faded]. There is no meaningful comparison possible with the unalloyed peace of the Self, which is unfathomable bliss beyond imagination and beyond possibility of conception by the mind.

Q: So, I should not take a rest at all whilst practising Vichara*?*
B: What do you suppose is *Vichara*? Do you think it involves repeatedly asking yourself the question Who am I? like a well-trained parrot? The actual import of *Vichara* is to effect subsidence of mind in the Heart. The investigation is certainly to be undertaken the moment a thought arises, but it is pursued only to the extent that thoughts present themselves. When thoughts do not arise, the mind must be kept a prisoner of the Heart cave. You are always at rest, only you do not know it.

Thoughts ruin your rest. So, remain without thinking. There is no question of taking rest during one's practising of *Vichara*. *Vichara* is practised only so that we can take rest eternally. Whenever some thought arises to ruin the mind's natural state of *nivritti*, kill it then and there by wielding the axe of *Vichara*. *Vichara* is not to be thought of as *sadhana* performed so that one may acquire or obtain something. *Vichara* is the weapon used to axe down whatever and whenever something arises to ruin one's natural state of ceaseless rest. Where then is the question of taking rest from *Vichara*?

Which Method Appeals to You

Q: For the past week, I have been delighting myself in listening to Bhagavan's soothing spiritual discourses in the Hall. I also have been meaning to ask Bhagavan the same doubt for all these days. I am a man who is utterly new to spiritual practice. Should I begin with Vichara*? Or should I begin with an easier method, such as watching the breath, for instance, and move on to* Vichara *once my mind has acquired sufficient maturity?*

B: No method is per se easy or difficult. Depending upon one's temperament, what one finds easy the next man finds difficult. The thing to do is to stick to what fascinates you. Never mind which method is best. Which method appeals to you?

Q: I like to meditate on the picture of the Lord which portrays Sri Krishna *playing the flute and standing in the midst of the* jamun *[Indian blackberry] orchard, with a few cows standing in the background. But Bhagavan has opined that* Vichara *is the only means to pierce and sunder the veil of ignorance. So, I tend to castigate myself that I am following a method, which, according to Bhagavan, does not lead me to Realisation.*

B: Who said that I disapprove of other methods? You may go on following your present method until you yourself feel, intuitively rather than intellectually, that the time has come for you to give up the *sadhana*. At that point in time the mind will automatically begin to gravitate towards incessantly reflecting upon 'I'. Fascination with 'I' leads to spontaneous *Vichara*.

***Vichara*, if not done for its own sake, does not bring forth a successful result. If a splinter of wood is stuck in your gum, your tongue will, of its own accord, go on trying to uproot it, without the need for any conscious effort on your part. *Vichara* will succeed only when there is that degree of spontaneity. The tongue knows that the splinter is a foreign body and must go. It will go on fighting until the alien appendage comes loose. Likewise, the mind must be able naturally to discern the ego, to which it owes its apparent existence, as being an unnatural and alien entity.**

This clarity will come only after prolonged practice *[abhyasa]*. That *abhyasa* may take up any form which appeals to you. Whatever road you are pursuing now will of its own accord lead you to *Vichara* when the moment is ripe, provided you are sincere and unrelenting in your effort.

What Is the Ego?

Q: When thoughts occur, I should revert my attention back to pure consciousness. That is the point of Vichara. *Is that right?*
B: What you mention is without doubt *Vichara*. But there is more to *Vichara*.

Q: Please explain.
B: Once the practice of *Vichara* has brought about a sufficient degree of ripeness (maturity or steadiness in introversion), the mind is loath to think thoughts and is now content to remain merged in the Beingness of the Self. Even then, however, there is the subtle 'I' who observes the fact of the mind remaining so merged. Catch hold of him and incessantly scrutinise him and when he vanishes, *Jnana* alone remains.

Q: Has Bhagavan said that the meditation 'I am *Brahman*' *is counter-productive?*
B: Yes.

Q: Why so?
B: Rather than meaninglessly endeavouring to concentrate on the Absolute Self, which is beyond the pale of understanding or perception by mind or through mental faculty, work with what you have. See what the ego is. What is this 'me'? That is the investigation needed. There can be no investigation into the Absolute. Work not with what is unknown but with what you readily have, the ego 'I'.

All living beings desire to be happy always,
without any misery.
In everyone, there is observed supreme love for
oneself, and happiness alone is the cause of love.

Love is the feeling of the mind being
submerged in the Shining of the Heart.

Love for objects can never provide satiation.
Realisation is not about acquiring something;
it's about Being what You Already Are.

When you are asked to abandon all your ideas,
that is precisely what you should do.
If you feel tempted to ask for a formula,
know that there is none. Just BE.

The more the 'I'-sense wears down, the more you
find yourself able to unselfishly Love.

When the mind stays in the Heart, the 'I'
– which is the source of all thoughts –
will go, and the Self, which always exists,
will shine.

Bhagavan Sri Ramana Maharshi

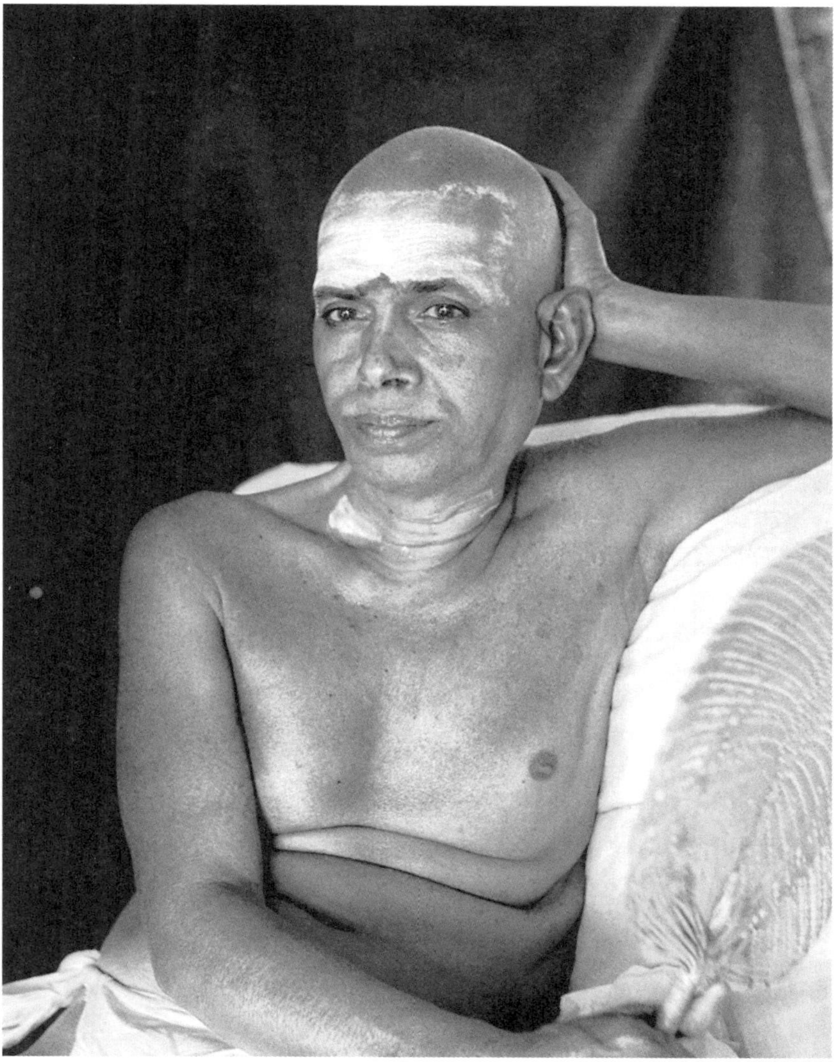

End Pages

Glossary

Ramana Maharshi Books

Open Sky Press Books

Arunachala Pilgrimage Retreat

Glossary

Abacharam
Offence
Abhyasa
Practice
Adhishtanam
Fundamental underlying reality or substratum
Advaita
Not two, non-duality
Advaita Vedanta
Philosophy of non-duality
Agraharam
Traditional South Indian Brahmin village or neighborhood
Aham Brahmasmi
I am Brahman (I am consciousness)
Aham Sphurana
'I'-pulsation
Ahamkara
Ego, I am the doer
Ahamkara Vichara
Enquiry into the nature of the ego
Aham Sphurti
Uninterrupted flash of the 'I'-Consciousness
Ahamvritti
'I'-thought, the most basic assumption of an 'I'
Ajata Advaita
Non-dual philosophy that there is no birth, and no creation
Ajnachakra
Third Eye Chakra
Akhandabrahmachari
Lifelong celibate
Akritopasaka
One who has not practised worship
Amrita nadi
Subtle energy channel through which the consciousness of the Self flows between the spiritual heart and the crown of the head
Ananya Sharanagati
Unconditional Surrender
Annamalaiyar Temple
Main Shiva Temple in Tiruvannamalai
Antarmukabhavam
State of inward-facing consciousness
Arivu
Knowledge, awareness, intelligence, or wisdom
Arunachala
Holy mountain (incarnation of Shiva)
Asat
Untruth
Ashwatthama
Prominent figure in the Mahabharata, one of the seven immortal beings
Atmasakshatkaram
Self-realisation
Atma / Atman
The eternal, non-personal Self
Atmajignasa
Enquiry into the nature of the Self
Atmalakshya
Having the Self as the aim
Atmasakshatkaram
Direct experience of the Self
Atma Vichara
Self-enquiry
Atmaswarupa
The true form of the Self

Avatarapurusha
Divine incarnation
Avidyamaya
Illusion caused by ignorance

Bhakta
A devotee of God
Bhakti
Unselfish love for God, devotion
Bhavatarini
A form of Kali, the Divine Mother who takes one to liberation
Bhishma
Son of King Shantanu (Mahabharata)
Bhima
Central character in the Mahabharata, son of King Pandu and Kunti, known for his strength
Bhoga Vasanas
Tendencies, desires, or attachments towards worldly pleasures and sensory experiences
Bhutas
Ghosts
Bimbithachittam
Reflective consciousness
Brahma
The creator God in Hinduism
Brahmashirsha Astra
Devastating divine weapon mentioned in Hindu epics, particularly the Mahabharata
Brahmashironamaka Astra
Symbolic spiritual concept for ego dissolution and Self-realisation
Brahman
The eternal Reality, the Absolute Existence
Brahmajnana
Knowledge (Realisation) of Brahman
Brahmajnani
Person with knowledge of Brahman
Buddhi
The subtle intellect, power of discrimination

Chidakasha
Pure space of consciousness
Chidhabhasa
Universal Self reflected through the mind
Chidjadagranthi
Knot of ignorance that binds consciousness to the body and mind
Chit
Consciousness, awareness
Chittaikagrata
One-pointedness of mind
Chittam
Mind, memory, conscious awareness
Chittashakti
Creative power of consciousness
Chittavritti
Fluctuations of the mind, thoughts that clutter the mind

Darshan
Auspicious sight of a deity or saint
Dattatreya
The first Avadhuta, an Avatar of Brahma,Vishnu, Shiva combined

Dhoti
Traditional garment worn by men in India
Dhrik
Gaze (of the Guru)
Dhyana
Meditation
Diksha
Spiritual initiation

Gandharvas
Celestial beings known for their musical and artistic abilities
Gayatri Mantra
Prayer directed towards the Supreme Consciousness
Granthi
Knot between the sentient and the insentient
Granthinasam
Destruction of the knot
Guru
Teacher
Guruvarutkataksham
The grace-filled glance of the Guru

Hasta Diksha
Initiation through touch by the Guru
Hatha Yoga
System of physical yoga techniques
Hridayagranthi
Knot of the heart
Hridaya
Heart, the spiritual center in the body
Hridayapundarikam
Heart–lotus, spiritual center of consciousness

Indra
Hindu King of heaven and gods
Ishwara
The supreme Being
Itihasas
Refer to the two great epics of ancient India: the Ramayana and the Mahabharata

---

Jada / Jadam
Insentient, inert matter, devoid of consciousness
Jagrat
Waking state (not being asleep)
Jagrat-swapna-sushupti
3 states of consciousness: Waking state, dreaming and deep sleep
Jagrat-sushupti
Experiencing the peacefulness of deep sleep in the waking state
Jamun
Indian blackberry
Japa / Japam
Meditative repetition of a mantra
Jarasandha
Prominent antagonist in the Mahabharata
Jiva
The indvidual soul
Jivanmukta
Liberated soul, released while living
Jivatman
Individual soul
Jnana
Spiritual knowledge

Jnana-anveshaka
Seeker of knowledge
Jnana marga
Path of knowledge
Jnanasakshatkara
Profound, intuitive experience of the true nature of reality
Jnanasiddha
One who embodies perfect knowledge
Jnanasiddhi
Attainment of perfect spiritual knowledge
Jnana Vichara
Contemplation of wisdom
Jnanayoga
Path of wisdom
Jnanopadesam
Imparting of spiritual knowledge or instruction in wisdom
Jnani
The Self-realised sage, one who has perfect knowledge

Kaivalya
Liberation from creation and rebirth / isolated oneness
Kevala Nirvikalpa
Temporary experience of non-dual awareness
King Shishupala
King of Chedi, cousin of Krishna
Koupeenadhari
One who wears a loincloth
Koshas
Five layers / bodies that cover the True Self
Krishna
A Supreme God in Hinduism, eighth Avatar of Vishnu
Kritopasaka
One who has practised worship
Kundalini Shakti
Dormant spiritual energy at the base of the spine
Kundalini yoga
Physical practice that focuses on the awakening of Kundalini
Kurma
Initiation through thought or subtle energy
Kuselar
Childhood friend and devotee of Lord Krishna

Lakshyam
Aim, destination
Lord Annamalai
Form of Lord Shiva worshipped at the Arunachaleshwarar Temple in Tiruvannamalai

---

Mahanubhavar
Great enlightened Being
Mahasamadhi
Final union with supreme consciousness, death of a realised saint
Mahaviksheenaka
The great destroyer
Manolayam
A state where mind structures are hazily projected

Manonasam
Destruction of the mind
Manonivritti
Mind turned inwards
Mantra japa
Repetition of a mantra
Matrubutheshwara
Shrine of Bhagavan's mother
Maya
Illusion, power which manifests the world
Moola-avarana
Covering / obstructing the source
Mounatapas
Effort to Self-realisation in silence
Muktapurusha
Liberated soul
Murti dhyana
Meditation on a form of God
Mukti
Liberation, freedom from rebirths
Muni
Sage / hermit

Nadis
Energy channels
Nan Yar
Who am I?
Nashamagiyamanam
Dead mind
Neti
Not this
Neti-neti
Neither this, nor that
Nijaswarupam
One's true form or Essence
Nirgunopasana
Meditation on the formless Brahman
Nirvikalpa
Without thoughts
Nirvikalpa Samadhi
State of being temporarily absorbed in the Absolute
Nishchal Das
Prominent 19th-century Indian sage who wrote *Vichara Sagara* – an influential text on Advaita philosophy
Nityapratyaksha
Eternal direct perception or ever-present awareness
Nivritti
Introverted mind
Nivrittiyanamanam
Denuded mind

Pakkuvam
Ripeness
Panniru Thirumurai
Sacret Tamil text
Parabhakti
Supreme devotion, unconditional, selfless love and complete surrender to the divine
Parabrahman
The supreme Self, supreme Brahman
Paramatma
The Absolute Atman, supreme Self
Paripakvi
Fully ripe person
Parithranaya sadhunam
For the protection of the righteous
Pranayama
Yogic breath control

Prarabdha
Inevitable karmic consequences
Prarabdha karma
Accumulated past karma responsible for current life experiences
Pratyaksha
Direct experience
Prema purna thaya jnanam
The wisdom arising from complete love
Punya
Merit, spiritual goodness
Puranas
Genre of ancient Indian literature that contain narratives of cosmology, mythology, history, legends, and religious teachings
Purnapakkuvam
State of total maturity
Purva samskaras
Old latent mind tendencies, habits

Rajas
One of the three gunas: passion, activity
Raja yoga marga
Royal Path, Path of Meditation and Self-discipline
Rakshasas
Supernatural, often demonic beings
Rudraksha
Seed of an Indian tree, tear of Shiva

Sadhaka
One who engages in spiritual practice
Sadhaka's vairagya
A spiritual practitioner's detachment
Sadhana
Spiritual practice
Sadhvasthu
The one true existence
Sagunopasana
Worship of a deity with form
Sahaja
Union with the divine, spontaneous enlightenment
Sahaja Swayam Prakasha
The natural Self-luminosity
Sahajajnani
Liberated sage, Self-realised being
Sahajajnanastithi
Established or dwelling in Brahman
Sahajastithi
Natural state
Sahasraram
Crown chakra
Samadhi
Union with reality, tomb of an enlightened being
Samsara
Cycle of birth and death caused by karma
Samsarasagaram
Ocean of samsara
Samskaras
Mental impressions, psychological imprints
Sankalpa
Personal will, desire
Sannyasa
Renunciation of worldly life
Sarvadhikari
Ashram manager

Sarvagnar
One who knows everything
Sastra
Authoritative spiritual scriptures
Sat
Truth, absolute existence
Sat Chit
Absolute existence consciousness
Satguru
True Guru
Satya Yugam
Golden Age
Sayujya
Complete union with the divine
Shaktipada
Transmission of spiritual energy from the Guru
Shankara
Famous scholar and teacher of Advaita Vedanta (8th Century)
Shankaracharya of Sringeri
Head of a monastic centre established by Adi Shankara
Shanti
Peace
Sharanagati
Surrender
Shathavari
Asparagus racemosus
Shiva
A supreme God in Hinduism
Shlokas
Sanskrit verses
Shunyam
Emptiness, void, or nothingness
Shunyastithi
State of emptiness
Shuka
Highly revered Vedantic sage, son of Vyasa (author of the Mahabharata)
Siddhapurusha
Perfected being, often with supernatural powers
Siddhi
Spiritual power
Simhasanam
Seat of supreme realisation
Spandabhraja Samadhi
Absorption in bliss, union with reality
Sparsa
Initiation through touch
Sphurana
Pulsation
Sri Krishna Paramatma
Lord Krishna in his supreme, transcendental form as Paramatma, as Supreme Soul or Supreme Being
Sri Ramana Gita
Devotional and philosophical text dedicated to Sri Ramana Maharshi
Sri Vidyaranya's Panchadasi
Renowned 14th century Sanskrit philosophical text on Advaita Vedanta
Stithaprajna
Firmly established in wisdom
Summayirutthal (Summa Iru)
Effortless Consciousness, naturally being still
Sushumna
Central energy channel in the body
Sushupti
Deep sleep
Svagruni
Self-luminosity

Swami
A Hindu ascetic, also used as title for renunciate spiritual teachers
Swapna
State of dreaming
Swarupa
Essential nature
Swarupa Jnana
Knowledge or realisation of one's true nature or essential Self

---

Tamas
Darkness, ignorance
Tapas
Austerity, effort to achieve Self-realisation
Thannunarvu
Self awareness, Self consciousness
Turiyatita
The ultimate state of consciousness

Upadesha
Teaching, instruction
Upadhis
Limitation, external attributes or limitations that seem to affect the pure consciousness
Upanishads
Sacred scriptures in Hinduism, last part of the Vedas
Uttatra
Son of King Virata of Matsya Kingdom from the Mahabharata

Vairagya
Detachment, renunciation
Vasanas
Habits of the mind
Veda Vyasa
Sage who wrote the Mahabharata
Vedanta
The culmination of Vedic knowledge
Vedas
The oldest and most important scriptures in Hinduism
Vedic Rishis
Ancient seers and sages of India
Vichara
Self-enquiry
Vichara abhyasa / sadhana
Self-enquiry practice
Vichara marga
Path of Self-enquiry
Vipareetajnana
False understanding
Vishaya
Sense objects
Vishaya vasanas
Desire for sense objects
Vritti
Structures of the mind, mental habits
Vrittijnanam
Temporarily merged in the absolute, but the mind's identity still kept unharmed

---

Yoga marga
Path of yoga
Yudhishthira's Rajasuya yajna
Significant event in the Mahabharata

Aham Sphurana

The Trilogy on Bhagavan's Teachings

Available in a Box Set of Three

In 2021, Open Sky Press received the July, August and September 1936 manuscript of Aham Sphurana. Our first step was to curate a selection of the most profound teachings from the text, which we compiled into the Book Aham Sphurana. Inspired to offer deeper explorations of the two central paths recommended by Ramana, dedicating an entire volume to each – Self-enquiry and Surrender – we created this edition first, the Vichara Book. The Surrender Book completes the trilogy, highlighting his life and teachings in a comprehensive way.

Aham Sphurana – A Glimpse of Self Realisation

Fascinating dialogues and stories of Sri Ramana Maharshi recorded by Sri Gajapathi Aiyyer in the summer of 1936, at Ramana Ashram. This book contains a selection from the complete manuscript *Aham Sphurana*. This selection, a brilliant treasure, speaks for itself. Beside the detailed teachings on Self-enquiry, Surrender and Jnana, it exposes a new glimpse of Bhagavan's personal day-to-day life at fifty-six, in his middle age.

ISBN 978-1-9163211-7-5

ISBN 978-3-943544-82-4
Available by mid 2025

Sharanagati – Surrender

For Bhagavan, Surrender, or *Sharanagati*, is a direct and powerful path to dissolving the ego and experiencing the peace of Self-realisation. This volume offers a deeper exploration of surrender as a spiritual practice, drawing from a selection of Bhagavan's teachings that emphasise its essential role in the journey toward liberation. Through practical insights and reflections, *Sharanagati* guides readers on how to fully let go, trust the divine, and live in alignment with the true Self.

Would you like to support translations?

If you are interested to help spread Bhagavan's teachings worldwide and have experience with translating and / or proofreading, please feel free to get in touch with us.

Arunachala Pilgrimage

Arunachala, the Holy Mountain, has been a powerful place of pilgrimage for two thousand years. It attracted the young Ramana after his Self-realisation. Later, when Sri Bhagavan Ramana Maharshi became a famous teacher of Advaita Vedanta, an ashram was established around him at the foot of the mountain. It became a popular destination also for Western spiritual seekers and the interest has continued into the present.

Many people visit Ramana Ashram, where the presence and peace of Bhagavan remains omnipresent. It is possible to sit at Bhagavan's Samadhi shrine and the shrine of his mother. Vedic chanting is still performed daily. The shrines of Major Chadwick, Annamalai Swami and cow Lakshmi can also be visited.

The editor of this book, John David, has been offering an annual spiritual retreat at the foothill of Arunachala in January yearly for more than twenty-five years. It is accommodated in a modern ashram with its own retreat kitchen. Satsang meetings, meditation and yoga take place on the ashram roof with a direct view of Arunachala.

www.johndavidsatsang.international/india